Why Data Science Projects Fail

The field of artificial intelligence, data science, and analytics is crippling itself. Exaggerated promises of unrealistic technologies, simplifications of complex projects, and marketing hype are leading to an erosion of trust in one of our most critical approaches to making decisions: data driven.

This book aims to fix this by countering the AI hype with a dose of realism. Written by two experts in the field, the authors firmly believe in the power of mathematics, computing, and analytics, but if false expectations are set and practitioners and leaders don't fully understand everything that really goes into data science projects, then a stunning 80% (or more) of analytics projects will continue to fail, costing enterprises and society hundreds of billions of dollars, and leading to non-experts abandoning one of the most important data-driven decision-making capabilities altogether.

For the first time, business leaders, practitioners, students, and interested laypeople will learn what really makes a data science project successful. By illustrating with many personal stories, the authors reveal the harsh realities of implementing AI and analytics.

Douglas Gray is a practitioner, leader, and educator with over 30 years of experience leading award-winning teams at industry luminaries in Analytics, including INFORMS Prize-winning American Airlines and Walmart. His teams have delivered advanced game-changing solutions in airline operations, healthcare, and omnichannel retail supply chain domains which deliver hundreds of millions of dollars in business value and economic impact annually. He teaches Analytics and AI Strategy at Southern Methodist University (SMU) in the Executive MBA, Executive Education, and MS Data Science programs, and has published over a dozen articles on Analytics best practices and applications.

Evan Shellshear is an expert in artificial intelligence with a Ph.D. in Game Theory from the Nobel Prize winning University of Bielefeld in Germany. He has almost two decades of international experience in the development and design of AI tools for a variety of industries having worked with the world's top companies on all aspects of advanced analytical solutions from optimization to machine learning in applications from HR to oil and gas, and robotics to supply chain. He is also the author of the Amazon best seller, *Innovation Tools*.

Chapman & Hall/CRC Data Science Series

Reflecting the interdisciplinary nature of the field, this book series brings together researchers, practitioners, and instructors from statistics, computer science, machine learning, and analytics. The series will publish cutting-edge research, industry applications, and textbooks in data science.

The inclusion of concrete examples, applications, and methods is highly encouraged. The scope of the series includes titles in the areas of machine learning, pattern recognition, predictive analytics, business analytics, Big Data, visualization, programming, software, learning analytics, data wrangling, interactive graphics, and reproducible research.

Recently Published Titles

Spatial Statistics for Data Science
Theory and Practice with R
Paula Moraga

Research Software Engineering
A Guide to the Open Source Ecosystem
Matthias Bannert

The Data Preparation Journey
Finding Your Way With R
Martin Hugh Monkman

Getting (more out of) Graphics
Practice and Principles of Data Visualisation
Antony Unwin

Introduction to Data Science
Data Wrangling and Visualization with R Second Edition
Rafael A. Irizarry

Data Science
A First Introduction with Python
Tiffany Timbers, Trevor Campbell, Melissa Lee, Joel Ostblom, and Lindsey Heagy

Mathematical Engineering of Deep Learning
Benoit Liquet, Sarat Moka, and Yoni Nazarathy

Why Data Science Projects Fail
The Harsh Realities of Implementing AI and Analytics, without the Hype
Douglas Gray and Evan Shellshear

For more information about this series, please visit: https://www.routledge.com/Chapman--HallCRC-Data-Science-Series/book-series/CHDSS

Why Data Science Projects Fail

The Harsh Realities of Implementing AI and Analytics, without the Hype

Douglas Gray
Evan Shellshear

CRC Press
Taylor & Francis Group
Boca Raton London New York

CRC Press is an imprint of the
Taylor & Francis Group, an **informa** business
A CHAPMAN & HALL BOOK

First edition published 2025
by CRC Press
2385 NW Executive Center Drive, Suite 320, Boca Raton FL 33431

and by CRC Press
4 Park Square, Milton Park, Abingdon, Oxon, OX14 4RN

CRC Press is an imprint of Taylor & Francis Group, LLC

ISBN: 978-1-032-66133-9 (hbk)
ISBN: 978-1-032-66030-1 (pbk)
ISBN: 978-1-032-66136-0 (ebk)

DOI: 10.1201/9781032661360

Typeset in Palatino
by SPi Technologies India Pvt Ltd (Straive)

Dedication

Doug: To my parents, my wife, and my sons without whose love and support I would have achieved far less. To all of my professors at Loyola, Georgia Tech, and SMU who provided me with the educational foundation for my professional career. To all of my leaders, colleagues, and students throughout my career with whom I have been on the journey of delivering business value and economic impact, and continually learning through failure and success. To the current and future generations of data science practitioners and leaders for whom this book is intended.

Evan: To every modeler starting their journey and wanting to know what they really need to know. To my family, friends, and those who look out for me and support me on my journey, without which I would never have achieved anything.

Contents

About the Authors

Douglas Gray is a practitioner, leader, educator, and advisor with 30+ years of experience in data and analytics, IT/software, e-commerce, and consulting. He and his teams have won multiple industry awards, including Teradata EPIC Award, FICO Decision Management Innovation Award, Alteryx Best Business ROI Award (2), Drexel LeBow Analytics50 Award (2), and AGIFORS Operations Best Innovation Award.

He has been a member of two INFORMS Prize-winning organizations: Walmart (2023) and American Airlines (1990). Doug was an early team member at award-winning American Airlines Decision Technologies (AADT), which pioneered numerous innovations driving substantial economic impact in the use of analytics in the airline industry, solving commercial and operational problems across the enterprise. At Sabre, Doug served as the founding CTO of Travelocity, the world's first real-time, internet-based travel reservation system. Doug is currently a Director of Data Science at Walmart Global Tech—US Omni Retail Tech, where he leads teams and programs that increase operational efficiency and cost effectiveness focused on end-to-end fulfillment, delivering 9-figures of business value and economic impact annually.

Through his own company, Blueprint Technology Advisors, LLC, d.b.a., Optima Analytics, he advises executive leadership teams on best practices of applying technology and analytics to corporate strategy and digital transformation, and implementing analytical sciences-based organizations and capabilities.

He has taught business analytics and AI strategy at SMU's Cox School of Business and SMU's MS in Data Science program as an adjunct professor since 2016. He has published over a dozen articles and research papers on analytics applications, and has been an invited keynote, guest speaker, and panel discussion participant at industry conferences and universities worldwide.

He holds an MBA from SMU's Cox School of Business (Beta Gamma Sigma), MS in Operations Research from the Georgia Institute of Technology's Stewart School of Industrial & Systems Engineering, and a BS cum laude in Mathematical Sciences (Statistics) from Loyola University Maryland (Pi Mu Epsilon).

Evan Shellshear has more than 15 years of experience in the development and application of complex algorithms and analytical solutions to a variety of industries from HR to oil and gas, and robotics to supply chain. He has worked in a variety of analytical fields from computational geometry to optimization, statistics, and AI.

He has a dual BA and BSc from the University of Queensland, Australia, a Diplom (Masters) and PhD in Game Theory from the Nobel Prize-winner founded Institute of Mathematical Economics at the University of Bielefeld in Germany.

He has authored more than two dozen peer-reviewed articles in journals and conferences, and almost 100 articles in leading blogs, magazines, and news outlets. He is also the author of the Amazon bestseller, Innovation Tools, and co-author of a number of other books, such as the bestselling 20 Beautiful Men and AI in Medicine (Springer).

Evan has served on multiple advisory boards of state and nationwide institutes, and has multiple accreditations across a number of digital platforms. In addition to his day job as a CEO and managing director, he is currently an adjunct professor at the University of Queensland and Queensland University of Technology teaching topics from business analytics and AI to strategy to both undergraduates and executives.

Foreword

This book is important. Analytics and AI have seized the popular imagination and have been applied within many organizations over the past couple of decades. For the most part, this has been a welcome development. Making decisions based on data and analysis generally leads to better outcomes than those made on intuition or experience. Analytics, data science, and now artificial intelligence (ADSAI, as the authors put it) have led to better marketing offers, more optimized supply chains, better human resource management, and greater productivity by knowledge and creative workers.

The authors, both of whom have worked in data science roles in organizations for many years, are in full agreement with me on the potential value of the field. But they have done it a great service by focusing on the many ways in which data science projects can go astray. As they note, data science projects are complex, and they demonstrate that there are multiple ways in which they can fail to deliver value to organizations.

Such in-depth analyses of "why things fail" in the analytics and AI space are somewhat rare (other than Doug Gray's multipart series on the topic in INFORMS *Analytics* magazine). Earlier in the history of analytics in business, the emphasis by me and others was on persuading people of the virtues of thinking and acting analytically. We naturally wanted to emphasize success and stories about it.

However, the other side of the coin—failure and how to avoid it—is just as valuable, if not more so. Now that data, analytics, and AI are an accepted aspect of many businesses and organizations, we need to increase the rate of success in producing projects and products that employ those resources. And pointing out the ways in which organizations fail is very helpful in that regard.

It's also somewhat more pleasant to read about failures than to read about big successes. It is comforting to observe that the undoubtedly smart people involved in these exemplary failures still managed to screw up. When we read about great success, we question whether we could pull it off ourselves. When we read about failure, we tend to think, "Thank God I haven't done anything that bad."

For it is now no secret that many data science projects and products fail. As the authors of this book illustrate, there are many different estimates of just how often that happens—77%, 80%, 85%, 87%, or 90% of the time, or whatever. I have always been a bit suspicious of the specific claims involving high percentages of data science failure, even though I have sometimes cited them myself to make one point or another. I'm not sure that a careful enumeration and examination of projects was made in any of these analyses, and the definition of failure isn't always clear in them, e.g., failed to deliver business value versus failed to be deployed to production. Regardless of the actual universal percentage of ADSAI project failures, or the reasons behind them, failures are all too common, and need to be addressed through greater education, increased awareness, and different approaches to data science projects, which this book does.

The fact is that sometimes data science projects should fail. It is an experimental discipline, after all, and not all predictive models will be accurate enough to be useful. In fact, as the British statistician George Box put it, "All models are wrong, but some are useful." Sometimes they are wrong enough to be of no use at all, and they should be discarded. I don't consider that a failure if it is done before a lot of time and money are devoted to deploying the model into production.

But what I really like about this book is that it largely focuses on the types of failure that go beyond the model, not predicting the future very accurately. The authors define failure as being unable or unwilling to implement the model fully, not solving a business problem or creating useful business insights, or not generating measurable business or economic value. This definition opens up the possibilities for failure (and improvement) to a broad range of organizational factors including poor fit with strategy, lack of skills, poor data, a dysfunctional development process, and so forth. Like the authors, these areas are where I see the most failures, and the power of this book lies in its focus on them.

Unfortunately, many data scientists are not trained in identifying or resolving these types of issues. We've begun to realize that data scientists are not unicorns who can do all data science-related tasks equally well. The authors suggest a strong focus on "translators," and I strongly agree that translation skills are necessary. I have found somewhat more organizational receptivity to the idea of "data product managers" than to "translators," but translation between business and ADSAI people and issues is a major focus of both groups.

In short, whether you are an analytics or AI leader, a data scientist, or simply a business professional or manager who believes in the power of data-driven, model-based decisions and actions, this book will help you be more successful. You'll learn not only how to fail, but more importantly, how to avoid failure. If you are aware of all or most of the mistakes and missteps addressed in this book and you manage to avoid them, you will be a highly capable practitioner or overseer of the science and art of analytics.

Thomas H. Davenport, PhD
Distinguished Professor, Babson College and
Fellow, MIT Initiative on the Digital Economy
Author of *Competing on Analytics* and *All in on AI*

Introduction

This may not be the best way to start a book—especially one encouraging the use of analytics, data science, and artificial intelligence (ADSAI). But despite all the grand ADSAI success stories, we felt we had to.

We have to show what happens when things go wrong, very wrong—starting with a story that highlights the major themes we'll be addressing in this book: the things that differentiate AI success from AI failure. We begin with the story of a usually healthy woman we'll call Jenny.

It was flu season when Jenny fell ill in late 2022, so when her temperature spiked to over 102°F (38.9°C), she didn't think much of it. Jenny was an active 42-year-old who kept fit and stayed on top of her health, among other things. It didn't seem consequential that her fever occurred a few days after she hurt herself doing some final gardening for the season—what happened next did.

After two days of trying to recover in bed, Jenny's breathing became more labored and she felt her heart racing even when she was lying down. Jenny's partner became concerned and encouraged her to see her general practitioner or go to the hospital, but Jenny had felt worse in her life and decided to stick it out until her health improved.

But she didn't get better.

The next day, Jenny was really struggling and surmised this wasn't the flu. Normally a slim, average-height woman, she now looked emaciated and weak. Her partner transported her to the car and instead of taking her to the GP, raced her to the emergency department. Upon entry, the medical team recognized her symptoms, did a blood test, and a concerning white blood cell count confirmed the life-threatening challenge she was facing.

The hospital staff knew the clock was ticking and they needed to act quickly. The problem was, Jenny's illness was one step ahead. Her symptoms continued to worsen over the next 36 hours, with blotchy skin, inflamed limbs, and abdominal pain. Jenny's mental state was poor and she was now struggling to breathe.

The doctors rushed to get her condition under control. This was when Jenny's partner heard something that made time stop and his head spin. The specialist said they were concerned that Jenny's organs might be failing and her liver and kidney were not working as they should.

Her condition had deteriorated dramatically and it wasn't clear if Jenny would make it through this bout of what originally looked like the flu. But it wasn't the flu, it was *blood poisoning*. When Jenny injured herself in the

DOI: 10.1201/9781032661360-1

garden, she inadvertently infected herself through a scratch on plant thorns, which carried bacteria that her body failed to deal with after the injury. The bacterial infection exceeded her body's capacity to destroy the pathogens and they multiplied. Something as innocuous as a bit of gardening had turned into a battle for her life.

Jenny was now suffering from *sepsis* and whether she would survive wasn't clear.

The Sepsis Scourge

If there is one area that receives an inordinate amount of attention from analytics and AI, it is medicine. At the time of publication, there are at least *eight published books* with the exact title *Artificial Intelligence in Medicine*, let alone hundreds of variations on this theme (one of the co-authors, Evan, has even contributed a chapter to a book with that title). New AI breakthroughs are announced on a nearly weekly basis. Algorithms to detect tuberculosis (TB), skin cancer, heart arrhythmias, cancerous tumors, MRI-based trauma, even COVID-19, and many, many more, often claiming to be *better* than a clinical expert.

However, for those rushing headlong into this space, it is a veritable testing ground for clearly demonstrating why ADSAI projects are so difficult to undertake and why data science projects fail as often as they do. One area that has clearly demonstrated this analytical challenge is—Jenny's ultimate diagnosis—sepsis. Bruised egos and spent money litter the pathway of attempted solutions, highlighting a number of the principles relevant to the rest of this book.

Sepsis is a serious clinical condition that represents a patient's uncontrolled response to a severe infection and, in spite of much research and many clinical interventions, still has a very high mortality rate. Normal immune and physiologic responses eradicate pathogens (e.g., the bacteria causing the infection) and in an ideal scenario, the first contact of the pathogen with the immune system should eliminate the invader and quickly return the host to a stable condition (so-called homeostasis). The course of a sepsis infection is due to the inappropriate regulation of these normal reactions.[1]

Sepsis can be a vicious, debilitating clinical condition that substantially alters the lives of those afflicted. Although it can begin with flu-like symptoms, sepsis can lead to septic shock, which occurs when the septic process has become so extreme, it leads to multiple organ dysfunction as well as low blood pressure and poor perfusion (circulation of fluids), meaning that the heart, brain, and other parts of the body are not getting enough blood. A deadly state of affairs.

Estimates vary, but the general consensus is that when someone enters septic shock, roughly 35% of cases end in death within 30 days, increasing to about 40% after 90 days.[2] Globally, approximately 10 million people succumb to this fatal illness each year, and in the United States, it is *the number one preventable killer in hospitals* (i.e., caused by infections arising in the hospital). Every year, 1.7 million US adults develop sepsis, which kills about 270,000 people annually.[3]

Years of research have not put a significant dent in its mortality rate for infected patients. Is there nothing we can do against this horrific killer?

For the reasons above, sepsis is a common target for medical researchers with the goal of finding ways to both identify and treat it. Because we can collect so much data from a patient stationed in a hospital bed, it is no wonder that AI researchers have turned their attention to trying to solve this challenge. Because of the scale of the ailment caused by this pathogen, there is also a significant economic interest in developing solutions for it, resulting in many companies and hospitals wanting to commercialize their research to put an end to this devastating illness.

One such company that has done so is Epic. How Epic approached its solution to sepsis leads us into the central theme of this book—*why AI, data science, and analytics are much more complex and far more challenging than the current hype may lead you to believe.*

An Epic Challenge

Epic Systems is America's largest electronic health records (EHRs) company,[4] storing medical information for 250 million US patients (75% of the population) in 2021.[9] In true startup spirit, Epic was founded in 1979 by Judith Faulkner (with co-founder Dr. John Greist) shortly after she received her master's degree, with a $70,000 investment from friends and family.[5] They first called the company Human Services Computing.

However, this is when its similarities to startups end. Unlike most startup companies, Epic has never taken investment from venture capital or private equity, nor acquired another company, and Faulkner has stated they will never go public.[5] It remains one of America's largest private healthcare software companies (based on estimates of its revenues).[6]

As a private company, Epic is a testament to America's innovative drive and continual push to commercialize promising technologies. Since its humble beginnings from the founder's basement, the company has amassed an estimated 25% of the EHR market in the United States,[4] and now has revenues of greater than $3 billion (growing double-digit each year)[7] with an estimated 13,000 employees as of 2023.[6]

Generally, it is difficult to find out what happens at private companies beyond their own press releases, which is the case for some of the products Epic has developed, including the one relevant for our purposes in this book. So, unlike our other stories coming later in the book, this one will be based on the external reports and analysis of others.

Over the last decade, Epic has had a long history of working with and developing sophisticated technologies. Since its first partnership with Nuance (maker of AI-based speech recognition software products now owned by Microsoft) to assist disabled US military veterans (using AI to help schedule medical appointments[8]), the Epic team has developed a portfolio of 20 or so of their own proprietary AI algorithms.[9] These technologies help identify certain illnesses, prevent cardiac arrest,[10] predict the length of hospital stays and no-shows,[11] and—the focus of this story—a flagship product centered on better sepsis management.

In 2013, Epic began its research and development into the management of blood poisoning and finally launched its finished product in 2017[12] (based on a number of promising early results), the so-called *Epic Sepsis Model (ESM)*.[13] Based on the software company's claims, the new sepsis model could discriminate between two patients, one who had sepsis and one who did not, better than existing systems. Being able to do so ensures that the sick patients are correctly identified and the non-endangered patients are not unnecessarily flagged. The team at Epic claimed that the system was "reducing sepsis mortality by one-fifth."[13]

The uptake was likely as Epic had hoped. According to estimates, in 2021, 180 hospitals were possibly using the model to support clinical decision-making in the United States.[9]

Based on statements by Emily Barey, MSN, then-director of nursing at Epic, in an interview with Healthcare IT News, the chief nurse said[36]:

> When Epic designed our sepsis model, we looked to improve on common sepsis scoring methods, such as SIRS … What we found when we did our initial analysis was that our model helped identify about 10% more septic patients in the timing window, when compared with the SIRS model.

With 10 million lives on the line, even a 1% improvement in the treatment of sepsis could lead to an additional 100,000 lives saved. Based on Epic's research and their own public statements, there was a clear argument to adopt the algorithm in as many hospitals as fast as possible. But this hasn't happened[12]. So why isn't Epic's sepsis model available everywhere? Or, if not Epic's model, why not a different one?

It's not just a question of competition (other systems do exist), it is much deeper than that, and it comes to the core of this book's purpose. Resolving the Epic challenge leads to why we wrote this book in the first place.

A Focus on Failures: The Purpose Behind Our Literary Venture

For both co-authors, this book is a *passion project*, to demonstrate the *reality* of ADSAI projects that is replaced by hype too often. To reach our goal of demonstrating a higher level of sophistication and nuance in analytics initiatives, we are hoping to achieve a number of objectives with this book. Some of these are:

- Encourage and help analytics practitioners avoid an overemphasis on technology and techniques, and lean into the human aspects and "soft skills" dimensions that are critical to ADSAI project success, i.e., increase awareness of the critical *art* versus the known *science* aspects of AI projects.

- Illustrate what everyone intuitively *knows*, but perpetually seems to *forget*: ADSAI projects need the same best practices as every other project, e.g., increase the importance of well-known concepts, such as communication, change management, and project management, which are too often overlooked in ADSAI projects.

- Emphasize fundamentals and demonstrate the critical importance of basics, such as understanding the *real* business problem, diligently considering business priorities, estimating business value and economic impact, and setting realistic expectations for outcomes *before* jumping into coding and modeling.

- Raise awareness to both practitioners *and* executives that models are relatively easy to build in a coding notebook in as little as a day or an afternoon, but models embedded in production systems and business processes are more difficult to develop, deploy, and operate by *an order of magnitude or more* in time, cost, and resources due to integrations with complex IT ecosystems, creating data platforms and pipelines, and then the really difficult part of ongoing operation, support, and maintenance.

- And much more.

More than anything, we want to counter the ADSAI hype with a dose of realism. We firmly believe in the power of mathematics, computing, and analytics, but if false expectations are set and practitioners and leaders don't fully understand everything that really goes into ADSAI projects, then a stunning 80% (or more) of analytics projects will *continue* to fail,[15] costing enterprises and society billions of dollars, and leading to non-experts abandoning one of the most important data-driven decision-making capabilities altogether.

But our focus is not solely on the *business* people. We want to increase awareness and understanding among *practitioners*, both citizen and professional data scientists, that there is a lot more to their craft than technical skills—something most practitioners already know but seem to forget in the enthusiasm and excitement of model and algorithm development.

Most importantly, we want to help companies become more successful and more effective in implementing ADSAI initiatives. We'd like to balance the hype and exaggerated promises with sensibility and a broader understanding of what is really needed, and to do this we decided to focus on *failures*. Why? Because *failure is an extraordinarily effective form of feedback*. This is not just our opinion, we'll see research later that shows you learn more (from us) this way, than concentrating on success.

In addition, the reason for our focus on the blunders is that there are many great books, such as *Competing on Analytics* and *All in on AI* by Thomas Davenport, PhD, that address in detail what good and excellent companies do right and also help companies without any experience kick off their ADSAI journey by learning from the best. However, based on our research, what is missing is not the coverage of successful strategies but the discussion of unsuccessful ones. The majority of companies struggle to implement their ADSAI programs, and often it is not clear why.

Many analytical disasters may use the techniques of successful companies and with so much focus on what successful companies do, we need to be sure that these strategies are what differentiate the winners from the losers. Without a proper review of the less than successful projects, how do we really know what works? Some inexperienced companies may be doing the same things as excellent companies, so how do we know what is really critical to success? We need to discuss failures to make sure we aren't kidding ourselves.

Our thinking has also been influenced by pioneers in other fields of thematically related failure topics, such as Henry Petroski, author of *To Engineer is Human*. Petroski discusses why designs based on the extrapolation of successful experience alone can lead to failure. He states that latent (i.e., not deliberate) design features that were not important in earlier systems can become overlooked, and these design flaws can dominate the behavior of more complex systems that evolve over time, i.e., focusing too much on success leads to blind spots.

Petroski's book provides a number of historical examples, such as the repeated and recurrent failures of suspension bridges. In 1883 the Brooklyn Bridge became the longest suspension bridge in the world at the time, the success of which didn't help in preventing disasters like the Tacoma Narrows Bridge, which fatally twisted itself apart and collapsed in 1940. The lessons learned from the Tacoma Narrows Bridge failure, and others, *were* generalized and applied across a broad spectrum of engineering structures and complex systems, leading to a permanent imprint on our collective experiences, likely more than any success did.

Petroski stresses that we need to understand how failures happen and incorporate this learning into the design process. Failure analysis influences the way engineers hypothesize, push the limits, and develop new systems and structures. He writes:

> I believe that the concept of failure…is central to understanding engineering, for engineering design has as its first and foremost objective the obviation of failure. Thus, the colossal failures that do occur are ultimately failures of design, but the lessons learned from these disasters can do more to advance engineering knowledge than all the successful machines and structures in the world.

It is not only Petroski who believes this is the case. In an important study published in 2013 in the journal *Management Science* by a team of researchers from Harvard University, University of North Carolina at Chapel Hill, and Emory University,[16] the authors showed that how we learn appears more complicated than you may think and failures play a key role in this. The scenario they considered was one in which the result of failure is death and the result of success is a longer and more satisfying life—heart surgery.

In a study of more than 6,000 cardiac surgery procedures that used a new technology, the researchers of the paper found that "individuals learn more from their own successes than from their own failures, but they learn more from *the failures of others* than from others' successes."

Of course, this is not limited to cardiac surgery; studies of organizations show the importance of failures for the process of learning.[17] However, for us to learn from a failure, we need to contextualize the failure and understand the reasons for it. This way, we can apply it to other situations not identical to the original situation and also recognize when to use the lesson in context. A great way to do this is by *telling stories*. We have taken this lesson to heart and will demonstrate in this book a number of stories about how failures occurred in real-life scenarios, providing the *insider details* of many failed projects, thereby sharing the lessons learned with you.

To figure out why ADSAI projects fail, we reviewed what our practitioner and researcher peers were telling us. We examined the *contexts* in which they failed, categorized them, and tried to understand why the failure occurred. By doing so, we are providing you with an inside track to learning from projects that most people don't ever see except for those working on the project. We are going to change that and bring you "inside the tent"—beginning with Epic.

The Epic Battle

Before we unpack Epic's AI tool, let's first return to the question: Why haven't more hospitals adopted Epic's system?

Over decades of collective failures, hospitals have learned that it is wise to carefully consider new approaches to treating patients. It is well known that incorrect lab results or unexpected side effects due to a wide variety of contraindications can turn obvious-seeming treatments into a pandora's box once opened to the broader public.

For a great example of this, consider the medication Vioxx, created by Merck. Vioxx's active ingredient, Rofecoxib, is a nonsteroidal anti-inflammatory drug approved in May 1999 by the US Food and Drug Administration (FDA).[18] Even though it went through clinical trials and the rigorous pharmaceutical drug approval process to ensure safety, it became a case study on the "safe" release of new drugs, from both a regulatory and commercial perspective.

Based on promising lab results, the medication was taken up quickly across the United States in the early 2000s, becoming a true blockbuster drug for Merck. Millions were prescribed the drug, and at its pinnacle, more than 80 million people worldwide were using Vioxx to treat arthritis and other conditions causing chronic or acute pain. Merck was estimated to generate sales revenue of US$2.5 billion from Vioxx.[19]

However, the increased usage revealed Vioxx's hidden danger. Soon after its launch in May 1999, reports of increased risk of heart attack and stroke began to alarm doctors across the United States. Because of its widespread usage, the issues were discovered early and culminated in Vioxx being voluntarily withdrawn from the market in September 2004, but not after causing up to an estimated additional 140,000 cases of serious heart disease.[20]

As investigators dug into the post- and pre-launch data, they discovered irregularities with the selection and reporting of clinical trial results that were used to gain FDA approval. It turns out that the Merck team was aware of the fourfold increased risk of acute myocardial infarction (heart disease) caused by Vioxx when compared to the control drug, but attributed this to a supposed protective effect of the control drug naproxen, telling the FDA that the difference in heart attacks was "primarily due to" this assumed protective effect.[21] It seems that Merck knowingly tried to interpret its data in a manner that suited them best. After all of the facts were revealed, the perceived deception permanently damaged Merck's reputation and consumer trust in the brand.

For Merck, the saga didn't end there. Lawsuits began piling up and in 2007, Merck agreed to pay nearly $5 billion to settle thousands of legal challenges.[22]

Knowledge of disastrous medical interventions, like Vioxx, is why medical staff in hospitals want to ensure the safety of any proposed new drugs, procedures, or technologies before they are widely implemented. The problem is, unlike Vioxx that went through FDA approval, in the Epic Sepsis Model (ESM) case, the scientific foundations are somewhat less clear. For example, there were no FDA clinical trials before its launch[23] because it is an AI tool, so no FDA review was needed. There was also no formal system in place to monitor its safety or performance across different sites after the rollout.

(Since the launch of ESM, the FDA has developed decision support software guidelines, which were released in September 2022.[24])

In addition, before launching ESM there was little public research and proof beyond an oral presentation at an American Medical Informatics Association Symposium,[25,26] and a publication in the journal *Critical Care Medicine*.[27] It is also not clear whether ESM was subjected to third-party testing before its initial release.[28] This lack of extensive peer-reviewed, independent assessment meant that clinical staff had good reason to take a measured approach to the tool's adoption.

As with Vioxx, doctors and clinicians faithfully used ESM only to discover in 2021 that the tool seemed less helpful than originally believed, as claimed by an independent study in *JAMA Internal Medicine*.[14]

Epic's earlier claim that their software reduced mortality by one-fifth by more quickly identifying and treating patients in the early stages of sepsis was based on a successful trial period and rollout in 2015 at Lee Health in Fort Myers, Florida.[13] This claim, among others made by Epic, was scrutinized by a team from the University of Michigan in the *JAMA Internal Medicine* article.[14] The authors gathered data on the Epic Sepsis Model from the time period of December 6, 2018, to October 20, 2019, and examined the electronic health records of 38,455 patients at Michigan Medicine (the University of Michigan health system); of whom, 2,552 (6.6%) experienced sepsis. The authors then analyzed the outcomes of interventions with the ESM system.

What they discovered was *not* what was claimed by the Epic team. Instead of the accuracy metrics reported by Epic, the Michigan team discovered that, for their case, the performance of the system was *about 20% lower* than claimed:

> The ESM identified 183 of 2,552 patients with sepsis (7%) who did not receive timely administration of antibiotics, highlighting the low sensitivity of the ESM in comparison with contemporary clinical practice. The ESM also did not identify 1,709 patients with sepsis (67%) despite generating alerts … for 6,971 of all 38,455 hospitalized patients (18%), thus creating a large burden of alert fatigue.[14,29]

This performance meant that "to find patients developing sepsis in the next 4 hours, they would need to evaluate 109 patients to find a single patient with sepsis."[14]

On its own, the accuracy results don't seem to agree with what Epic claimed, and the additional alerts seemed to cause unnecessary work for medical staff. Was Epic about to face a litany of legal proceedings and billions of dollars of losses, like Merck?

To understand the results, we need to compare them to baselines of what hospitals have in place so that we can form a proper opinion. For example, the University of Michigan study compared the ESM tool to contemporary clinical practice (based on timely administration of antibiotics). However, there are many other systems that can be used and may perform differently in the given circumstances, such as the Targeted Real-time Early Warning System (TREWS).[30] The TREWS approach predicts which patients will develop septic shock by training a supervised learning machine learning model on 54 potential features available from measurements in Electronic Health Records (EHRs) and uses this trained model to generate TREWScore risk predictions.

In reviewing the literature, one can find that the TREWS approach has been compared to the ESM model. According to research presented in *Nature Medicine* by a team from John Hopkins University School of Medicine in Baltimore,

> A recent evaluation of the Epic Sepsis Model, one of the most widely deployed sepsis early warning systems, found that only 12% of alerts occurred on sepsis patients and only 33% of sepsis cases were flagged by the system. In contrast to these three studies, our companion paper found that 82% of sepsis cases were flagged by the TREWS alerts and 38% of alerts with an evaluation were confirmed by a provider.[30]

Compared with TREWS, ESM was flagging almost **50% *fewer* real sepsis *patients and was less specific about the patients it identified* (i.e., many of the flagged cases were not in fact sepsis cases). Assuming doctors have been able to convince hospitals to replace their current systems with Epic's ESM (which we'll see later is likely the case), with 10 million lives to be saved, instead of being made aware of 8 million of them, we'd only be on top of approximately 3.3 million, *leading to over 4.7 million more cases like Jenny's that escalate without an early intervention*. Based on this data, it is very likely not a good outcome.

False alerts, also prevalent in Jenny's case, are not quite as big of an issue as missed interventions; however, alert fatigue is known to lead to delayed treatment and patient harm, and an article from the Canadian Medical Association Journal cites a report indicating there were 566 alarm-related deaths between 2005 and 2008.[31] In Jenny's case, this means that limited resources would be unnecessarily wasted preparing a patient for sepsis treatment, leading to medical staff missing a *real alarm* because they were attending to too many false alarms, causing further fatalities.

Independent investigations conducted by the medical news outlet STAT also found that Epic has been paying hospitals *up to $1 million* as part of their honor roll program to encourage the adoption of predictive algorithms.[9] While it sounds as though Epic is supporting a good cause, this program could certainly create a conflict of interest.

The *JAMA Internal Medicine* article, along with the many follow-up opinion pieces and investigations, led to so much negative attention for the Epic team that the White House even cited issues with the system in its Blueprint for an AI Bill of Rights stating:

> A proprietary model was developed to predict the likelihood of sepsis in hospitalized patients and was implemented at hundreds of hospitals around the country. An independent study showed that the model predictions underperformed relative to the designer's claims while also causing 'alert fatigue' by falsely alerting likelihood of sepsis.[32]

In spite of the above, many hospitals still use Epic's Sepsis Model, but why? Shouldn't hospitals be dropping the tool in light of the independent research? Shouldn't there be a general rejection given what we've learned? Or is it not that simple?

Beyond the Clickbait: When Headlines Just Scratch the Surface

As you would expect, the situation is not as clear as a single peer-reviewed article and the ensuing media coverage would have us believe.

When we started looking into the details, we found that just following the negative publicity led to superficial and likely incorrect conclusions. So we didn't just do that. We used our analytical backgrounds to examine the reasons in detail and, in our opinion, the causes for the initially unclear results are not due to incompetence, profiteering, or other motives often ascribed to Epic.

For example, Epic countered the findings in the news coverage, noting that the researchers in the JAMA publication did not calibrate the model for their specific patient population and data, defined sepsis differently than Epic's model, and failed to acknowledge that two articles assessing the product's performance had previously been published.[28,33]

Additionally, other issues can arise that cause implementation challenges and make it difficult to compare new findings with Epic's original results. A report by STAT[34] showed how *data drift* can cause a significant drop in performance, caused by changing the so-called "coding of illnesses"—classifying illnesses into predefined buckets, which assists with things such as hospital funding—which is exactly what happened after Epic's development period. In 2015, many new specific codes were introduced, but if a user was to run the model ignoring the new codes, the original performance claimed by Epic would likely remain, as was discovered in the independent study by STAT.[28]

Other issues, such as the change in internal processes (e.g., if and when microbiology tests are ordered), could also have a negative impact on the algorithm's performance because it seems that one of the critical inputs to the model was the result of a microbiology test.

These points seem to be valid.

Another STAT report stated that, of the hospitals they spoke with and also for publications other than *JAMA*, hospitals did report a *benefit* for patients after fine-tuning the ESM model. Most importantly, none of the health systems that found flaws in Epic's sepsis algorithm reported that its use resulted in harm to patients. In fact, some hospitals said they generated positive results after customizing the tool and limiting its use to certain circumstances.[34]

As far as the $1 million payment to encourage hospitals to use the Epic algorithm, although it does seem to create a potential conflict of interest, when we look at the details, we see that this conclusion may not be so clear. Epic states, "its incentives are designed to reward implementation of technologies—whether developed by Epic or another company—that can improve patient care."[35] Financial inducements tied to pharmaceutical prescriptions and other interventions are common in healthcare, so Epic following this practice is not an indictment of the algorithm. To qualify for the payment, hospitals must adopt an early-warning algorithm for sepsis, whether a homegrown model or one from a third-party developer. In this light, it does not seem like such a bad incentive program, especially if the outcome is better decisions, regardless of which system is used.

Since launching, ESM has gone through many updates, and the 2022 version corrects several problems: Epic now recommends that its model be trained on a hospital's own data prior to clinical use.[28] Epic also mentions re-engineering the algorithm and changing the data inputs (e.g., significantly reducing the number of variables used to predict danger), adjusting the definition of sepsis onset and its guidance for tuning the algorithm to local patients.[34]

Soon after the *JAMA* article was published, Emily Barey came out with a statement highlighting the article published in the peer-reviewed journal *Critical Care Medicine*. The researchers from Prisma Health in South Carolina found a 4.3% reduction in deaths when comparing outcomes of septic patients before and after the implementation of Epic's algorithm. Therefore, although, theoretically, false alerts and missed cases do occur, practically, lives like Jenny's are being saved, contrary to what we thought earlier.

Barey further stated: "MetroHealth found they were able to deliver antibiotics to their septic patients in the emergency department almost an hour faster and those patients had a shorter length of stay and lived longer."[36]

On the surface, this is great news, but how do we balance it with the false alerts? According to Barey, "Our own analysis found our model not only was more sensitive to identifying positive septic patients, but also alerted for 27% fewer patients when compared with common sepsis scoring methods, like SIRS."[36]

These claims do not contradict the work done by the *JAMA* team, instead, it shows the complexity of using data science tools.

We can see that based on the differing data inputs and population characteristics, and the definition of sepsis and other in-field details, the performance of the algorithm changed. Hardly a surprising result. Epic also compared its algorithm to other methods such as SIRS[36] (thereby ensuring a fair baseline):

> UCHealth in Colorado found something similar. Their implementation of the Epic model had 19% fewer alerts in comparison to the Modified Early Warning Score. This is good news for clinicians. That's a lot less noise in sepsis alerts.

So what should hospitals do? Not all hospitals use ESM, and for those who use a system with a performance worse than the Epic Sepsis Model, the performance gains would be beneficial. If a hospital isn't using TREWS, or even if a hospital is using TREWS but isn't achieving the same results as John Hopkins University, then the Epic system may be beneficial.

Where do these conflicting reports of positive and negative results and new versions of the model leave us? Can we trust the new version? What does this story tell us about AI projects in general?

Data-Driven Projects Are Complex

The sepsis early warning detection story is an example of ADSAI, which when deployed does not lead to a clear-cut win for the algorithm. This is common because ADSAI projects are complex.

After properly looking at the numerous articles covering Epic's sepsis model, we could see that many factors were at play causing the later challenges in the algorithm's usage—data quality, varying definitions, and more. In this case, the outside observer caught a glimpse of the challenges faced by a model in production due to its exposure to the world outside of the company walls. However, the *real problem* is not what the public sees (like with Epic), it's what's going on behind company walls when it comes to data-driven projects.

If the real-world part of the commercialization process (business-as-usual usage after model deployment) seems difficult, then the part most people don't see is, by some estimates, creating four times more mayhem.[15] If, as a reader, you feel that Epic's Sepsis Model is complicated and difficult to get right in real life, then imagine things being *four times more difficult*—you are now experiencing what data scientists in many companies face today.

This is a much greater problem than the alert fatigue created by a sepsis alert system. This is the misallocation of resources, time, and money leading to much greater loss of life and opportunity on a grand scale. For all the

ADSAI systems that stagger out of the gate into the blinding light of reality, *four more never make it.*

This is an enormous amount of wasted effort.

In our experience, the cost of developing a robust ADSAI system depends on the scope of the problem and the scale of the company, but a *properly developed system* typically requires an investment of between US$200,000 and up to $50 million (some of the systems we feature here cost 10 times more than the upper estimate to develop). If for each successful project, four more are wasted, then we are looking at from US$800,000 to $200 million wasted *per successful project*—this is the critical problem that we need to address immediately.

To understand the scale of how much financial waste will occur across the globe in the immediate future if we do nothing, let's look at an estimate of the AI investment figures predicted by the year 2030, produced by leading research organization Statista:

> [A]ccording to Next Move Strategy Consulting, the market for Artificial Intelligence (AI) is expected to show strong growth in the coming decade. Its value of nearly 100 billion US dollars in 2021 is expected to grow twenty fold by 2030, up to nearly two trillion US dollars.[37,38]

If 80% of this is financial waste, it is a monumental misinvestment of our limited resources. We must do something. Now.

If we end up wasting more than $1 trillion on ADSAI project failures, it will not only waste an incredible sum of money, but it will also adversely affect people's attitudes toward one of the most powerful approaches to assisting decision-making: the data- and model-driven approach! People will lose confidence in ADSAI, and society will split into two parts: The smaller group of successful analytics advocates and the vast majority who have been burned by a poorly executed data science project, never again to believe in this decision-making approach.

To help turn the majority into believers and prevent more project failures, this book will reveal the complex and more subtle underlying problems that keep ADSAI teams working hard day and night trying to develop innovative products to solve major challenges, like sepsis. That said, we promise not to throw you into a trough of despair with the realization that you are more likely to fail than succeed. This book is going to temper the hype and provide you with a realistic view of the challenges data scientists and companies face. We will take you to the front lines with detailed descriptions, leaving you in a situation with much more accurate expectations and in a much better position to make a decision about that next ADSAI project.

The stories that you'll read here are rarely told, nor can they be told by many people. We are often sold the hype and promise of AI without knowing how extremely difficult and challenging it really is to create and deploy an ADSAI system. How complex is it?

To give you an idea, if you've ever done a small-scale pilot to test an AI idea (which many, many companies have), for the managers who think they can easily roll out their pilot project, from a cost perspective the production system can be up to *100 times more costly* than the pilot. A study published in *Sloan Management Review* reported that[41], "A good rule of thumb is that you should estimate that for every $1 you spend developing an algorithm, you must spend $100 to deploy and support it." We'll dig deeper into this later.

Begin Your Journey to Outsmart Failure

Join us as we explore the primary types of failures that arise in ADSAI projects. As a part of this journey, we will share with you something you won't get anywhere else: *Our personal insider stories* that only we can describe, giving you insights into what is so very difficult and challenging about ADSAI projects. Stories of rushed attempts at doomed projects, corporate politics, the blind leading the blind, and wishful thinking, leading to some of the most wasteful uses of resources and money. You'll be privy to things that are not typically written about in books on ADSAI. We'll tell you the behind-the-scenes details that few people ever find out, and we'll help you learn in one of the most effective ways possible—*from the failures of others*. They've failed so you don't have to.

It is important to note that these issues and failures target ADSAI projects. The categorizations of project failures from an IT, project management, or other perspective have been wonderfully covered in many other books such as *Project Recovery* by Harold Kerzner.[39] We are focused on the excitingly hyped world of analytics, data science, and artificial intelligence.

To make the journey more comprehensible, we will use a common framework aligned with the *People, Process, Technology (PPT)* framework[40] to group the themes encountered by our peers into an easier to understand and easily recognized set of topics.

We see the majority of failures arising because some companies lack experience and knowledge and quickly buy into the ADSAI hype, so we begin by addressing that part of the problem: The first section of the book focuses on the challenges faced by analytically immature organizations. We then group the themes according to the PPT framework, with the addition of the strategy rubric to begin the analysis:

1. Strategy
2. Process
3. People
4. Technology

Within each of these sections, we analyze the main themes discovered from our research and personal experience.

In the final section of the book, we turn our attention to the more analytically mature companies that, as we will estimate later, are probably failing only half as much as the analytically immature organizations. But even analytically mature companies are also likely failing at an unacceptably high rate, and there are always new projects with new challenges that have caused very skilled practitioners before us to fail. We can learn from these, no matter our level of expertise.

Throughout the book, we use the terms analytics, data science, and AI (ADSAI) interchangeably even though we know that this is not strictly correct. It will allow for a smoother presentation of the ideas, and, in any case, many projects combine all three in their development.

Everyone loves to brag about a big success, so you will see that in many of the books we reviewed, the identities of successful companies are named without hesitation. Unfortunately, because of the nature of failure and companies being less than happy to lend their names to a failure (even if it does help others learn and become more successful), we are largely unable to share the names of the organizations featured in our tales. So, we will invent names of people and companies where required, but our hope is that companies will recognize that once a failure has happened, then it has happened—it is visible on the balance sheet, cash flow statement, or somewhere else. There is no denying it, and ideally, we should be able to talk about and learn from it. We hope in the future, companies will be more willing to share their failed attempts at ADSAI so we can all learn more. As Kerzner states in his book:

> When a project is completed successfully, we go through excruciating pain to capture best practices and lessons learned. Everyone wants to broadcast to the world what they did well on the project to achieve success. But the same is not true for project failures. For personal reasons, people are reluctant to discuss failures even though more best practices can be learned from failures than from successes. People fear that failures may be used against them during performance reviews.[39]

Failure is feedback. Failure is not something shameful, it is something from which to learn and grow.

By presenting these stories and learning from our failures, we think we will be able to soften the ADSAI hype and reveal the full breadth of skill required to use these methods, techniques, and technologies in a way that will help you succeed. As Emily Barey from Epic said[36]: "I think it is important to underscore that this was people, process and technology working in concert. The Epic early warning system was only the first step."

When companies recognize this complexity and avoid the hype, the results can be amazing. Barey continues: "MetroHealth's team-based workflow was effective enough that the trial ended early, and the flags were turned on for all patients presenting to the ED."

Critical Thinking: How Not to Fail

At the end of each chapter, instead of simply stating what the main points to think about are, we will raise them as questions to enable you to ask these same types of questions in your organization and hopefully apply the lessons learned. Here are some questions based on this Introduction:

- If analytics projects are data-driven, then why aren't answers simply and objectively right or wrong? How did the Epic Sepsis Model case reveal that it isn't clearly one or the other? So, what role do such models really have in the end-to-end decision-making process?
- When rolling out a new ADSAI tool, what lessons can we learn from Epic's challenges?
- Why can't we just focus on successes and ignore the failures when trying to decide what leads to analytical success for organizations?
- Why do you think ADSAI projects are more complex than pure IT projects?
- What is the advantage of using a framework like PPT (+ Strategy) to frame our findings? Why not just create something new?
- Why do you think people are so reluctant to discuss the lessons arising from failures rather than from successes? What can we do to change that?
- Why do you think learning from failures could be more impactful than learning from successes? What about analytics projects makes learning from failures particularly important?

Notes

1. Stearns-Kurosawa, D. J., Osuchowski, M. F., Valentine, C., Kurosawa, S., & Remick, D. G. (2011). The pathogenesis of sepsis. *Annual Review of Pathology-mechanisms of Disease*, 6(1), 19–48. https://doi.org/10.1146/annurev-pathol-011110-130327.
2. Wikipedia contributors. (2024, February 18). *Sepsis*. Wikipedia. https://en.wikipedia.org/wiki/Sepsis.

There are a variety of results on the mortality rate caused by sepsis. For example, Wikipedia states a number of published results, such as "Sepsis will prove fatal in approximately 24.4% of people, and septic shock will prove fatal in 34.7% of people within 30 days (32.2% and 38.5% after 90 days)." It also states: "The risk of death from sepsis is as high as 30%, while for severe sepsis it is as high as 50%, and septic shock 80%. Sepsis affected about 49 million people in 2017, with 11 million deaths (1 in 5 deaths worldwide)."

3. Richardson, L. (2021, December 16). Artificial intelligence can improve health care—but not without human oversight. *The Pew Charitable Trusts*. https:// www.pewtrusts.org/en/research-and-analysis/articles/2021/12/16/artificial-intelligence-can-improve-health-care-but-not-without-human-oversight.

4. Kovalenko, P. (2023, September 6). Epic vs Cerner: EMR / EHR Comparison Guide. *Langate*. https://langate.com/epic-vs-cerner-emr-ehr-comparison-guide.

5. Moukheiber, Z. (2012, April 18). Epic Systems' tough billionaire. *Forbes*. https:// www.forbes.com/sites/zinamoukheiber/2012/04/18/epic-systems-tough-billionaire/.

6. IBISWorld—industry market research, reports, and statistics. (n.d.). https:// www.ibisworld.com/us/company/epic-systems-corporation/406798/.

7. Dyrda, L. (2022, July). Epic's revenue up 13% in 2021, hit $3.8B. *Beckers Hospital Review*. https://www.beckershospitalreview.com/ehrs/epic-s-revenue-up-13-in-2021-hit-3-8b.html.

8. Nuance and Epic Join Forces on Artificial Intelligence to Revolutionize Disabled Veterans Accessibility to Health IT (2017, February 21). *Businesswire*. https:// www.businesswire.com/news/home/20170221005625/en/Nuance-and-Epic-Join-Forces-on-Artificial-Intelligence-to-Revolutionize-Disabled-Veterans-Accessibility-to-Health-IT.

9. Ross, C. (2021, July 26). Epic's AI algorithms, shielded from scrutiny by a corporate firewall, are delivering inaccurate information on seriously ill patients. *STAT*. https://www.statnews.com/2021/07/26/epic-hospital-algorithms-sepsis-investigation/.

10. Ochsner and Epic use machine learning to prevent adverse events. (2018, June 4). Epic. https://www.epic.com/epic/post/ochsner-epic-team-machine-learning.

11. Murray, S. G., Wachter, R. M., & Cucina, R. J. (2020, January 31). Discrimination by Artificial intelligence in a Commercial Electronic Health Record—A Case Study. *Forefront*. Health Affairs. https://doi.org/10.1377/forefront.20200128.626576.

12. Ross, C. (2021, September 27). Epic's sepsis algorithm is going off the rails in the real world. The use of these variables may explain why. *STAT*. https://www.statnews.com/2021/09/27/epic-sepsis-algorithm-antibiotics-model/.

13. Reducing Sepsis Mortality by One-Fifth with Epic. (2019, March 18). Epic. https://www.epic.com/epic/post/reducing-sepsis-mortality-epic.

14. Wong, A., Ötleş, E., Donnelly, J. P., Krumm, A. E., McCullough, J. S., DeTroyer-Cooley, O., Pestrue, J., Phillips, M., Konye, J., Penoza, C., Ghous, M., & Singh, K. (2021). External validation of a widely implemented proprietary sepsis prediction model in hospitalized patients. *JAMA Internal Medicine, 81*(8), 1065-1070. https://doi.org/10.1001/jamainternmed.2021.2626.

15. O'Neill, B. T. (2019, July 23). Failure rates for analytics, AI, and big data projects = 85% – yikes! *Designing for Analytics*. https://designingforanalytics.com/resources/failure-rates-for-analytics-bi-iot-and-big-data-projects-85-yikes/.

16. KC, D., Staats, B. R., & Gino, F. (2013). Learning from My Success and from Others' Failure: Evidence from Minimally Invasive Cardiac Surgery. *Management Science, 59*(11), 2435–2449. https://doi.org/10.1287/mnsc.2013.1720.

17. Dahlin, K. B., Chuang, Y., & Roulet, T. J. (2018). Opportunity, Motivation, and Ability to Learn from Failures and Errors: Review, Synthesis, and Ways to Move Forward. *The Academy of Management Annals, 12*(1), 252–277. https://doi.org/10.5465/annals.2016.0049.

18. Wikipedia contributors. (2024, February 2). *Rofecoxib*. Wikipedia. https://en.wikipedia.org/wiki/Rofecoxib.

19. Reuters. (2006, December 7). Merck sees slightly higher 2007 earnings. *The New York Times*. https://www.nytimes.com/2006/12/07/business/07drug.html.

20. Bhattacharya, S. (2005, January 25). Up to 140,000 heart attacks linked to Vioxx. *New Scientist*. https://www.newscientist.com/article/dn6918-up-to-140000-heart-attacks-linked-to-vioxx/.

21. *Wayback machine*. (n.d.). https://web.archive.org/web/20150324043011/http://www.fda.gov/ohrms/dockets/ac/01/briefing/3677b2_06_cardio.pdf.

22. Vioxx: The downfall of a drug. (2007, November 12). NPR. https://www.npr.org/series/5033105/vioxx-the-downfall-of-a-drug.

23. Richardson, L. (2021, December 16). Artificial intelligence can improve healthcare—but not without human oversight. *The Pew Charitable Trusts*. https://www.pewtrusts.org/en/research-and-analysis/articles/2021/12/16/artificial-intelligence-can-improve-health-care-but-not-without-human-oversight.

24. Center for Devices and Radiological Health. (2022, September 28). *Clinical Decision support software*. U.S. Food and Drug Administration. https://www.fda.gov/regulatory-information/search-fda-guidance-documents/clinical-decision-support-software.

25. *Curriculum vitae*. Bennett, T. (2021, April 14) https://som.cuanschutz.edu/FIMS/Content/faculty/22381/TBennett_CV_modular_external.pdf.

26. Bennett, T. D., Russell, S., King, J., Schilling, L., Voong, C., Rogers, N., Adrian, B., Bruce, N., & Ghosh, D. (2019). Accuracy of the Epic Sepsis Prediction Model in a Regional Health System. *arXiv*. https://arxiv.org/pdf/1902.07276.pdf.

27. Cull, J. D., Blackhurst, D., Kothari, S. N., Pellizzeri, K., Spoor, K., Manning, B., & Brevetta, R. (2021). 1235: Validating the EPIC Sepsis Inpatient Predictive Analytic Tool as a Sepsis alert system. *Critical Care Medicine, 49*(1), 621. https://doi.org/10.1097/01.ccm.0000730828.10165.13.

28. Ross, C. (2022, October 24). Epic's overhaul of a flawed algorithm shows why AI oversight is a life-or-death issue. *STAT*. https://www.statnews.com/2022/10/24/epic-overhaul-of-a-flawed-algorithm/.

29. Muoio, D. (2021, June 22). Epic's widely used sepsis prediction model falls short among Michigan Medicine patients. *Fierce Healthcare*. https://www.fiercehealthcare.com/tech/epic-s-widely-used-sepsis-prediction-model-falls-short-among-michigan-medicine-patients.

30. Adams, R. J., Henry, K., Sridharan, A., Soleimani, H., Zhan, A., Rawat, N., Johnson, L., Hager, D. N., Cosgrove, S. E., Markowski, A., Klein, E., Chen, E. S., Saheed, M., Henley, M., Miranda, S., Houston, K., Linton, R. C., Ahluwalia, A. R., Wu, A. W., & Saria, S. (2022). Prospective, multi-site study of patient outcomes after implementation of the TREWS machine learning-based early warning system for sepsis. *Nature Medicine, 28*(7), 1455-1460. https://doi.org/10.1038/s41591-022-01894-0.

31. Jones, K. (2014). Alarm fatigue a top patient safety hazard. *Canadian Medical Association Journal*, *186*(3), 178. https://doi.org/10.1503/cmaj.109-4696.
32. Blueprint for an AI Bill of Rights: Making Automated Systems Work for the American People. (2022, October). The White House. https://www.whitehouse.gov/wp-content/uploads/2022/10/Blueprint-for-an-AI-Bill-of-Rights.pdf.
33. The JAMA article (14 above) states: "only limited information is publicly available about the model's performance, and no independent validations have been published to date, to our knowledge."
34. Ross, C. (2022, February 28). AI gone astray: How subtle shifts in patient data send popular algorithms reeling, undermining patient safety. *STAT*. https://www.statnews.com/2022/02/28/sepsis-hospital-algorithms-data-shift/.
35. Rindisbacher, S. (2021, August 26). Epic Systems' AI algorithms scrutinized; concerns highlight need for health tech whistleblowers. *Phillips & Cohen*. https://www.phillipsandcohen.com/epic-systems-ai-algorithms-scrutinized-concerns-highlight-need-for-health-tech-whistleblowers/.
36. Siwicki, B. (2021, September 14). Epic's director of nursing discusses new research on its sepsis early. *Healthcare IT News*. https://www.healthcareitnews.com/news/epics-director-nursing-discusses-new-research-its-sepsis-early-warning-model.
37. Thormundsson, B. (2023, October 6). Artificial intelligence (AI) market size worldwide in 2021 with a forecast until 2030. *Statista*. https://www.statista.com/statistics/1365145/artificial-intelligence-market-size/.
38. Next Move Strategy Consulting (NMSC). (2023, January 1). Artificial Intelligence Market Size and Share | Analysis - 2030. Next Move Strategy Consulting. https://www.nextmsc.com/report/artificial-intelligence-market.
39. Kerzner, H. (2014). *Project Recovery: Case Studies and Techniques for Overcoming Project Failure*. John Wiley & Sons.
40. Morgan, J. M., & Liker, J. K. (2006). *The Toyota Product Development System: Integrating People, Process, and Technology* (1st ed.). CRC Press. http://ci.nii.ac.jp/ncid/BA78367969.
41. Massachusetts Institute of Technology. (2020, September 28). *Getting serious about data and data science | MIT Sloan Management Review*. MIT Sloan Management Review. https://sloanreview.mit.edu/article/getting-serious-about-data-and-data-science.

1

Analytically Immature Organizations

A top 200 company on any major stock exchange should not be one that gets caught up by a well understood and repeatedly solved analytics challenge. However, this is precisely what happened to an enterprise when a team of external accounting consultants thought their familiarity with numbers gave them an automatic ability to run an analytics project like pros. The sad part was that the outcome delivered was anything but professional.

Our story began when a large retail chemical manufacturing conglomerate, that we'll call ChemCo, engaged a local accounting company with a small analytics team to create a holistic supply chain model to provide detailed costs for all items in their warehouse. The impetus for the engagement was to review the whole process—from sourcing to warehouse management—through an analytics lens. This would allow ChemCo to take a product all the way to the retail shelf and calculate the profit margin based on the full cost of handling and delivery. The vision was then to apply an optimization engine to the whole process and use this AI tool to optimize the cost of their supply chain.

In most instances, the self-belief of the consultants in their ability to solve this problem would not be enough to sign off on starting the project. A partner in the local accounting firm must approve projects in the interest of protecting key relationships. However, in this case, a senior manager successfully convinced the supply chain partner to take on the ChemCo project. The partner was likely unable to properly judge the project due to lack of experience with data-driven decision-making, and the senior manager was supremely confident that they could optimize the whole process.

The basis of this confidence was a number of LinkedIn videos about how to carry out such an optimization project. Given how easy the videos made it look, the senior manager guaranteed that the engine would run in real time, and by doing so, oversold the ease of solving the problem as well as its final functionality. The partner could see a tool like this being a win for their relationship with the client. After the project was sold to ChemCo, the client demonstrated the only wisdom in this story by requesting a proof of concept for one of the product warehouses before the accounting team could roll it out company-wide.

The accountants began creating a model to identify all touch points in the supply chain and to analyze the delivery, pick, and place of each item, using this information to accurately estimate the true, full cost of the product. If the

DOI: 10.1201/9781032661360-2

cost of any of these steps were to change, they could re-calculate this part and then re-optimize the delivery pathway to the store shelf. If no other path was better, this information could be used to re-price an item on a shelf to maintain a desired margin.

To build the proof of concept, three months of data was collected from one of the small warehouses, which nonetheless amounted to millions of rows of data. ChemCo managed their company's data on SQL databases and the audit team's lack of experience led them to believe they could use SQL scripts to run the whole optimization solution. So they jumped right in and began exporting data in CSV files from ChemCo's database, then uploading them to an SQL database in their own environment to begin developing and testing code.

The local LinkedIn-trained "expert" wrote a couple thousand lines of code to price 10 of the products in the warehouse. Although inexperienced, the coder was able to complete this ahead of schedule, which unfortunately significantly boosted his confidence. Upon later review, it was discovered that our newly minted data scientist had copied and pasted the code each time and simply changed the name of the product in the copied chunk of software, resulting in a few hundred buggy lines of code per product. Not only was the copy-and-paste methodology a grand software engineering mistake, but the suspicious simplicity of the system also meant that either this auditor was a genius and figured out an incredibly smart solution, or (more likely) was incredibly mistaken.

At this point, a glimmer of hope emerged, and before they deployed the copy-paste code confetti, someone within the accounting business decided that these algorithms should be reviewed and it was passed to a senior analyst. Unfortunately, the only "senior" part about this individual was his title (the food chain in this organization is graduate, analyst, senior analyst, assistant manager, manager, senior manager, director). A more capable organization would have known to ask someone more senior than the "senior" analyst, with enough experience to make a proper judgment. Of course, the senior analyst didn't pick up any issues with the code and approved it, extinguishing the moment of hope and bounding toward the point of no return. The fact that ChemCo lacked both a testing and development environment didn't concern the accounting experts, resulting in the program being sent for implementation into a production environment with no tests whatsoever—a trojan horse with a ticking code bomb.

The algorithms were designed to pick up all the live, current data from the central database, review for a particular time range, and optimize that operating period. However, the time range of analysis was not entered (someone forgot) and although the intention was to use this program for three months of data (a few million rows), it would end up pulling out hundreds of millions of rows of data for the more than a decade of data stored in the database. Trying to extract this from the database would cause a company-wide meltdown; this central storage is used for everything. Hitting "run" on the software would kill everything by overloading the database with queries, taking down the point of sale (i.e., scanners in the stores), finance, and anything relying on real-time data.

If this code bomb were to go off, it would also bring down the entire production system of ChemCo. They would no longer be able to look up prices. People working with chemicals would end up not knowing the chemical properties of their inputs and could inadvertently *kill someone* trying to work around this technical glitch. The impact on ChemCo's reputation would be disastrous and likely cause their stock price to enter free fall. There was *one* chance to fix it, before our consultants' hubris wiped out 1,000 times more value than their little proof of concept was worth.

The AI Hype

In February 2023, the US Federal Trade Commission (FTC) issued a stark warning to companies slapping the AI label on everything they sell to try and increase sales and ride the AI hype train. Entitled "Keep Your AI Claims in Check," the blog post[1] warned organizations about exaggerating the abilities of their AI systems or using the term AI to describe their offering when it is not present. The FTC saw that the AI hype was spiraling out of control and told companies to check themselves.

It would be valuable for many consultants to heed this admonishment, such as those working with ChemCo, who bought into the hype and underestimated the challenges of delivering a quality analytical tool. Ignoring the FTC's advice must happen regularly because, as we wrote in the introduction, 80% of analytics projects face a situation of failure, and the audit team for ChemCo was certainly in that 80%.

As we will see later, this trend has been around for decades and doesn't seem to be improving. The question is, in spite of all the frameworks and the well-trained and highly paid nature of the audit team, why do so many data science projects keep failing? The answer to this question revolves around the challenges faced by analytically immature organizations.

To help us understand why so many ADSAI projects fail, we want to briefly return to the Epic Sepsis Model (ESM) and ask ourselves the question: What separated the early adopters of ESM from those who decided to wait? This will help us understand why some companies rush headlong into analytics projects, lacking experience and knowledge, and others hold back, fully understanding that there may be challenges ahead.

There is very likely a variety of reasons for the differential rate of adoption (some good, some bad), but for the ESM system and the hospitals who chose not to utilize it, the diagnostic results probably weren't clear enough. The system obviously needed more iterations, warning labels, and better clarification of appropriate use, which were introduced later.

Both co-authors have worked in organizations trying to commercialize analytics technology, and we clearly understand the difficult balance for an entity like Epic that is trying to achieve both a business and clinical outcome. They need to get the product out the door (not just to make money but to gather critical customer feedback) and simultaneously make a decision about their confidence in the tool.

Many companies face similar challenges, like the ChemCo audit team that was trying to profitably deliver a project and ultimately would realize that it was much harder to do than it appeared in the LinkedIn videos. Although there seemed to be initial benefits to using the Epic Sepsis Model, and caution was still warranted, the early-adopter hospitals may have been simply attracted to the AI hype due to lack of experience and knowledge, much like the ChemCo audit team.

However, the issue isn't just companies excited by AI and jumping onto the bandwagon—it is often a two-way street in the world of analytics. Epic's team likely recognized the business value of the AI hype and wanted to capitalize on it but fell victim to some of the common failures plaguing data science projects. We'll delve into a few of these issues here, continuing our medicine theme to give you a flavor of what is to come later. It will become clear that all of these examples apply to most other applications of AI as well.

Building on the Epic case study, one reason their medical application struggled was the data challenges of training a more robust model based on a rigorous, broad-based experimental design. Such a design would embody a much more representative and diverse patient group, or achieve something similar by training on a hospital's own patient database to account for demographic differences (as was suggested by Epic after the criticism, we'll also discover the importance of this later). Epic's experience in healthcare would have given the company a better understanding of the environment in which it operates than most and it still struggled, so what about the hundreds of AI startups trying to disrupt healthcare? Their data-driven algorithms are only as smart as the designers who build them. If those people are not experts in medicine, how good can their models truly be?

Although neurosurgeons may not understand the details of how an AI algorithm works, they do learn the nuances of brains, which allows them to provide a holistic perspective on the health of an individual's gray matter. The problem with AI used in scenarios of interest to neurosurgeons is that many classification algorithms are only trained to recognize things like tumor or no tumor, healthy or unhealthy. The AI then needs to classify a brain scan into one of these buckets, even if the classification makes no sense.

For example, the world-renowned AI company based in San Francisco, OpenAI (the developers of ChatGPT), created a pioneering research tool that combined natural language processing (NLP) and image classification, calling it Contrastive Language–Image Pre-training or CLIP.[2] Given an image, it can help predict which text is most likely to belong to the image.

For example, for a histology image of a piece of brain tissue between glass slides, we can discover which text is most likely to belong to the image (e.g., healthy brain tissue or cancerous brain tissue). The CLIP homepage once showed a scan of a brain and the labels "healthy brain" and "brain with tumor" (when checking at the time of writing, the homepage showed other types of correctly classified medical image scans). Its goal is to demonstrate its impressive accuracy after training on a set of brain images using a neural network. However, because this is all the algorithm knows, its impressive performance turned into dismay when the algorithm was used with pictures of wagons and it was 76% sure that the white wagon was a healthy brain and 80% sure the red wagon was also a healthy brain.[3]

We're certain OpenAI was aware of this and its proof of concept never laid claim to correctly identifying unintended inputs. However, exciting headlines produced by proofs of concept, like CLIP, can lead nonclinical research teams to claim that their system will put some clinical professionals out of a job, but then fail to deliver on the hype. This is not a claim made by newcomers who lack knowledge of AI, it is one made by some of the best recognized AI experts in the field who seem to get caught up in the hype.

As the CLIP examples hint, radiology has been under constant threat of mass unemployment by AI. Because of the large repositories of images to train deep learning algorithms, such as ImageNet,[4] tasks that require image classification have been low-hanging fruit for applications of artificial intelligence. In 2016, machine-learning pioneer Geoffrey Hinton unleashed a bold proclamation:

> I think if you work as a radiologist, you are like the coyote that's already over the edge of the cliff but hasn't yet looked down … People should stop training radiologists now. It's just completely obvious within five years deep learning is going to do better than radiologists…. It might be 10 years, but we've got plenty of radiologists already.[5]

So, how has AI-powered medicine advanced since Hinton's prediction nearly a decade ago?

At the University of Alabama in Birmingham (UAB) and other academic medical centers,[5] the radiology faculty now uses AI-enhanced tools as a routine part of care. Computer-aided detection and triage software have the *potential* to reduce turnaround time by automatically highlighting positive findings within images (e.g., Qure.ai[6]). Natural language processing tools, trained on millions of radiologists' reports, can generate written conclusions based on these notes.

It seems that AI-based radiology tools are being used, but does this mean we should stop training radiologists, as Hinton claimed? We really don't think that is such a great idea.

By looking at the world through only a technological lens and enjoying the hype it creates, we miss everything else that can cause AI overexcitement to miss the mark. For example, although these AI healthcare tools are being implemented, there is in fact a global radiologist shortage,[7] driven in part by worker burnout. Jordan Perchik, MD, a fellow in the Department of Radiology at the UAB Heersink School of Medicine, said in a publication on the university's website that: "The amount of imaging is going up 5 percent per year, and we're not training 5 percent more radiologists per year."[5] Given other continuing challenges in radiology departments (such as budget cuts), we don't see AI filling this gap.

In fact, in medicine, the situation can be quite counterintuitive, as the co-authors have experienced themselves. One of the co-authors developed the first-ever operating theater scheduling optimization tool to be implemented in a hospital (although research papers on a similar tool had been produced and proof of concepts tried, this tool was actually implemented). This tool promised to increase efficiencies by optimally allocating patients to limited theater slots, leading to greater throughput. But what did this mean for public hospitals? Increased costs, because they would now be processing more patients in less time. Dr. Perchik confirms this in radiology: "The most commonly used AI tools are ones that speed up scans, paradoxically increasing the workload for radiologists."

The AI hype cycle in radiology has quieted somewhat, as the dramatic results from early proof-of-concept (POC) studies have failed to pan out in real-world settings as initially predicted by AI leaders such as Hinton. Data science tools might be good at telling you whether a brain looks healthy if you show it an image of a brain (or even a red wagon), but after playing around with such algorithms, doctors often quickly discover that image recognition algorithms can be brittle and inconsistent. This is a well-known problem in deep learning.[8]

In addition, taking into account existing workflows, which may not easily accommodate AI software and therefore lead to an efficiency loss, it is no surprise that only around 30% of radiologists reported using any type of AI in 2020.[3,9] This trend is expected to continue despite the fact that as of early November 2022, there were 200 FDA-approved radiology AI algorithms ready for use.[5]

One reason for this slow uptake could be poor performance. Only 5.7% of the surveyed radiologists reported that AI always works, whereas 94% reported inconsistent performance.[3] This augurs a very different evolution to Hinton's claim.

AI's inconsistent performance is confirmed by other experts in both radiology and across healthcare. In a recent interview, AI guru and Coursera founder Andrew Ng said, "Those of us in machine learning are really good at doing well on a test set, but unfortunately deploying a system takes more than doing well on a test set."[10] He continued,

> We collect data from Stanford Hospital, then we train and test on data from the same hospital, indeed, we can publish papers showing [AI systems] are comparable to human radiologists in spotting certain conditions. It turns out [if] you take that same model, that same AI system, to an older hospital down the street, with an older machine, and the technician uses a slightly different imaging protocol, that data drifts to cause the performance of [the] AI system to degrade significantly. In contrast, any human radiologist can walk down the street to the older hospital and do just fine. So even though at a moment in time, on a specific data set, we can show this works, the clinical reality is that these models still need a lot of work to reach production....All of AI, not just health care, has a proof-of-concept-to-production gap.

This gap is redolent of the issues faced by Epic.

The American College of Radiology concurred with Ng: "A large majority of the FDA-cleared algorithms have not been validated across a large number of sites, raising the possibility that patient and equipment bias could lead to the inconsistent performance."[3]

But radiology is not alone with its challenges. Another healthcare example that made headlines was the promise of disrupting the treatment of diabetic retinopathy from the team at Google Health. Similar to Epic's model, this was technology without any form of FDA approval when it was rolled out, so the Google team chose not to launch it in the United States—it was launched in Thailand with high expectations.

The technology behind the invention was developed by Google Health's AI team, who claimed to be able to identify signs of diabetic retinopathy from an eye scan with more than 90% accuracy—the level of a human specialist.[11] Like most image classification systems, in order to ensure accuracy, the deep learning model was trained on high-quality data. The Google team would reject low-quality images; however, in the real world, such quality couldn't be guaranteed. The problem was that in Thailand, nurses would scan dozens of patients every hour potentially in poor lighting conditions, leading to more than one-fifth of all images being rejected by the algorithm, which was trained on only high-quality data.

This led to real-life results that were anything but impressive, or worse, no result at all. The system had to upload images to the cloud for processing and poor internet connections would cause delays. "Patients like the instant results, but the internet is slow," said one nurse. "They've been waiting here since 6 a.m., and for the first two hours we could only screen 10 patients."[12]

More than for any other company, you'd think Andrew Ng's advice would have helped guide the Google team—he worked there for two years within the Google Brain team!

Another famous example of the Proof of concept (POC)-to-production gap was Watson Health, IBM's moonshot to apply AI in healthcare. Watson was supposed to revolutionize everything from diagnosing patients and recommending treatment options to finding candidates for clinical trials.[13] Despite the potential benefits of Watson, healthcare providers were hesitant to adopt the technology. This was due to a number of factors, including the high costs of AI technology, the privacy concerns, and the regulatory hurdles. Watson Health ended up being an example of IBM's marketing machine functioning far more effectively than its AI team. The list of such high-profile AI disasters in medicine goes on and on. These examples clearly contribute to the enormous hype problem surrounding AI in healthcare, setting false expectations and playing down the complexity of the algorithms involved.

What's more, these issues go far beyond healthcare. The AI Incident Database has a growing list of more than 2,000 AI catastrophes that reached the light of day and then failed loudly enough that the press picked up on them.[14]

So why does the deployment, testing, and rollout of so many AI tools seem so complex and fraught with challenges? Why don't we (the co-authors) believe in the sales and marketing pitches of the IBMs of the world? To answer these questions, we turned to thousands of our peers around the world.

Mapping the Terrain: Prior Insights

Both co-authors have experienced their share of successes and failures. Even though our combined experience amounts to almost 50 years of executing data science projects for a wide variety of industries, before we began espousing our own theories, we turned first to our peers to find out what *they* think are the major challenges of ADSAI projects. We wanted some data to back up our hunches.

We did this in three ways:

1. We looked at what fellow practitioners wrote in blog posts, white papers, podcasts, videos, and similar outlets.
2. We looked at peer-reviewed articles published in scientific journals and conference proceedings.
3. We interviewed and talked to our peers to hear their stories.

In the first case, we individually reviewed and read more than 100 pieces of content. In the second case, our combined research (including the research of others) covered more than 2,000 peer-reviewed research articles. Third, our peer interviews and discussions spanned dozens of leading practitioners. Although our research was very broad, upon analyzing the comments and experiences of others, certain themes very quickly repeated themselves with a long tail of other sporadic issues.

Now that we had our data and reasons for failure, the next step was to find if someone had already addressed the challenges in a cohesive format such as a book. There are many experts who have thought deeply on this topic and tried to map out the successes and failures in order to provide guidance. Has another author already covered these findings and presented them in the needed format?

When we discuss our research, we have to first mention the guru of corporate analytics, Thomas Davenport, who has written, co-authored, and edited 23 books. Davenport's focus is typically on best practices and what he has learned from working with the *most analytics-capable* organizations around the world. What we found in the literature touched on many of the topics explored in Davenport's books, however, our focus is not on the top 1% of organizations but the other 99% (although the prolific author has also provided guidance for new entrants to the analytics scene, such as *Keeping Up with the Quants*).

Davenport doesn't have a monopoly on this line of literature and so clearly, in a similar vein, there are many, many other books (*The Humachine, Behind Every Good Decision*, and more) that also look at what is considered industry wisdom and expound on principles for success. In addition, many of these books also analyze the problem from a non-algorithmic perspective, delving into human biases, or even asking the question, "what is data?"

For example, author Gary Klein has published many insightful books culminating in one that is most relevant here, *Streetlights and Shadows*, which expounds on the benefits of expertise over analytics and the situations in which one should be preferred over the other. This is a critical complement to our work, but only provides one facet of why analytics programs fail—an overreliance on analytics.

Books such as *Sensemaking* by Christian Madsbjerg take a very different approach by focusing on the humanities side and the data beyond the quantifiable 1s and 0s in our spreadsheets and databases. He discusses what we miss by not looking beyond our digitally collectable data and raises our awareness of the data *not considered*, which could also cause a project to fail. But this again is only one piece of the puzzle.

There are many other books that briefly touch on topics related to ours but nothing answered the questions we had as practitioners, nor revealed the failure reasons that our research had shown us. We saw a significant gap in the literature and aim to fill it here.

During our literature review, we also discovered a plethora of frameworks, guides, and so-called best practices. Given the proliferation of such blueprints, we wanted to first check whether the tide of failures had been stemmed by these recommendations, because if they were working, there would be no need for this book. Unfortunately, what we discovered dashed our hopes.

What Happened to Best Practices?

As the uptake of data science tools increases, as well as the failures, a clear need to share best practices has evolved. This has occurred in organizations at multiple levels from strategy to choosing the right tool for the right problem. What is perplexing is that in spite of this, there are no clear signals that the adoption of so-called best practices has worked. Why?

Before we answer, we'll briefly review what is available to the aspiring data-driven organization from the strategy level right up to the choice of tool (see Figure 1.1 for the dependencies, represented vertically from bottom to top, between the levels).

At the Data Foundation (management/strategic) level, there are a number of data frameworks that come together to make analytics possible, beginning with Data Management Maturity Models,[16] developed to help organizations assess and improve their data management capabilities. These frameworks typically consist of a number of categories such as governance, architecture, data quality, metadata, data warehousing, business intelligence, and document and content management.

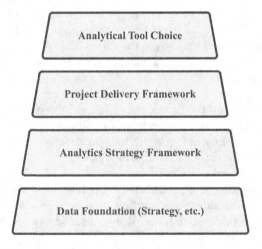

FIGURE 1.1
The hierarchy of frameworks to building an ADSAI capability.

With a strong data foundation aligned to the company's strategy, organizations are able to more easily exploit their data to begin making data-driven decisions. But the need for guidance doesn't stop there. Because the data alone won't answer business questions, numerous analytics strategy frameworks have been developed to build upon these data foundations and increase the chances of ADSAI projects succeeding.

For example, the **DELTTAA** (**D**ata, **E**nterprise, **L**eadership, **T**argets, **T**echnologies, **A**nalysts, and **A**nalytical techniques) framework developed by Davenport in his book *Competing on Analytics* (2017) teaches the reader what companies look like at each stage as they advance from what Davenport terms "Analytically Impaired" to "Analytical Competitors." In addition to his framework, we are aware of another half-dozen open and proprietary methods[17] based on different practitioners' experiences as well as many *ad hoc* systems used in a variety of organizations. There is no lack of choice.

After the data and analytics strategy creation, for data science project delivery, there are an equal number of project delivery frameworks practitioners can follow to deliver on their objectives. These begin with some of the older frameworks, such as Knowledge Discovery in Databases (KDD), which were developed using the perspectives of the day to recommend planning out the entire project, and delivering it in one go, so-called Waterfall methods.

The issue with Waterfall methods is that they do not cope well with significant changes, uncertainty, and ambiguity at the beginning of or during the project—things that are invariably synonymous with data science projects. Hence, new frameworks emerged that were more iterative with many feedback loops, the so-called Agile methodologies.

As Agile approaches became more popular, processes with an Agile or iterative inspiration emerged, such as CRISP-DM,[18] CPMAI,[19] Data Science Process Flow (DSPF),[20] or the Data Analytics Lifecycle,[21] as well as a proliferation of approaches developed in books (with more or less aspects of agile), such as *Keeping Up with the Quants* by Davenport, *Guerrilla Analytics* by Enda Ridge, *Modeling for Insight* by Robert J. Batt and Stephen G. Powell, *The AI Playbook* by Eric Siegel, and more.

Going the next level up, if you've picked your delivery approach, then you have to choose what analytical tool to apply to your problem. There are hundreds of books to help you diagnose and then decide which approach to use (e.g., regression, decision trees, linear programming, transformers, etc.) based on all the technical aspects of a problem that one could possibly face, for example, deterministic vs. stochastic, predictive vs. prescriptive. It is in this area that most data scientists spend the majority of their training (as we will see in the People chapter and our discussions on university analytics program curricula), and it is not until they begin working in the field that they realize how much more a data scientist must cover than knowing which analytic tools to use, when, and how.

Each of the aforementioned approaches has its pros and cons based on the individual company's circumstances. Therefore, there isn't one particular framework that we would recommend for all readers. What is clear, however, is despite all of this work and all of these frameworks, we are not seeing a reduction in project failure rates.

In fact, in a blog post published by Data Science Process Alliance, using a meta-analysis of the failure rate from 2014 to 2019,[22] the author claims failure rates beginning at greater than 70% in 2014 and increasing to claims of almost 90% by 2019. Even if we admit the obvious uncertainty and potential lack of rigor in these types of claims, they don't paint a picture of the numerous analytical frameworks making an obviously visible dent in the failure rate—irrespective of the number of new companies launching analytical efforts that may lack any experience (because frameworks exist for them too!).

This shows that despite all the good intentions of decades of recommendations, project outcomes are likely not improving. Previous advice and publications that focused on frameworks, processes, and approaches to reduce the number of failures don't seem to have achieved their goal. We need a new and different approach, one that brings readers and practitioners into the trenches of data science and has them view the gory remains of thousands of failed projects.

Where should one focus one's energy?

By analyzing the literature covering thousands of peer-reviewed articles and hundreds of blogs and other content, we see that generally if you pick the wrong tools, the project is not likely to succeed. However, even if the right tools are chosen, if you choose a *poor approach* to deliver the project, then your clever tool selection will likely be in vain. Even worse, if the required strategic/management support isn't there, then even with the right tools *and* a good project approach, the developed solutions may never see adoption or generate business value.

This insight influenced how best to present the results of our research to the reader to gain the maximum value from this book. However, before we present our research findings and the way we will structure them, there is one final thing we need to do that the reader is probably thinking should have come first: Define a common understanding of what ADSAI project failure even means.

What Counts as an ADSAI Failure?

It is important that we align our understanding of the topics in this book—most importantly, what we mean by *failure*.

Scope, timeline, quality, and budget are typical metrics of (IT) project success and are relevant to this ADSAI context as well. However, for our purposes, success or failure means taking into account the following:

- Was the model fully implemented? That is, deployed to production as a decision support system that continually generates value.

- Was the model then utilized to solve a business problem (that the organization cares about), answer a key business question, or make a decision? (I.e., Is anyone using the model and has it improved their circumstances? Did it generate valuable insights and prove useful? What was the outcome relative to the original intent of the project?)

- Were tangible, measurable business value, and/or economic impact generated/manifested?

Each of these points was used as a guide for our investigations because a concrete scientific definition would likely lead to its own failure of applicability to scenarios of interest. In addition, failure, and success, can be very fluid, relative terms measured along a continuum, with success at one end and failure at the other. If a project fails to be completed and also doesn't reach any measurable value or is canceled outright without anyone the wiser, well, that is a clear failure. However, sometimes projects can be completed and even implemented without accomplishing all of their original intent, and as such, could be judged either a *moderate* success or a failure.

As a part of our research, we realized that there was a second concept that we needed to explain to elucidate our common understanding of failure. This is the difference between an analytically mature and analytically immature organization. There are dozens of maturity frameworks and definitions (even ones created by the co-authors[23]) and, like our definition of failure, we will follow the work of others.

An analytically *immature* organization is typically one that lacks most of the requirements to deliver on analytics projects, such as high-quality data, in-house analytical skills, senior stakeholder buy-in, etc. These are topics that we will address in the coming chapters. If a company (especially at the strategy level) well recognizes, and continuously experiences, the failures presented in the following chapters, then it is likely analytically immature.

Analytically *mature* organizations are ones that don't typically suffer from the failures in the coming chapters. Usually, there will be senior stakeholder buy-in and a desire from the top as well as a strategy to leverage analytics to improve decision-making. This generally leads to these companies having the needed human and technological resources, regular experience applying analytics, and realizing at least some commercial benefits from these activities.

With the above concepts and our analysis, we also realize that there are enough frameworks and methodologies created by much more talented and skilled authors than us and we won't try to create a new one here. We will, however, provide relevant suggestions after unpacking a failure, but you won't discover the five steps to analytical wisdom. We will try to point you in the direction of the existing content and discuss existing approaches to solving the challenges raised. So although our focus is on failures, in this book, you will still encounter stories of success to build upon the lessons learned from our less successful peers.

Our Thesis

Now that we are on the same page, what has our research shown us? What did we discover after digging through such an inordinate number of articles, opinions, and journals?

To disappoint those looking for a quick answer, what we discovered was complicated and not simply a one-liner for failure avoidance. To unpack it, let's start with an endemic problem revealed by Kaggle's annual data science survey.[24]

Kaggle claims to be the world's largest data science community. It was founded in 2010 as an online community to run data science competitions, and its annual surveys consistently show that roughly 60% of respondents (i.e., data scientists who respond to the survey) have less than two years of work experience. Ignoring the response bias with this survey, it gives us a moment to pause and think about who is doing data science in the world. This finding gets our thesis rolling, starting with a suspicion on the lack of experience to know how to run a data science function from the top of the organization (strategy level) down.

The problem with missing skills at the top level is that when experience or knowledge is lacking and something is popular (e.g., the hype surrounding AI), we can sometimes see a deference to the technical gurus. In his book (mentioned earlier), *To Engineer is Human*, Petroski states that too many engineering programs are beyond any form of basic verification (something managers are too often happy to accept) and once the numbers are crunched, engineers tend to rely on the results rather than their own judgment. He then makes a point that has become almost prescient with the rise of cloud-based AI tools: Powerful tools ably assist analytically immature people to amplify their errors. Petroski states this in the chapter "From Slide Rule to Computer" almost 50 years ago:

> [I]nexperienced engineers are tempted to work beyond their competence because of the availability of powerful software, and once the numbers are crunched, engineers tend to rely on the results rather than their own judgment, e.g., the roof of the Hartford Civic Center, which was designed using a computer model to analyze the stresses. So confident were the designs that they brushed aside the questions of workmen who had noticed a large sag in the roof well before it collapsed under the snow and ice of a January 1978 storm.

This capability gap is causing a large schism between the analytical haves and have nots, i.e., the analytically mature versus the analytically immature, or what Davenport called the Analytically Impaired (organizations that lack several of the prerequisites for serious analytical work, such as data, analytical skills, or senior management interest) versus Analytical Competitors (organizations that routinely use analytics as a distinctive business capability, taking an enterprise-wide approach with committed and involved leadership, and have achieved large-scale results).

This lack of experience, together with the marketing hype and excitement surrounding ADSAI caused by the high-profile successes of the analytically mature, means new companies are jumping on the analytics bandwagon without realizing the complexity of ADSAI projects—there is no vision or strategy, just a reaction to the hype. Expectations run high and ADSAI initiatives are seen as disruptive, instead of incremental, by executives who don't understand what data science really does. When leaders think of a project, they dream big and target their biggest problems instead of starting with something commensurate with their experience and current ADSAI maturity.

This means that when an analytically immature organization begins a project, the first and main factor they underestimate is *data issues*, including a lack of one or more of the data sources centralized for analysis (in a data lake, data lakehouse, or other platform/framework), data quality, data access, data relevance, metadata, data lineage, and data management/processing tools. This underestimation is one of the greatest causes of failure and is a challenge for all companies. Every time.

Less mature organizations often also lack a well-defined use case that aligns with the company's strategy. They want to use AI and leave it to the wrong people (e.g., the data scientists) to figure out where to use it. Unfortunately, data scientists typically aren't trained in management or commercial issues so they invariably fail in trying to solve both the commercial and technical side of the business challenge. Many data scientists also very likely don't understand the proper way to engage end users and stakeholders in a business (this is not a skill taught at universities in data science courses as we'll see in later chapters). Therefore, they probably don't understand how to extract the requirements needed to deliver a project that adds value.

This means that data scientists will presumably pick the wrong project, and picking the wrong project will most likely produce a poor return on investment (ROI) as well as not align with the business strategy. As mentioned, commercial training, strategic planning, and stakeholder engagement aren't part of data science degrees or training. In addition, many data scientists often don't understand the domain of the company with which they have started working (most of them will be new to the business domain and workforce as shown by the Kaggle study), so they probably have a hard time interpreting their results in light of the business environment.

Because companies are reacting to hype and hastily launching into AI development, by delivering projects in this way (unplanned and left to data scientists), the organization's leadership team most likely doesn't properly understand the initiative (because they haven't defined it and just want to use AI). So they don't get 100% behind the project because they aren't 100% bought in. Leadership continues to do their day jobs and probably won't set the project up for success (or even have defined it), have the right processes in place or set the right expectations, and won't even know what is required to get started. To top it off, they won't have set business targets with clear commercial goals that would help get proper buy-in from end users, superiors, and peers.

What's worse, many companies starting out don't properly resource their teams due to lack of experience, knowledge, and access to experienced data scientists. The aforementioned Kaggle surveys show that around 70% of those working in data science probably have less than three years of experience.

Due to a lack of understanding and the desire to keep up with the hype, immature companies are also treating AI projects like IT initiatives because it's the closest context they know. They focus on the technical IT side of the project and give it to their IT teams; however, ADSAI projects are much more complex, with significant and even more important human elements than IT projects, especially considering that they can completely change (or, on rare occasions, completely eliminate) job functions and decision-making processes within a business.

This then leads to no organizational support throughout the project (managers don't know what is required), not utilizing the final product (if there is one), and unengaged stakeholders (data scientists aren't taught how to engage end users). Change management is not carried out because the data science team doesn't know how or possibly even realize it is needed, and in an immature organization, resources aren't allocated for it. Because the data scientists are inexperienced, they don't understand all the effort required to get the model to production (they are new to real-world projects and only have completed proofs of concept). Projects take longer than the original optimistic estimates, and stakeholders lose interest or it fails altogether.

Our thesis paints a gloomy picture for analytically immature organizations and if read widely, would question why any company, except the most capable, would ever embark upon such a journey. This book is designed to help these former organizations change course.

We believe that for more mature companies that have significant experience, the failure rate is low (see our calculations in a moment to see just how low), but still much higher than what it should be. Even in an organization with good processes, the talent coming in will likely need to be retrained to address the "people" side of their work (i.e., nontechnical "soft skills"). Again, these are things that universities aren't teaching data scientists in spite of a decade of poor data science outcomes.

The obvious solution to much of this includes better processes, strategies, project management, and so on, but the problems go beyond data science. They touch on any new innovation because the world will continue to develop new technologies that technically trained people will be required to implement in organizations that are not ready for it, and for which the technically trained people are not capable of delivering the critical nontechnical side. The irony is that the nontechnical training required has existed for much longer than the new shiny technology and such people-focused courses are available at most universities (just typically outside of the department teaching the data science courses).

If we want to practically resolve this, then it requires many changes—a fundamental one being that we change what we teach data science and analytics students to give them the best chance to succeed. Too much of too many academic degrees is focused on the *technical* with little to absolutely no emphasis on any nontechnical skills, beyond a final capstone in which a student is thrown into the deep end of a business problem. At the time of writing, most students will enter an AI immature organization surrounded by a majority of people with only a few years of technical experience, who have had to learn people skills on the job, fumbling through one failed delivery after another, and losing trust and faith in their capabilities along the way.

We've just described many of the main themes of what can go wrong in ADSAI projects based on our research. However, companies will obviously differ in which parts they get right. Therefore, to help organizations get the most out of this book by focusing on areas in which they see the most failures, we have grouped the above points into four main categories based on the People, Process, Technology (PPT) division we mentioned in the previous chapter. We do this so each lesson is more easily recognizable to the reader as we look into the details of each and unpack what went wrong. We add strategy to the PPT categories and present them in the following order:

1. Strategy
2. Process
3. People
4. Technology

To come up with this order of importance, we categorized each failure reason raised in our literature review to one of the four themes and plotted them on a yearly basis as to how often each theme occurred. As our goal is to understand the importance of each theme over time, to avoid a year where simply many articles were written, we count how often each theme arose in a given year and divide that by the total number of articles published in a given year. This gives a relative importance of each theme (see Figure 1.2).

Looking at the data over the years, we see that *process issues* seem to be the most commonly cited in studies and blog posts, likely being one of the most common causes of failure, then strategy, and finally people and technology.

Although the most common issues lie in the process stage, we look at the *strategic level* first because it is the company's highest level of decision-making and defines everything that comes after. Then, we take the next most important area, the *process* side, and finally dive into the *people* and then *technology* aspects last.

But how sure can we be that we've covered everything?

In a final step to validate our research we asked one of the greatest repositories of human knowledge ever created, what does it think causes the failures of ADSAI projects? We turned to the astounding knowledge base called ChatGPT (GPT-3.5) and asked what it thought, using the following prompt:

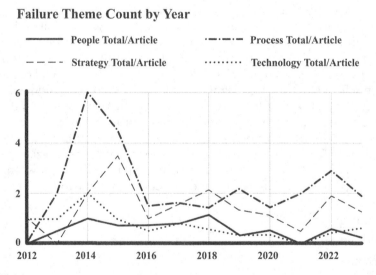

FIGURE 1.2
A graph of the weighted failure mentions in the literature by year and type.

> The failure rates in data science projects are so extremely high in companies (greater than 85% according to reports) and we have many frameworks to help do projects successfully, so why do we still see so many failures? People know the reasons for failure so why do we still fail?

It returned the following response (abbreviated to just the headline points):

1. Lack of clear business objectives
2. Poor data quality
3. Inadequate data infrastructure
4. Lack of appropriate skills and expertise
5. Inadequate communication and collaboration

These comments beautifully supported our research, with its five main reasons aligning with our research, as will be seen shortly. The stored knowledge of *billions of parameters trained on trillions of text tokens* seems to agree with our findings, with not much left to doubt. Even the order of ChatGPT's response largely corresponds to our findings.

The next thing we did was group the themes by whether they were issues facing mature or immature organizations, based on the co-authors' combined experience to classify the issues as mature or not. For analytically immature organizations, the issues written about appear more often than those facing more mature organizations, as expected. (As stated before, values for each year in Figures 1.2 and 1.3 on the line graphs are not whole numbers because we divide the number of mentions by the number of articles and some articles mention many issues that could affect multiple categories this avoids a year with an unusual number of people writing articles skewing the data.)

The numbers in Figure 1.3 corroborate the idea that as a company improves its maturity, it can reduce its failure rate. If we take these time series of failures as a proxy for organizations' success rate, then calculations will show that about 95% of all weighted mentions point to a failure attributed to an immature (or both) organization and 45% of all weighted mentions attribute the failure to a mature organization (or both). If this is reflective of real life, then by becoming a more mature organization in the way you approach analytics, you can potentially *halve* the number of failures.

So how can we use this data to properly figure out how often analytically immature organizations fail based on 80% of all AI projects failing?

To estimate this, we reviewed the data in a white paper covering how organizations are "Closing the Gap Between Ambition and Action" in AI in *MIT Sloan Management Review*[25] as well as other project failure rate data.[15] Using this, we can conservatively assume that 80% of data science projects fail (both mature and immature organizations). In addition, analytically mature organizations make up around 23% of all companies (according to the MIT Sloan article), meaning approximately 77% of all companies are analytically

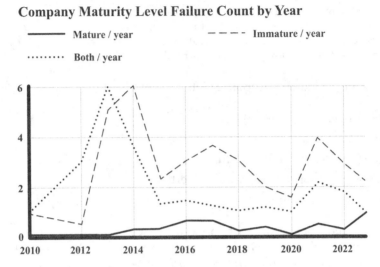

FIGURE 1.3
A graph of number of failure mentions in the literature by year and company maturity.

immature. If we use Figure 1.3 to draw the conclusion that the failure rate at analytically immature organizations is twice that of mature organizations, then the real failure rate of the analytically immature organizations is actually around 90%.[26] This means, for the majority of companies, the true failure rate is even higher than the alarming 80%!

Such a high failure rate is going to badly damage the ADSAI industry if it continues, so the groundwork must be laid in a way that is palatable and maximizes the chances for organizations to improve their experiences with data science. If this failure rate continues, companies will label ADSAI as "snake oil" and a false promise, not realizing the effort required to deliver on such initiatives.

For immature organizations, we strongly recommend staying away from the hype, *because 9 out of 10 times, you will fail to deliver the desired outcome*. The following chapters will outline some of the biggest failures awaiting you. Don't make these mistakes, and learn from the failures of others—we've cited research earlier that shows this is one of the most effective ways to learn.

Although we've talked a lot about analytically immature organizations, for mature organizations, we will share some of our decades of experience as to what we *still* see going wrong and what was learned from these experiences. Our estimated 40% failure rate for analytically mature organizations is still too high and our goal is to help reduce this further.

To finish this chapter, we'll answer the key question: How do projects typically finish for analytical immature organizations?

Facing Challenges

How a project finishes for an analytically immature organization (i.e., failure) was something that ChemCo was unfortunate enough to experience, but luckily in their case, the damage was less than it could have been.

As the accounting team was about to roll out their SQL script to ChemCo's database to optimize their supply chain cost structure, the senior manager happened to have a discussion with another analytically interested director over lunch and explained what they were doing. This conversation occurred early in the week and the senior manager flagged that the optimization script was to be delivered at the end of the week. Once the director heard what was planned, he asked some simple questions, like, have you tested this in a test scenario using IT infrastructure similar to the planned production environment?

The answers to these questions shocked the director because not only had they not tested the program in a test IT environment, as flagged earlier, it turns out that ChemCo didn't have any testing protocols at all, and normally deployed new, untested changes directly to their live working database. So, no red flags were ever raised by the accounting team's proposed approach. ChemCo had the excuse of being analytically immature; however, the consultants selling the services are supposed to know better. Not only was the software never properly built and tested, but no more thought was involved than simply handing over the script to the client and letting them figure it out.

The answers (or non-answers) to the ChemCo director's questions quickly revealed the senior manager's lack of understanding and the imminent disaster facing them.

The accounting firm director immediately stopped the delivery of the code and let his superior, the business partner, know about the impending disaster (no longer a database one, but now a reputational one). The partner was so angry that he sent the messenger (the director) out of his office without allowing him any further comments. The accounting company's policy demands its employees have a can-do attitude (bring solutions not problems), so hearing the bad news was not taken well. As a result, the partner pulled the plug on the project, recognizing that admitting defeat was better than sending a stock-market-wrecking SQL script to the client. A painful blow to the partner's ego and bottom line, but a much smaller failure than what they would've faced at the end of the week if the code had been deployed.

The problem with ChemCo began at the top level. An entire strategic layer of analytics maturity was missing. This is the first step to get right to avoid ADSAI project failure, so we start with that in the next chapter.

Critical Thinking: How Not to Fail

- Why do you think so many people believe the AI hype? Do you see this hype as any different to previous technology hypes?
- Clinical staff are some of the best educated in the world, so do you truly believe that a lot of the failed AI projects are due to hype? If not, why else?
- When analyzing the reasons for failure, we turned to the online publications of our industry peers as well as peer-reviewed articles. What value do you think the thought pieces of our practitioners have compared to the scientific studies?
- Despite all the analytics frameworks, why could it be that failure rates are still so high?
- What do you think is the disadvantage of giving a specific definition of failure? Especially when it comes to doing a meta-analysis?
- In this book, we won't cover the behavioral science topics of biases (e.g., confirmation bias, hindsight bias, etc.), so we leave it to the reader to consider, what type of known biases could contribute to data science project failures? Which are the most important?
- When it comes to a failure, out of the three possibilities of budget, cost, or scope, which aspect of project failure do you think is least painful and causes the least distress to senior managers? To data scientists? Is there a mismatch?
- What important topic do you think was missed in our thesis (there were many not presented here as we focus on what we saw as the major items)? If you added it, how much difference do you think it would make to the overall number of failed projects? Would it be significant?
- If all companies were analytically mature, how much less investment would be lost compared with the current situation?
- For a large-size company trying to reinvent itself by leveraging ADSAI to create a competitive advantage, how would you justify the investment to reduce the chances of failure? When does the investment stop making sense for an analytically immature firm? What area would you invest most in (strategy, process, people, or technology)?

Notes

1. Atleson, M. (2023, February 27). *Keep Your AI Claims in Check*. Federal Trade Commission. Retrieved December 15, 2023, from https://www.ftc.gov/business-guidance/blog/2023/02/keep-your-ai-claims-check.

2. Radford, A., Sutskever, I., Kim, J. W., Krueger, G., & Agarwal, S. (2021). CLIP: Connecting text and images. OpenAI. https://openai.com/research/clip.

3. Smith, G., & Funk, J. (2022, July 20). AI has a long way to go before doctors can trust it with your life. *Quartz*. https://qz.com/2016153/ai-promised-to-revolutionize-radiology-but-so-far-its-failing.

4. ImageNet. (n.d.). https://www.image-net.org/.

5. Windsor, M. (2022, December 5). This radiologist is helping doctors see through the hype to an AI future. *UAB Reporter*. https://www.uab.edu/reporter/people/achievements/item/9925-this-radiologist-is-helping-doctors-see-through-the-hype-to-an-ai-future.

6. Qure AI | AI assistance for Accelerated health care. (n.d.). https://qure.ai/.

7. Henderson, M. (2022, May 10). Radiology facing a global shortage. Radiological Society of North America. https://www.rsna.org/news/2022/may/Global-Radiologist-Shortage.

8. Heaven, D. (2019). Why deep-learning AIs are so easy to fool. *Nature*, *574*(7777), 163–166. https://doi.org/10.1038/d41586-019-03013-5.

9. Stempniak, M. (2022, February 11). Only 30% of radiologists currently using artificial intelligence as part of their practice. *Radiology Business*. https://www.radiologybusiness.com/topics/artificial-intelligence/30-radiologists-artificial-intelligence-practice.

10. Perry, T. S. (2022, August 18). Andrew NG X-Rays The AI Hype. *IEEE Spectrum*. https://spectrum.ieee.org/view-from-the-valley/artificial-intelligence/machine-learning/andrew-ng-xrays-the-ai-hype.

11. Beede, E., Baylor, E., Hersch, F., Iurchenko, A., Wilcox, L., Ruamviboonsuk, P., & Vardoulakis, L. (2020). A Human-Centered Evaluation of a Deep Learning System Deployed in Clinics for the Detection of Diabetic Retinopathy. *CHI '20: Proceedings of the 2020 CHI Conference on Human Factors in Computing Systems*, 1–12. https://doi.org/10.1145/3313831.3376718.

12. Heaven, W. D. (2020, December 10). Google's medical AI was super accurate in a lab. Real life was a different story. *MIT Technology Review*. https://www.technologyreview.com/2020/04/27/1000658/google-medical-ai-accurate-lab-real-life-clinic-covid-diabetes-retina-disease/.

13. Konam, S. (2022, March 2). Where did IBM go wrong with Watson Health? *Quartz*. https://qz.com/2129025/where-did-ibm-go-wrong-with-watson-health.

14. AI Incident Database. (n.d.). https://incidentdatabase.ai/.

15. O'Neill, B. T. (2020, October 28). Failure rates for analytics, AI, and big data projects = 85% – yikes! *Designing for Analytics*. https://designingforanalytics.com/resources/failure-rates-for-analytics-bi-iot-and-big-data-projects-85-yikes/.

16. Spruit, M., & Pietzka, K. (2015). MD3M: The master data management maturity model. *Computers in Human Behavior*, *51*, 1068–1076. https://doi.org/10.1016/j.chb.2014.09.030.

17. Steenbeek, I. (2023, March 22). Data Management Maturity Models: a Comparative Analysis. *Data Crossroads*. https://datacrossroads.nl/2018/12/16/data-management-maturity-models-a-comparative-analysis/.

There are many others listed here focusing more on data management than analytics, but this is a core foundation for analytics so it is worth listing them here: DAMA-DMBOK, DCAM, CMMI CERT-RMM (Data Management Maturity Model) by CMMI, IBM Data Governance Council Maturity model,

Stanford Data Governance Maturity Model, Gartner's Enterprise Information Management Maturity Model), and more.

18. Shearer, C. (2000). The CRISP-DM model: The new blueprint for data mining. *International Journal of Data Warehousing and Mining, 5*, 13-22.

19. Cognilytica. (n.d.). Cognilytica Courses. https://courses.cognilytica.com/cpmai/.

20. Gupta, S. (2022, August 10). Data Science Process: A Beginner's Guide in Plain English. *Springboard Blog*. https://www.springboard.com/blog/data-science/data-science-process/.

21. UNext Editorial Team. (2023, March 1). Data Analytics Lifecycle: An Easy Overview for 2022. *UNext*. https://u-next.com/blogs/hr-analytics/data-analytics-lifecycle/.

22. Hotz, N. (2022, November 13). Why big data science & data analytics projects fail. *Data Science Process Alliance*. https://www.datascience-pm.com/project-failures/.

23. Shellshear, E. (2021, April 13). Australia's Data Analytics Challenge [Video]. YouTube. https://www.youtube.com/watch?v=fRSTdUGxy4g.

24. See for example some of the following sources:

   Kaggle. (n.d.) 2018 Kaggle Machine Learning & Data Science Survey. https://www.kaggle.com/datasets/kaggle/kaggle-survey-2018;

   Mooney, P.T. (2018, November 12). 2018 Kaggle Machine Learning & Data Science Survey. https://www.kaggle.com/code/paultimothymooney/2018-kaggle-machine-learning-data-science-survey.

   Mooney, P.T. (2020, November 19). 2020 Kaggle Data Science & Machine Learning Survey. https://www.kaggle.com/code/paultimothymooney/2020-kaggle-data-science-machine-learning-survey.

   Mooney, P.T. (2021, October 14). 2021 Kaggle Data Science & Machine Learning Survey. https://www.kaggle.com/code/paultimothymooney/2021-kaggle-data-science-machine-learning-survey.

25. Ransbotham, S. (2017, September 6). Reshaping business with artificial intelligence. *MIT Sloan Management Review*. https://sloanreview.mit.edu/projects/reshaping-business-with-artificial-intelligence/.

26. To calculate this, we used $0.77*(2x) + 0.23x = 0.8$, where x is the failure rate of a mature organization, and we estimate that they fail half as much based on our data presented in the graphs. We then figure out how many organizations are immature vs mature (i.e., the 2x multiplied by the 0.77, which comes from the MIT article in reference 26), and this will equal the estimated 80% (0.8 on the right side of the equals sign).

2

Strategy

> If you try to tell someone else how to do their job better using sophis-
> ticated mathematics and computers without thoroughly understanding
> how they do their job today, including all of the problems and challenges
> they encounter, then you sir/madam are a fraud.

**—R.E.D. "Gene" Woolsey, PhD, Professor, Colorado School of Mines,
and Operations Research Academic, Practitioner & Consultant**

With large datasets, sufficient available funding for quality IT resources, and
industry trends pushing for data-driven decision-making, retailers should
be in a great position to take advantage of the latest analytical offerings.
Especially well into the 21st century.

Examples of retail AI successes are touted everywhere, from Amazon
automating its warehousing (and the ensuing purchase of Kiva systems)
to Walmart's inventory optimization of Pop-Tarts in the face of Hurricane
Frances in 2004. However, there are other areas in which retail analytics seems
to go astray, and a commonly problematic application is in personalization.

For example, Target's story of predicting a teenager's pregnancy (and then
proactively marketing prenatal products to her via mailer coupon packs)
before her parents found out has now become part of analytics community
folklore—possibly an example on how *not* to manage personalized offers.
Unfortunately, AI personalization projects that go astray are far more common than the few you may encounter in *The New York Times Magazine*. It
happens all the time, but most people never see it because the consequences
are only known to those involved and quickly swept under the rug. But not
in this book.

Before we delve into an example of what can go wrong, we must admit
that analytics-driven personalization is a challenging undertaking. Analytics
empowers marketing to individuals by allowing it to efficiently scale up its
reach to millions of people. However, the data used to train the algorithms
that do the personalization are never perfect, and therefore, guaranteed to
cause issues. Especially when we carry out so-called hyper-personalization
marketing activities. Before we begin our first failure story on personalization, to help understand the difference between the variety of personalization tactics (i.e., hyper vs. others), we'll describe here what they typically do.

Many analytically driven personalization programs will segment a company's customers into similar groups of individuals; the similarity could

DOI: 10.1201/9781032661360-3

be related to their purchasing habits, demographics, weather, time of year, behaviors, choices, and more. Millions of customers are segmented into distinct groups with the goal of having members of one group as similar as possible to each other, but at the same time, as different as possible to members of the other groups. (Typically, the data scientist on the team defines what "similar" and "different" mean on a case-by-case basis.) By doing this, you can have more confidence in applying one offer to one group (due to their similarity) and a different offer to another group (due to their difference to the first group). These groups could be anywhere in size from hundreds to millions of people.

The world of hyper-personalization begins when we decrease these group sizes to the ideal number: one. Hyper-personalization means that each individual will receive an offer unique to their circumstances. The challenge is that the data collected on someone based on their transactions or estimated demographics are never 100% correct (or even enough), which means that sometimes this approach is going to miss the mark.

Even if aspirations are not of the hyper type, personalization programs are difficult to roll out and require a lot of coordination from many layers of an organization, and in the case of a large global retailer with billions in revenue on the line, this was where things went wrong. The project not only damaged the global retailer's reputation among the world of analytics consultants, but also destroyed employee goodwill and cost the protagonist of our story their job.

RetailCo's Strategic Nightmare

The ravages wrought by COVID-19 created an extremely stressful time for retailers worldwide. In early 2020, many brick-and-mortar retailers believed that the coronavirus would mean the end of their business, and millions would lose their jobs. People were locked down and unable to physically visit shopping malls and main streets, effectively killing their local businesses' largest revenue stream.

That was until the flood of online consumers caused stock-outs across home gym equipment, running shoes, and other products for organizations that had a website and delivery capability. The new work-from-home trend led to incredible supply chain headaches but also record profits for organizations. Simultaneously, the pandemic accelerated the digital and analytics trend like nothing else in the history of mankind. This was humorously illustrated by a meme circulating at the time that asked the viewer to select which of the following was responsible for their digital transformation: (a) CEO, (b) CIO, or (c) COVID-19.

It was around this time that our particular organization, let's call them RetailCo (disclaimer: it is not Walmart), was embarking upon an ambitious journey to transform their customer relationships. They had recently appointed a number of new senior executives, and the personalization program was intended to become one of their big analytic successes. We'll follow the journey of one of their senior executives, an exceptionally talented and award-winning leader with years of experience in delivering analytically focused outcomes in global enterprises. For the sake of anonymity, let's call him Ben.

Before RetailCo began its journey, the company seemed to be in a good position to launch a personalization program. They had all the data (albeit not well organized), lots of information about customers, and the hypothesis that they could do something with that information to improve everyone's experience—a win-win-win (relationship, customer, and company). Sell more, sell at a better price, and satisfy the customer.

The key to achieving this win-win-win scenario was breaking free of the blanket discount monotony and thinking harder about what each product meant to each customer. By looking at customer-item purchase frequencies and reconsidering the discount approach to rarely purchased products (i.e., the long tail of products), the company was able to find an angle that would benefit all parties.

RetailCo's hypothesis about their stores (in one of their retail chains) was that because the demand profile is long-tailed (in the products purchased by specific customers) and very geographically, weather, and temporally segmented, there was an opportunity to do something with the data to create a better customer relationship.

They also "knew" this could work because they had seen it work before. For example, analysis done by The Weather Channel looking at hair products in the United States[1] showed that if you have long hair and a cold snap comes, there are products you can use to protect your hair, but you need to know ahead of time to serve appropriate ads, which is exactly what The Weather Channel allegedly did. Targeting people this way proved to be quite successful.

Simultaneously RetailCo realized they could use their customer data to improve communication with shoppers. When this marketing is done well, the customer notices that they are seeing what interests them rather than being spammed. For example, when using an Electronic Direct Mail (EDM) marketing strategy (i.e., personalized e-mail), customers won't consider it "junk" if the message includes value-adding information. Again, a win-win-win for the company and its long-term relationship with customers, as well as a direct improvement to the customer experience.

Ben could personally relate to this positive experience: He always opened clothing catalog e-mails from certain online brands because it was not junk mail to him—they did a good job of serving him products he was actually interested in buying. As long as the items were of interest, even getting an e-mail every other day didn't bother him.

His objective for RetailCo was clear: Leverage the existing data to build a better relationship with the customer, which also benefits the company. The business value of this program was recognized by everyone at RetailCo; it was time to do the commercial groundwork. Although they could quantify the targeted value by looking at benchmarks, RetailCo needed to answer basic questions, such as: Are they collecting the data they need for personalization algorithms? Is it technically possible? Could the recommendations be integrated into existing processes? The answer to each question was "yes." However, making sure the rest of the executive team understood personalization was a difficult undertaking.

As a member of the Executive Leadership Team (ELT), Ben was required to run information and training sessions to help the rest of the ELT understand how their flavor of personalization would work. Often, a fellow executive (e.g., the supply chain leader) who always did things "old school" would counter Ben's approach with their own perspective, suggesting how *they* would do it and providing *their* numbers, business case, and pros and cons. These comments opened the door for the entire ELT to then get involved with their *own* suggestions, which were not necessarily helpful. And so began the dreaded "decision-making by committee"—when people provide unsolicited advice on matters they don't understand. This has since become a common problem for AI due to its familiarity caused by hype.

To try and help convince the ELT of the merit of his version of the proposal, Ben quantified his business case from all angles, many times over, providing high-, medium-, and low-value outcome scenarios. He even took the lowest of the low estimates to be conservative and proved that it could still work. He also spoke to many peers in the retail space to bolster his arguments and further convinced his ELT colleagues that it would work. Ben even partnered with one of the top global analytics consulting firms to tackle this project, both parties seeing the incredible value it could deliver.

With the business case locked in, budget approved, and consulting partners chosen, it was time to begin the innovative and promising project. Plans were drawn up, resources allocated, and RetailCo turned their attention to the first part of the project—getting the data and locking in the needed IT manpower. Unfortunately, right here at the start, things began to fall apart.

The project began with high hopes. Everyone was excited and committed to the opportunity but as discussions advanced, it soon became clear that the IT team wanted to do a lot more work than was necessary, i.e., scope creep. The project plan was designed to start small by delivering minimal functional components to the marketing team to determine the system performance. However, many members of the IT team had previously worked in large organizations that had apparently preferred the Waterfall approach to project management. The computing specialists didn't want to embrace the notion of the *minimum solution* required to achieve the desired result.

(In corporate scenarios it can be very advantageous to build a minimum viable product (MVP) and show some value early.)

They argued that there would be a big upside to the business if they could properly execute the data management piece by implementing a holistic change—not just do what was necessary for the personalization project. Political games began, and the project no longer aligned with its initial scope; for example, IT argued to create a Customer Data Platform (CDP), which is not necessarily required for the customer loyalty (personalization) initiative. They argued that RetailCo would need a CDP in the longer term anyway, and the necessary work would be much cheaper if everything was done at the same time.

Even if that were true, it undermined the personalization initiative's momentum and priorities. Although it was not a bad idea to ultimately build and deploy a CDP, this type of diversion represented a huge undertaking and would massively extend the project scope. Instead, it would have been best to focus on the data needed for the project at hand. Then, down the road, RetailCo could scale up and out to a comprehensive CDP. However, the IT executive leading the team approved the CDP idea as part of the personalization project, causing a serious misalignment of the initial strategy.

In addition to the emerging IT challenges, the ELT meetings continued to reveal that the executives truly didn't understand the personalization program. Ben and his external partners at the global analytics consulting company continued to struggle to regain alignment, despite the fact that they repeatedly expounded the strategy and reasoning to the ELT.

The CEO of RetailCo was talented, but not data-driven, and he and the rest of the executive team didn't comprehend the effort required to run an AI system in production, and seriously underestimated the human capital needed. The development team explained that they, not AI, needed to define the actions (discount types, images, text content, etc.) for the personalization model to do its job—if it is given bad data, it will produce bad recommendations. But not being granted the dedicated people meant there was no ability to provide the AI with the needed inputs to define all the various actions. It seemed the other executives, who probably only read AI headlines, were misled into believing that this part of the project could in fact be done properly by only one or two people.

So, completely against Ben's wishes, the ELT set up a small committee to do a redesign of the technical project leadership and chose only two people who both had no experience in AI/ML. The CFO and CEO, neither of whom were in reality experienced enough to make such a decision, unfortunately, approved the two-person team (in place of the already staffed, experienced six-person team).

If the co-authors were to take a step back and lean in with their experience, they would both agree with Ben. A larger team is needed to keep the model tuned and the entire data and personalized recommendation system running smoothly. The personalization engine needs good marketing copy, and (at that point in time) this requires qualified people to create, edit, and deploy— it can't just be plugged in and let run into perpetuity. It needs proper structure and governance. The ML model (the "big AI brain") is only as smart as the quality and integrity of the information that is fed in to train and tune it.

The ML model relies on the information coming out of the data pipelines, and the IT system must cleverly deploy targeted messages (e.g., is it an e-mail or banner ad and how will it be served up?). This whole process and system flow needs to be executed by people who understand it and orchestrated by people who can make it work reliably. The first use case was for e-mail, but the other ELT members believed they didn't need all the originally allocated staff, in particular the senior managers to oversee the work. In reality, RetailCo needed an experienced, hands-on technical lead to run the project, so that the originally intended scope and deliverable would not be undercut in favor of other items not in scope. The project lacked a key resource.

In addition, when using AI, you need to let a project, and a model, run its course without everyone leaning in and getting involved too early, especially before reliable results are produced. The modeling process is experimental, more "R&D" than "systems development." ADSAI teams need to be prepared for and embrace the figurative "puff of smoke over the workbench," and have an attitude of *learning*, not just the algorithm learning from the data, but the organization learning from the process. Data scientists know the results won't be clear-cut straight away. The variability in the results will be both good and bad, but if you don't trust the process, you will never achieve the desired outcome.

Back to RetailCo, who now lacked a sufficiently resourced team with the right experience. What now happened was that when the AI didn't always improve a KPI or outcome as the inexperienced team members wanted, category managers leveraging the personalization engine lost faith and reverted to the old ways of doing things, and by doing so, adversely impacted the system. They sent out their prior standard e-mails because they were worried about hitting their team's targets in the short term. This ruined the scientific validity of the results and meant the system could never properly learn from its actions.

This lack of comfort with ambiguity and uncertainty is a problem because there will always be a period in which a model (and people) needs to learn and won't perform well. The ELT lacked the patience to understand that. The project team planned to test a small sample size to get an indication, but the retail chains couldn't adapt because they were worried about not hitting their targets to which their bonuses were tied and the ELT hadn't given them the flexibility in their KPIs to trial it. Competing priorities can mean holding the course with AI can be difficult.

For all of the reasons stated above, Ben realized that the personalization model experiment, let alone a system, would never work in the cultural and managerial environment at RetailCo. "Too many cooks in the kitchen spoils the broth" as it were: scope and resource allocation, decision-making by unqualified executives, a confounded and compromised experimental environment in which users revert to prior ways of doing business, and so on. Mentally and physically exhausted, Ben delivered the promised components and left the company.

The project was clearly going down the wrong path when Ben left (improperly handled data, overcomplicated data systems integration, etc.). From his perspective, the AI was intended to be *augmented* intelligence, not completely remove people from the process. But the ELT possibly had a vision fueled by the hype of an autonomous AI system making perfect decisions, requiring little to no human input. What began as a well thought out, promising use of analytics, ended as a strategic failure, the responsibility for which started at the top.

The Difficult and Critical Role of Strategy

Many things went wrong with the RetailCo personalization project, but the level where it all unraveled was the most important one—the *strategic* level.[2] The problems faced by Ben illustrate many of the main strategic failings (and others) that we discovered in our research.

Zooming into just the strategic reasons for failure for analytically immature organizations, our investigations revealed the main reasons include:

- Failing to build the *need* in the organization (e.g., poorly defined use case, no clear business value, no actionable insights, solution looking for a problem, etc.)
- Lack of (or lack of alignment with) a vision or strategy (e.g., a technical solution not aligned with a key business problem)
- Not clearly measuring success (e.g., what impact the deliverables should have)
- Lack of leadership/upper management buy-in and lack of alignment among the ELT

Unlike many of the examples we found in the literature, RetailCo actually got the most common strategic failing right: They knew the business case and it made sense. They also had a vision (although weren't truly aligned with it) and knew how they would measure success. The biggest stumbling block that caused this project to fail was the lack of leadership/upper management buy-in and alignment. We'll delve more into this later, but before we do, let's explore the number one reason that causes ADSAI projects to fail according to the analytics community: Rushing headlong into the analytics hype without thinking about what you are doing.

Failing to Build Organizational Need

A failure to build the need in the organization was the most commonly recurring theme in all of our research. It came up even more often than data quality issues. Both co-authors have also seen this. It was most thoroughly witnessed and understood by one of the co-authors, Doug, when transitioning from what was the best analytics team in the airline industry, attempting to take their experience and expertise elsewhere, but ultimately failing due to missing this key criterion for success (i.e., building the need). We'll tell the story from the beginning, starting with an incredible success within one of America's largest airlines.

Doug was fortunate to start his career in 1987 in the Operations Research (OR) Department of American Airlines (AA), where he was able to learn from the very best. Arguably one of the most successful analytics organizations in history by any measure, the OR Department quickly grew from 40 staff members to more than 500 in the period from 1987 to 1992. Led by Dr. Thomas M. Cook, it helped transform AA into the most technologically advanced airline in the post-US airline industry deregulation environment.

Most notably, AA's OR team—the world's largest private sector OR department—was recognized in 1991 when awarded two of the most prestigious prizes of the Institute for Operations Research and the Management Sciences (INFORMS): The INFORMS Prize (for effective integration of OR/analytics in an organization) and the Franz Edelman Award (for economically impactful application of OR/analytics). The 1991 Edelman Award was for Yield Management at American Airlines,[3] which delivered $1.4B in incremental revenue over a three-year period, with an additional projected $500 million annually in subsequent years. AA's OR team later earned Edelman finalist recognition for both Crew Schedule Optimization and Airport Arrival Slot Allocation Optimization. The Edelman Award is the equivalent of industry's Nobel Prize for Applied Mathematics. (Thomas Cook and his right-hand man Barry Smith, who spearheaded the implementation of American Airlines' yield management revolution, were also awarded the INFORMS Impact Prize in 2016 for their work in revenue management, which quickly spread and was adopted by other similar industries, including hotels, cruise lines, rental cars, passenger and freight railroads, and even self-storage facilities.)

American Airlines' pricing, yield, and revenue management system, known as DINAMO, designed for optimally managing pricing and seat inventory allocation to maximize revenue, was so effective, it was credited for putting PEOPLExpress Airlines *out of business*, according to its founder and CEO Don Burr.[4] The OR department at AA evolved on a grand scale over the period of 1982–2021; first, becoming a wholly owned subsidiary of American Airlines, called Decision Technologies (AADT), then merging and spinning off as a part of Sabre, i.e., Sabre Decision Technologies. Finally, it became Sabre Airline Solutions, which was (measured by global market share) the world's leading provider of airline decision support analytics software products and consultancy services (Sabre Airline Solutions was acquired by CAE, Inc., in 2021).[5]

Some critics have noted, and rightly so, that despite its tremendous success implementing OR deeply and widely throughout the airline, AA was still not consistently profitable in the 1980s and 1990s.[6] The profitability challenges were primarily due to a wide range of macroeconomic factors, for example, fuel costs and consumer travel habits, intensely competitive "fare wars," a business model that was in need of being streamlined post-deregulation, and a reliance on a variety of different (aging) aircraft types (and suppliers) that significantly increased fuel, maintenance, and crew training costs. AA's CEO Robert Crandall was famous for saying that he thought airlines were *horrible investments* (Richard Branson is quoted as saying that the fastest way to become a millionaire is to take a billion dollars and invest it in an airline) and that he *never bought a single share of any airline stock with his own money.* (He did, however, receive AA shares in his compensation package.) He was a self-described airline *manager*, not an airline *investor*. However, Crandall clearly saw that without his analytics competitive advantage, his could have been the company going bust and not PEOPLExpress. The impact of analytics at AA is best summed up by the following now-famous story.

Crandall was allegedly telling another notable airline CEO colleague all about his brand-new OR-based yield management (YM) system, and suggested he too should invest in the technology. Crandall's CEO buddy said, "But Bob, your airline is losing money and my airline is already more profitable than yours!" To which Crandall responded, "But just think how much more money we would have lost without the OR YM system!" The quote is legendary and may be apocryphal, but shares an insight into the potential that Crandall correctly saw with the system.

The endeavor of carrying over the OR and analytics know-how and expertise of AA to other companies, especially in other travel/transportation industry sectors, was not without its challenges. Wishing to build on the notable revenue management (RM) success at AA, AADT was contracted to build an RM system for a major passenger railroad company. The project, which was originally planned to take less than a year, ended up taking *six years* to complete and delivered a more rudimentary RM solution with less sophistication than originally anticipated. The schedule delay and scope change were due to a variety of, at first unforeseen, highly impactful issues, including:

- Lack of alignment to the overall company strategy driven by a low data maturity
- Historical data availability, quality, and integrity issues due to insufficient data collection policies, processes, procedures, and systems

- Myriad complex cultural differences and change management challenges encountered as a result of moving from a stodgy bureaucracy with predominantly manual processes to a modernized, automated, and optimized decision-making approach for pricing and seat inventory management
- Significant fundamental differences between the way in which airlines and passenger railroads operate and manage pricing and seat inventory controls

To say that RM systems are data intensive is an understatement. American Airlines' DINAMO RM system was "standing on the shoulders of a giant" in terms of data (i.e., Sabre Reservation System). The passenger railway had no such system for collecting, tracking, and storing massive amounts of historical data. This makes demand forecasting (the starting point of revenue management) very challenging, if not practically impossible. All of the data management infrastructure required to support the RM system had to be built from scratch, which *literally* took *years*. In addition, the culture at AA was founded upon technology, data, automation, and advanced analytics, unlike the culture at the passenger railroad company, whose management team had to adapt and adopt a new streamlined, automated, and optimized way of operating its business with respect to pricing and seat inventory controls.

The power of RM technology, while holding the potential to be economically transformational, is not always guaranteed to be organizationally transformational, let alone transportable. AADT ultimately delivered the solution for the passenger railroad and learned innumerable valuable lessons from the experience. The trials and tribulations were not in vain, because based on these learnings, AADT successfully delivered a revenue management system for another major national passenger railroad with much less difficulty several years later.

One of the senior executives at AADT told Doug many, many years later that, in hindsight, the company dramatically underestimated the difficulty level and practical viability of taking the models and solutions built for AA and "lifting and shifting them" over to other passenger airlines, let alone passenger railroads. The OR team quickly discovered that other companies did not want to simply buy what AADT had built for American Airlines. What they wanted was AADT's *uniquely formidable expertise* in applying OR, data, and analytics to solving *their* company's most complex problems, i.e., AADT's intellectual property in the form of "know how."

The team also discovered the *considerable difference* in the way in which airlines in the United States operate versus airlines in Europe, Latin America, and the Asia-Pacific regions. This includes the nature of their respective route structure and flight schedules, geographies over which they operate, and even cultural differences. For example, a notable Asia-Pacific airline factored in a measure of "equity" when building crew schedules to ensure that all flight crew, regardless of seniority, got an opportunity to fly the most desirable routes, such as to San Francisco or Los Angeles, with some reasonable frequency.

Failure to transfer analytics from an airline to passenger railroad falls into the category of a very sophisticated solution from one industry being applied to solve a seemingly similar problem for another company in a seemingly similar but still relatively different industry without fully understanding the details of the underlying target business environment with respect to data, process, and culture. However, most importantly, the biggest failure was not building the business need and just assuming that because it worked well in one industry it would work well in another. Given the importance of this topic, and how often it came up in our research, we are going to analyze this reason for failure from a variety of angles.

Not Understanding the Real Business Problem

As our research has shown and we've mentioned before, the number one reason data science projects fail is because business people and data scientists, individually and collectively, don't understand the real business problem at hand, and as a result, fail to develop a plausible business case. Often, a data scientist will collect data and build a model and, at best, come up with the right answer to the wrong problem (i.e., a problem or question that the customer did not ask to be solved). Communication is a big issue (we'll talk more about that later) and is part of the challenge here, but there are several foundational steps that data scientists must take before beginning a project to help ensure that the business problem being addressed is mutually identified and thoroughly understood.

First and foremost, data science fundamentally requires a high degree of intellectual curiosity to be done well. You cannot be a data scientist at arm's length. You will need to "get dirty" with the details of your company's industry and business. To be effective, a data scientist requires a good contextual understanding at three levels:

1. Industry and Segment
2. Corporation and Department
3. Domain Problem Space

Data science applications vary greatly across industries and their respective segments, including:

- Energy (oil and gas, electric, wind, solar, generation, transmission)
- Transportation (airlines, railroads, trucking, rental cars)
- Healthcare (provider: institution or private practice, insurer, device manufacturer, pharmaceuticals)

- Financial services (banking, credit cards, credit reporting, mutual funds, hedge funds, private equity, venture capital)
- Manufacturing (automobiles, steel, consumer packaged goods, semi-conductors, food)
- Retail (big box, hardware, clothing, housewares)

Each of these industries has their own unique economics, operating models, and competitive landscapes. As much as an executive should try to get past the AI hype to truly understand the reality of ADSAI, it necessarily behooves the data scientist to research and understand as much as possible about their industry to help them understand the business problem they will apply their expertise to.

Each corporation within a given industry segment has its own competitive and economic DNA (e.g., low-cost provider vs. premium high-margin provider, culture, and mode of operation). To support the development of the business case, the executive must work with their analytics team to share a common understanding around:

- What is the company's business model?
- What is the company's strategic competitive advantage?
- What is the company's core product and/or service offering(s)?
- How does the company make (or lose) money (e.g., unit economics, order-to-cash cycle, etc.)?
- What are the primary sources of sales, revenue, and cost (i.e., operating expense and capital expenditure)?
- What makes the company "tick," for example, how the firm operates and converts inputs into outputs?

The company's annual report and financial statements are a great source of in-depth, detailed information to help answer these questions. (If you don't have a background in business administration, then find a friend in accounting or finance to help you get started.)

Inside an organization, many different departments may be using data science (or not, depending on the company's data and analytical maturity). The approach to data science and the problems to be solved are as varied as the departments, including Marketing, Sales, Manufacturing, Operations, Finance, Accounting, Human Resources, etc.

Understanding the goals, objectives, business processes, metrics, operating plans, and roadmaps of each organization is paramount to apply data science. Data scientists need to know *how the work gets done*, including budgets, data, data systems, and software, and learn to speak the *language* of each department—and, yes, each will have their own vocabulary, terminology, and acronyms. The corporate world LOVES acronyms. Being a data scientist requires deep immersion in your industry, the company, and department to understand the domain problem space and be able to contribute materially. The goal is not to be the math geek with the fancy laptop, but rather to be a team member who digs in deep and helps solve problems using some really powerful, specialized skills and tools.

When Doug started working for the OR Department at American Airlines in 1987, fresh out of graduate school at Georgia Tech, all he knew about airlines was how to make a flight reservation, get a boarding pass, find his seat, order a drink, and claim his luggage. Over the subsequent six years, he learned all of the relevant facets of airport operations, airline operations, maintenance/inventory operations, and crew/flight academy operations. Whenever he had a new project, he *physically parked himself* in the problem area next to the people who did the actual work, for example, Airport Traffic Control Tower and Terminal Radar Approach Control facilities, as well as network operations centers, maintenance hangar, and office buildings, etc. He didn't leave until he understood how these employees did their jobs and what the problem at hand was that required a solution from him. Then, and only then, did he commence with data science modeling work.

Both an executive looking to implement an ADSAI project and the data scientist who will be supporting it should be crystal clear on the answers to a number of key questions related to the business need:

- What is the problem that we are trying to solve? (The answer to this must be clearly and succinctly stated—no jargon.)
- What is the key business question we are trying to answer?
- What is the desired business outcome?
- What is the end state of the model/system we need to build? How will it be utilized?
- What is the "target" for improvement (e.g., cost reduction, conversion rate increase)?
- What key performance indicators (KPIs) are relevant to measure economic impact?
- What experiments can we run to measure the before-and-after effect of the model?

Multiple meetings and whiteboard sessions may be required to adequately answer these questions, but it will be time well spent for all parties involved. As the old software engineering adage goes, "An ounce of design is worth a pound of debugging." Take the proper time needed at the start of a project, and you are less likely to fail in the end.

Because this is easier said than done, we continue to see the incredible failure rate of analytics projects. Given the analytics failure rates, we can see that only 20% of analytic insights will deliver on their desired business outcomes. Understanding the true business problem at hand will help your project make—and hopefully grow—that 20% success rate. But to have a chance at success, we need to choose a problem suitable for the ADSAI approach. How do we find such problems? We turn to that next.

The Problem with Selecting Good Business Problems

In early 2020, as the COVID-19 wave spread across the globe and wreaked havoc in its wake, on a chilly morning in New Zealand, a worried team of container packers questioned what they were doing. They read the news and saw the health disaster unfolding in Italy, but until their manager said "stop," they kept working.

They filled container after container of frozen and chilled lamb goods bound for Greece. Once loading was complete, the container ship began its month-long journey at the beginning of March. By the end of the month, the ship was approaching Greece when the head of sales received the call he had been fearing from his Greek counterpart.

The reason for this dreaded call?

They were canceling the entire shipment. Restaurants were locked down and they would not accept a single gram of the meat. At the end of the call, the head of sales slumped in his seat speechless. Tens of millions of dollars were at stake. What could be done?

It was at that moment he did something that few people would do—he turned to his analytics tool (developed by a team that worked with Evan) to find an answer, at the very time when most would rely on either their intuition or the highest paid opinion.

In this moment of analytical faith, an incredible answer was found—all in less than a minute (for what would have taken a week of manual Excel effort without the AI tool). The tool discovered another market in which the head of sales could sell his goods in two weeks, and at a higher price than in Greece. This was because Greece was a so-called gold customer, which meant they received priority sales, even if the price was lower. The head of sales found a bronze customer located in Asia who would accept the goods at a higher price that day.

While this organization was making good, data-informed decisions, at the same time, thousands of other organizations with similar tools and skills were failing. Why was one organization able to leverage its data when others could not? In the case of the lamb seller, they were solving a problem that was amenable to analytics and able to produce good, usable solutions.

What does an amenable problem look like? It fulfills at least three things.

1. **It is complicated**. The problem must not be too complex, but also not too simple. If there are many complex interactions with too much

uncertainty, then we are very likely in trouble (i.e., it will be too difficult). If the solution is always obvious, then we are also in trouble because it won't justify overinvesting in advanced analytics; simple automation will do. We need to find the "Goldilocks" balance of difficulty for which technical AI approaches yield accurate and useful insights. These types of problems are well known to acolytes of the Cynefin problem classification framework[7] and are rightly called complicated.

2. **It makes business sense**. If the analytics tool doesn't have an impact in a commercial way, it is likely to fail. The application of AI cannot be someone's pet project; the ROI must be there and be clear to the business, and best of all, align with the company strategy, i.e., the business case justifies the spend on AI (e.g., leveraging an AI tool at scale will add 10% to the bottom line) or there must be a good business reason (e.g., reducing key person risk). We will see this later with the eye-opening WayBlazer story in which the project simply failed to cross the commercial threshold.

3. **The investment is well understood**. This point is worth calling out separately as it is endemically underestimated. When estimating costs for the business case, ensure there is a buffer, because AI projects always cost more than anticipated. Even if external consultants build the tools for a fixed price, there could be unexpected additional expenses, such as internal team effort to connect the analytics techniques developed to the business use.

These high-level criteria are important to ensure long-term success but especially in business, a commercially sensible project is probably the most important out of all three. It is worth spending a bit more time on this point and unpacking what that means and how it can be easily assessed for ADSAI (and even general technology) projects.

Mike's Story: AI in the Outback

Few places on Earth can break people like the Australian Outback. Toughness is not enough to survive, let alone thrive there. You must be smart, resourceful, and innovative to even stand a chance.

In 2019, Australia experienced the culmination of a devastating nine-year-long El Niño weather pattern (characterized by long, severe droughts). Plants and animals die during a regular El Niño. In this particular one, it was common to see livestock strewn along the road where they had perished for want of food and water. Then, in the second half of the year, began one of the worst bushfire seasons Australia has ever seen that made a difficult situation impossible. An estimated 5 million hectares was burned to ash,[8] an area bigger than the whole of the Netherlands.[9]

Mike is a crop farmer—one of those tough-as-nails, wily, and innovative Australians who make their living in this environment. Reeling from these last catastrophes, and wanting to keep ahead of the next disaster, he began exploring smart farming techniques enabled by AI. The technology he found overlaid AI onto big data and would have been integrated into his irrigation, pest control, and soil management systems to allow for "precision farming."

In theory, by refining the focus of his practices from the paddock level to that of the individual plant, the technology could reduce wastage by up to 80%. That is a lot of extra (desperately needed) cash. Especially when you are trying to compete in a global market with little assistance from your government, against foreign farmers with lots of assistance from theirs, and in an environment in which very few crops will generally grow.

The tech salesperson's pitch to Mike was compelling. It showed a familiarity with the existential challenges faced by Australian farmers—supported by a clever application of AI generating potentially significant returns. However, the business case outlined by the salesperson raised doubts in Mike's mind. The initial investment would be $500,000 with additional costs of $80,000 per annum for data storage and processing alone, and this didn't account for maintenance and support.

To put this in context, in 2020–2021, average Australian farm cash income in US dollars—out of which the farmers pay their families' income—was about $137,500.[10] Profit was $79,000, which translates to a 1.6% rate of return on the farm assets (and the financial year 2020–2021 was fortunately a good one for Australian farmers). Within that, average expenditure on crop and pasture chemicals (herbicides, etc.) and fertilizer was $63,000. Adding water rights, expenditure totaled $100,000.

Assuming the technology performed at its absolute maximum (80% cost reduction) and did not add to any other costs, at the very best, it would be profit neutral for the average Australian farm going forward, after significantly putting the farm into deficit the first year. In short: If Mike's farm were roughly average, adopting AI may have thrown his family into serious financial difficulty.

Putting the Cart (Technology) before the Horse (Business)

The current AI hype is making investment decisions in its tools more difficult than ever before. The technology is at once enchanting, powerful, and increasingly pervasive, and everyone has something to say about it—from the 24-hour news cycle postulating whether AI and robots will eliminate millions of jobs and subsequently destroy humankind, to Elon Musk and his self-driving electric automobiles. Our opinion is that not enough people are looking at the main problem that this presents for businesses. Almost everyone is caught up in the *engineering* of what AI can do, whereas more people ought to be interested in its *value* in terms of the *business impact* it can generate, which brings us yet again to the AI hype problem.[11]

Although the development of some AI algorithms can mimic the operations of an intelligent mind, or better still, a super intelligent mind on narrowly focused tasks, at the time of writing, humans have yet to create a new form of intelligence to rival our own. However, we do have at our disposal technologies that offer the possibility of automating a broad range of human activities. This is not just the automation of manual labor on the production line, many of the major advances in AI—particularly in the past decade—have been in automating data processing and analysis.[12] One of the most thrilling (and terrifying) advances has been the advent of the GPT-4 platform from OpenAI, one of the most familiar, widely known tools that has proponents seeing a possible pathway to general intelligence AI. GPT-4 can write entire cogent essays, and even poems, from a single prompt, on virtually any topic. Other generative AI tools can compose "original" music scores, render "original" works of art, and create "original" videos (with sound) from a text prompt.

The current hype associated with AI is quite familiar to those with knowledge of the history of the technology and its past hype, and also a warning sign that business, government, and public expectations about the technology may be running ahead of reality. Renowned futurist Roy Amara famously said that, "We tend to overestimate the effect of a technology in the short run and underestimate the effect in the long run." Scientific advances in neural networks and machine learning, vast improvements in computing power, and the advent of distributed computing have brought about a qualitative change in the capabilities of the technology. But modern AI still has limits and is still expensive, especially when machines must be trained to learn specific and novel task sets.

The problem with AI is that the focus is on what it *can* do, not what it actually *does*. At present, the engineers are in the driver's seat, and their strength is not always business outcomes because they focus on *possibility*, i.e., the "how to do it" instead of the "why" or "how much" (value and cost). Economics realizes many things are possible, but also acknowledges that resources are constrained and must be directed to the best possibilities. Paraphrasing the famous words of Lionel Robbins: "Economics is the study of life as a relationship between ends and scarce resources which have alternative uses."[13] *Economics* needs to be put in the driver's seat when it comes to the question of AI adoption for any organization, and engineering should work under the hood. The question must not be the engineering of what AI can do, but rather the economics of what AI is worth in terms of value to business and society. We'll unpack why in order to pose a better solution to the challenge of restoring economics as the primary decision-making framework for AI adoption.[14] By doing so, we'll solve one of the big strategic reasons for failure, not clearly measuring success.

The Solution: Put Economics Back in the Driver's Seat

First, we need to firmly and simply establish the exact economic criterion for AI adoption. This is straightforward enough: An AI system should be adopted by an organization if, and only if, the profit obtained is greater than the opportunity cost of that profit.

The easiest errors to make in economic reasoning are forgetting about opportunity cost, focusing only on whether profit after adoption is positive, and so committing to a suboptimal decision. Opportunity cost is important—the value of the next best alternative. Typically, this is the profit achieved under the status quo, but it can also be the profit achieved by an alternative strategy (e.g., buying more fertilizer for Mike).

Consider the logic in Figure 2.1. Economists will recognize this formula as a particular case of a consumer (buyer) surplus-maximizing decision, in which a rational consumer looks at their set of decisions and chooses the one that maximizes their consumer surplus. The surplus concept is useful because it also helps explain why certain situations arise, such as the one faced by farmer Mike. When pricing AI products and services, AI producers analyze their potential customers' gains and then choose a price point to maximize their surplus (not their customers').

However, organizations can fail to factor in the total cost of ownership, which includes all the other costs that arise with such a system, including maintenance, repair, installation, failures, lower than expected results, etc. Mike needs to consider each of these factors, as well as the chance that the system could fail altogether, if he is going to make an optimal decision. Figure 2.1 is valuable as a "cue" for the economic mindset—a habitual yardstick to always call to mind when considering AI adoption. On its own, however, it is not enough guidance for decision-makers; it is too abstract. We need to be more specific.

The basic economic principle of AI adoption can be restated in what economists famously call "marginal" terms, meaning incremental or additional. What will be the change in profit obtained by AI adoption? Adapting this, we can unpack what should be the basic economic principle of AI adoption. It now becomes something more specific: AI should be adopted if, and only if, *relative to the next best alternative*, the marginal benefit (i.e., additional benefit

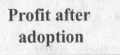 

FIGURE 2.1
The basic economic principle of AI adoption—of which, the right-hand side is extremely easy to forget.

over the current base) of its adoption is greater than its marginal cost (i.e., additional cost over the current base). The next best alternative (opportunity cost) will, again, typically be the status quo, but it could also be hiring another employee or outsourcing some tasks.

To make this as useful as possible, let's be even more specific. AI adoption can generate gains by improving the quality of our judgment. This leads to better quality decisions (typically through better quality predictions and prescriptions). From an organization's perspective, this means:

1. the organization has better allocation/utilization of its inputs; and
2. the organization has better quality/delivery of its outputs.

The first situation leads to lower costs and the second situation would lead to greater revenue. Other cases in which we improve the quality/delivery of the organization's outputs can simply lead to a better delivery of services; for example, in a hospital scenario, this can lead to more lives saved, hence an increase in the value of the so-called statistical lives saved. In addition, these outcomes may be directly or indirectly generated. In the latter case, the integration of AI may generate greater returns on existing assets by creating synergies that boost productivity. In Mike's case, the AI offered cost savings in the long term. By integrating AI into his irrigation, pest control, and soil management systems, he would have reduced wastage and enhanced the productivity of his existing assets, potentially reducing his required capital expenditures in the future.

On the other hand, the marginal cost of AI adoption consists of at least two main components:

1. Upfront cost of installation and setup
2. Ongoing operating cost of the AI system (including maintenance, repair, and support)

When these components are converted into expected Net Present Value (NPV), i.e., the current value of future discounted cash flows, we have the basis for an economically informed decision, as illustrated in Figure 2.2, which refines the previous criterion in Figure 2.1. To make the figure more applicable, instead of the general inputs and outputs perspective we mentioned earlier, we focus on the specific value drivers also mentioned to make the framework clearer. Figure 2.2 should be calculated for each alternative and then compared to make the best possible investment decision.

Figure 2.2 shows the economic principles of AI adoption and provides simple accessible cues for building and triggering a habitual economic mindset when thinking about AI adoption in organizations. To complete the system, we provide a decision tree for AI adoption (see Figure 2.3).

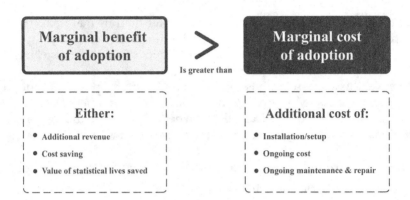

FIGURE 2.2
The economic principle of AI adoption unpacked: What are the changes in benefits and costs (relative to each alternative)?

The decision tree consists of three simple questions: Two are the responsibility of an AI salesperson to answer, one can be posed internally to the organization. The first question to ask the salesperson: What is the dollar amount or percentage gain that your AI system generates? If the salesperson cannot answer in terms of revenue, cost reduction, or value of a statistical life (or similar important output), a conservative rule of thumb is not to adopt the AI system (unless you have other strategic reasons that might be hard to estimate). If the salesperson gives a sufficient answer, the second question may be posed to the salesperson: What are the dollar costs of installation/setup, operation, maintenance, and repair? Again, if the salesperson cannot answer, a conservative rule of thumb is not to adopt the AI system. If the salesperson gives a sufficient answer, however, we proceed to the third question to be asked internally: Given the next best alternative to this AI system, are the marginal benefits of adoption greater than the marginal costs (compared to the alternative)? If no, pursue the alternative, if yes, adopt the AI system.

This might seem like common sense and relatively straightforward economic thinking, but as the saying goes, the funny thing about common sense is that it isn't that common. When we put the economic process for AI adoption in a decision tree, any given AI system will need to meet a high bar to be adopted. Three of the four options end in rejection. Keeping these three elements of an economic attitude in mind and adopting them are important steps for economics to lead the decision when it comes to organizational AI adoption. The problem is one of hype and expectations getting ahead of the reality of AI's value proposition. The solution is a simple heuristic to assess the potential value of AI systems as presented in Figure 2.3.

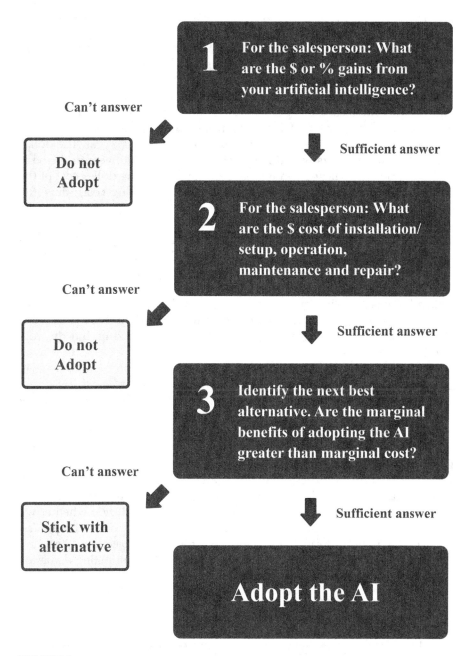

FIGURE 2.3
A simple, three-step decision tree for any AI adoption problem. Note the high bar that AI must meet to be economically valuable.

Resolving Mike's AI Investment Challenge

Applying this simple heuristic to Mike's situation, we can readily understand why he couldn't make business sense of the salesperson's pitch of AI-enabled precision farming.

As noted, the salesperson suggested that Mike would achieve cost savings of 80% (the salesperson got past the first decision point in our economic decision tree). We saw that if Mike's farm was roughly average, the relevant expenditures would have sat somewhere around $100,000/year. The dollar value of Mike's savings would have been around $80,000/year in the best-case scenario. The salesperson was also upfront about the dollar cost of the systems: $500,000 for installation, $80,000/year in ongoing costs; thus, the salesperson got past the second decision point.

However, we can immediately see why the salesperson failed on the third decision point: The best-case marginal benefit of adopting the AI ($80,000) was less than the marginal cost ($80,000 plus the installation cost). Mike would have made less profit than his opportunity cost (e.g., doing nothing) if he adopted the AI and would have eroded the meager 1.6% rate of return he was accruing on his assets. He may have even bankrupted his family by incurring a significant debt to purchase a profit-neutral technology. The technology (engineering) may have been amazing, but the economics were not.

Mike's story is one among many of the real examples that the co-authors encounter every day in practice. Because it is based on *economic reasoning*, our heuristic applies equally across the many industries readers may be working in.[15]

Putting economics back in the driver's seat (and engineering under the hood) allows us to resolve investment decisions as specific as whether a given farmer should adopt an AI system and as general as deciding among which biomedical priorities to allocate scarce research funds. Using an economic heuristic of worth, rather than an engineering heuristic of possibility, guides us to make better decisions and can help us decide whether we should even embark upon an AI project. However, for many companies, this isn't the issue, but rather, having many promising projects and deciding which to pursue. How can we efficiently prioritize the competing demands of the many business departments for AI attention?

Solving a Problem That Is Not a Business Priority

> Ruthlessly rigorous prioritization of (technology, data science) projects based on potential business value and economic impact is the best way to ensure meaningful, successful outcomes.

> **—Fortune 50 EVP and CTO**

Every single company has limited capital and human resources to invest in IT and data science. There are *never* sufficient budget dollars and people to fund and execute all projects. In cases we've observed in Fortune 50 companies, new project demand exceeds the available budget by 2–4x. Projects must compete for resources during each budget cycle based on their respective relative potential to generate incremental business value.

Data science projects are no exception and are ultimately judged on their ability to move the needle on economic performance. That said, in many companies, there is a lot of political wrangling and "pet project" machinations that affect the decision-making process regarding which projects get off the ground, i.e., the HiPPO projects (**H**ighest **P**aid **P**erson's **O**pinion).

Fortunately, there are multiple rational, fact-based, data-driven frameworks that help estimate, measure, and compare value to inform data science project decision-making.

In a Harvard Business Review article by Kevin Troyanos, head of analytics at Publicis Health, a heuristic rubric was offered to help prioritize business questions using a two-dimensional grid (see Figure 2.4):[16]

- x-axis (horizontal): Ability to activate or execute, implement, and deploy the solution
- y-axis (vertical): Potential to impact, or business/economic value

Working on **high-value key business question** (KBQ) projects with a high ability to activate and a high potential to impact are where businesses want to be operating the large majority of the time. Selecting projects that can be implemented, and also deliver significant, tangible, measurable business value and economic impact (e.g., cost reduction, operational efficiency or performance improvement, revenue increase, or customer satisfaction and experience enhancement) can be challenging, but is absolutely necessary for long-term success.

Curiosities should be completely avoided because they consume resources on projects that offer low ability to activate and low potential to impact.

Pipe dreams, sometimes referred to as "moon shots," offer high potential to impact but a low ability to activate. Sometimes companies embark on such projects—despite a low likelihood of success—on the fervent hope that they will succeed and deliver tremendous market leverage or competitive advantage. If the project fails, then they try to extract key learnings to feed into other less ambitious projects. (Our upcoming example of WayBlazer falls into this category, along with IBM Watson Health, another well-documented story mentioned earlier.)

Incremental improvements offer low potential to impact and a high ability to activate. These types of projects can be effective when an organization is just getting started with data science and looking for some "quick wins"

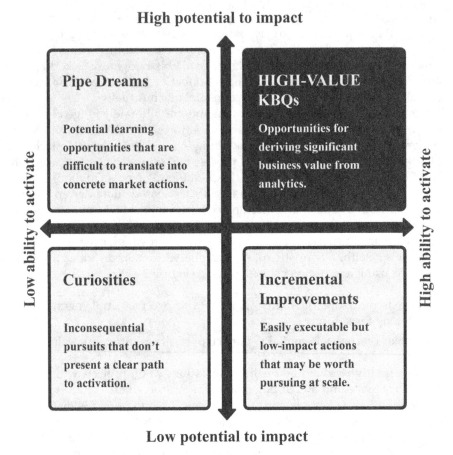

High potential to impact

Pipe Dreams

Potential learning
opportunities that are
difficult to translate into
concrete market actions.

**HIGH-VALUE
KBQs**

Opportunities for
deriving significant
business value from
analytics.

Curiosities

Inconsequential
pursuits that don't
present a clear path
to activation.

**Incremental
Improvements**

Easily executable but
low-impact actions
that may be worth
pursuing at scale.

Low ability to activate

High ability to activate

Low potential to impact

FIGURE 2.4
Two-dimensional heuristic key business question prioritization rubric based on an estimate of
the potential to impact business/economic value (y-axis) and the ability to activate, execute,
implement, and deploy the solution (x-axis).

Source: Publicis Health.

while they are building momentum and growing the capability to handle
larger, more complex, and higher value initiatives. The payoffs are not as
great, but if they add some measurable value and the team sharpens their
skills, then that is considered a win.

There will always be many views, perspectives, and opinions on how
best to prioritize and select among competing projects, so a more uniformly
applied, objective approach can help level the playing field. For those who
prefer a more *quantitative* approach to scoring and ranking ADSAI projects,
Doug has successfully utilized a process of ranking in a variety of software

and analytics product/solution development settings, and we provide a detailed description in the notes.[17]

Doug's approach combines each prospective project's business value potential, resource/cost estimation, and technical complexity into a project "score" to enable a quantitative *ranking* of projects to assist in deciding which initiatives to work on. The scores act as a surrogate quantification of the KBQ Grid for each project's potential to impact (value and cost) and ability to execute (complexity), and helps to reveal to managers the logic behind a decision to start the "fun" part—people debating and haggling over the individual and aggregate score for their respective project(s). (This process should be accompanied by a more rigorous financial analysis of projects using NPV, ROI, and IRR metrics.)

This is not just a theoretical exercise. When Doug was VP of Engineering & Product Management for a division of a $1.3B software product company, they had a list of 2,000 feature modification requests (FMRs). They estimated their capacity to complete about 500 FMRs in a new major product release. The team used Doug's ranking process (detailed in the chapter bibliography as mentioned before) to rationally, objectively, and as economically and efficiently as possible, narrow down the list of projects their engineering team could realistically do in one release cycle, and they proved it worked in practice for this team.

Because the selection of problems is such an important part of getting to the right business questions, let's dig into an example of a high-quality company that was a pioneer of ADSAI across the travel sector, but misjudged their solution's ability to activate and landed in the 80% of companies failing to deliver on their promise.

WayBlazer: Companies Will Not Always Pay for the Fancier Mousetrap

The innovation, and the ultimate unexpected shut down, of the trailblazing travel AI startup WayBlazer in 2018 has been well documented. Their story is additional proof that world-class industry leaders, proven powerful AI technology platforms, and venture funding from technology titans, including IBM, cannot guarantee success, or even at least the avoidance of failure.

WayBlazer was founded in 2014 by travel distribution technology industry luminary and former Sabre VP/CIO Terrell B. "Terry" Jones, who pioneered EaasySABRE and was founder, President & CEO of Travelocity.com, along with former IBM Watson General Manager Manoj Saxena. It was later led by travel and hospitality industry veteran Noreen Henry. WayBlazer set out to revolutionize and transform consumer online travel planning, shopping, and booking using voice and text NLP technology embedded into mobile, messaging, concierge apps, and advertising channels to improve customer experience and increase booking conversion rates.

WayBlazer focused on the trip planning aspect of travel. The business-to-business company developed AI technology to help brands improve customer engagement and conversion. For instance, WayBlazer worked with InterContinental Hotels Group (IHG) to power the voice component of its mobile app and Facebook Messenger interface. The company also partnered with Trisept Solutions on its Xcelerator product, an AI search engine for travel agents.

Former CEO Noreen Henry had an ambitious vision:

> Four years ago, we set out to blaze a new, innovative way for users to shop and book travel that leverages the power of AI to understand a traveler's unique trip intent and offer the most relevant personalized trip recommendations. Through a visually engaging chat platform, WayBlazer enabled major travel brands to engage customers through voice, messaging and even advertising channels to improve the customer experience and drive increases in conversion.[18]

Although the company's technology leader Saxena found success in other verticals with IBM Watson, travel proved challenging. Getting customers to change software platforms and integrate new technology wasn't easy, often taking ten months from test to contract with no immediate cash flow or guarantee that businesses would eventually sign up.[19] WayBlazer licensed IBM Watson technology to power its NLP capabilities and enable it to provide recommendations based on a traveler's specific context and intent.

In addition to WayBlazer, major companies such as Microsoft and Google began investing heavily in developing AI solutions for a variety of sectors, including travel. This would clearly challenge WayBlazer's sales activities. When asked if it was difficult for a startup such as WayBlazer to compete with these larger players, the later leader Henry said:

> We went head-to-head with a number of these companies and our ability to deliver real results very quickly with a small team at a low cost often proved its value and brands were willing to partner with us. But again, it takes time and B2B can be a long sales cycle. The large companies can go longer before needing to generate revenue from a niche solution.[20]

To survive these long sales cycles, according to Crunchbase,[21] WayBlazer received a total of $8.7 million in two rounds of financing, with the most recent round in May 2017 for $3.7 million, including a $5 million Series A investment from IBM.

Interestingly enough, Doug ran into Terry Jones at an Analytics/AI conference in 2019 in Dallas, where Terry was the keynote speaker, and Doug was a participant in a discussion panel. When Doug asked what exactly caused the outcome at WayBlazer, Terry said that despite successfully completing several POC projects with multiple big brand name companies, they just couldn't get enough customers to move forward fast enough and invest in the production implementation of the solution. Simply put, they ran out of time and money. In any new venture, the costs never fail to materialize, but the revenues are often less reliable.[22]

Multiple notable companies, including IHG Hotels & Resorts, Hilton, Marriott, Emirates Vacations, and Leading Hotels of the World, all signed on for POC projects, but getting them to step up and pay for a full-fledged production deployment of WayBlazer's groundbreaking technology in a timely manner turned out to be a bridge too far.[19]

All companies have limited capital and resources and must therefore rigorously prioritize their selection of investments in new, innovative technologies based on which ones will measurably, tangibly, and *substantially* increase their cash flow over that generated by their status quo incumbent technology platforms (in this instance, travel distribution websites and mobile apps). Organizations typically utilize metrics such as NPV, ROI, and internal rate of return (IRR) to compare competing projects; i.e., to try to build a proper business case.

Based on the commentary from the founders of WayBlazer, we can surmise with high likelihood that despite its clever, highly innovative AI-based technological tools for travel planning and exploration, WayBlazer's solution came up short on implementation project NPV, ROI, and IRR metrics. Their AI solution failed to generate sufficiently substantial incremental cash flows to offset the high costs of new technology acquisition, integration, and changeover. Compared with proven incumbent travel booking tools, the business value and economic impact of WayBlazer's solution was not sufficient to warrant the investment to integrate and productionize the newfangled AI product. WayBlazer did not make the final cut for those notable companies' AI and IT priorities and investments.[19]

For travel advisers, encouraged by the fact that they have outlived another startup, be advised that WayBlazer's reasons for failure were not inherently technological or market-driven, and its demise does not mean AI can't succeed in travel. You may not recall having heard about Duryea Motor Wagon Company—its failure as America's first commercial car company did nothing to discourage Henry Ford, Ransom Olds, or Kiichiro Toyoda (to say nothing of Elon Musk).

"A McKinsey & Co. report said that travel is dead last in implementing AI but also that AI's biggest opportunity is in travel," Jones said. "It's tough ... But travel companies need to wake up. If someone does implement AI, it'll be a real game changer. But we ran out of time at WayBlazer."[19]

Challenges in Aligning Vision, Strategy, and Measuring Success

Data scientists and leadership may have very different definitions of a "successful" project. Data scientists may believe that if they've solved the stated business requirement, then the project hasn't failed, whereas those on the business side may not see projects as successful unless they have created actionable insights that drive business growth or reduce cost. This can lead to significant alignment issues between the data science team's focus and what the business wants them to do—in fact, data scientists' responses to ADSAI project success surveys (mixed in with nontechnical respondents) might even suggest that the 80% failure rates are too low.[23] With such misalignments, even with access to "good" data, organizations may still struggle to convert it into actionable and commercially relevant insights. This creates a huge outcome discrepancy between access to data and the ability to extract value from it.

Again, the problem here lies at the start of the project in making sure the data science team and leadership collaborate to define a clear vision or strategy. If the strategy is mutually understood and followed throughout the project's journey, then ideally, both sides should agree upon whether the ADSAI project was successful in the end.

This problem was evident with our retail giant at the start of the chapter. It was clear that very little productive collaboration occurred at RetailCo. Their greatest challenge lay with the ELT. Because they were all senior leaders, experts, and in charge of their respective area, they each *thought* they understood what AI is about—unfortunately for all involved, the former has absolutely nothing to do with the latter. Some ELT members were trying to make decisions in situations about which they had practically no knowledge, experience, or expertise. Perhaps they had read something on LinkedIn and became "instant experts"—the Dunning-Kruger effect incarnate in all its glory.

People who are analytically inclined, if given a statement and shown that it is false, can admit it is false. The cultural environment in the ELT at RetailCo was different. Egos and a strong desire to maintain control played a big role in the personalization project's failure. Leadership behavior filters down to the departments, and people begin working in silos, which can be dangerous for ADSAI projects. The challenges with this particular project were not by any means analytical ones, rather, they were broader cultural and managerial issues, and behaviors driven by executives who were making scope and resource allocation decisions that served their own purposes, for example, controlling costs, trimming what they thought were excess resources, building out a CDP infrastructure, inappropriate task-to-resource assignments, etc. A clear lack of alignment.

Combine these issues and behaviors with executives wanting to treat a data science project like an IT project with legacy IT systems, and, with leadership slowing down progress with their Waterfall project management mentality versus a leaner, Agile MVP approach, and you have an analytics failure in the making.

From the start, the preference of our senior executive Ben was to build an *extraction* of the data instead of integrating data into RetailCo's systems with a stand-alone personalization engine, at least initially. This latter approach would be cheaper and faster, but it would require the business to think about and execute the project in an unfamiliar way (i.e., the culture shift and change management dread). The original business case was based on this latter type of approach. Without proper strategic alignment, the RetailCo data science project was never going to be a success.

We often came across this major failure in our research—not clearly defining success (i.e., defining or measuring it appropriately) or the final deliverables, or what's more, the actions one should take based on the insights. This is a typical symptom of AI hype—going all in without thinking, just because everyone else is.

On the flip side, instead of committing without thinking, the leadership simply does not support the initiative in spite of approving and confirming the importance of AI. It can be an insidious problem with the analytics team pushing ahead, full of uncertainty as to whether their funding will be cut, or even worse, if their work will become shelfware.

Lack of Leadership Buy-in

Finally, lack of leadership and upper management buy-in of the ADSAI agenda commonly occurred in our research as a major reason for project failure at the strategic level. It starts with complex cultural issues such as whether there is a norm of using evidence for decisions in the company, or an expectation that people will use expertise versus following the most expensive opinion (or HiPPO, as mentioned earlier). This is not the same as aligning the vision and strategy, this goes deeper—to struggling to achieve buy-in in the first place.

For example, does upper management mandate the use of analytical tools? (Often there must be 100% uptake to get the ROI on an ADSAI project.) Does management commit by devoting enough money in the form of sufficient resources and tool investment to even build capability? Part of the challenge here is that for this to happen, management needs to understand the benefits of using analytics over existing solutions (e.g., experience-based decisions) and be convinced (often with simple calculations) that the ADSAI project will deliver a good outcome. This starts at the top.

But even simpler than these more complex cultural issues, for leadership and management to buy into, invest, and support ADSAI, they must first understand what it is and isn't, as well as the true capabilities of what it can and cannot do. To achieve that understanding, executives need guidance from leaders who understand the company's business *and* have a track record in successfully applying ADSAI at enterprise scale; that is, at the company-, division-, or department-level. ADSAI is, in effect, a *strategic tool*, and like any tool, it must be properly operated and maintained, and most importantly, aimed at a *target*. When used this way, in the experience of both co-authors, AI typically leads to improvements in current operations (either revenue increases or cost decreases), and is just one of many ways to achieve better operations (e.g., companies could simply hire more staff to do more instead of using AI). A strategy for ADSAI starts with some key business questions, problems, or decisions of considerable importance that will uniquely benefit from an ADSAI approach (or at least be better than the alternatives, like we discussed earlier when analyzing opportunity costs). Addressing these will create significant measurable, tangible business value and economic impact.

Having leadership buy-in leads to a clear path to success. The American Airlines' business problem was Yield Management. At RetailCo, it was personalization. The primary difference between the two examples: At AA, senior executives gave the ADSAI team the latitude to operate and execute the strategy while holding them accountable to deliver results, which they ultimately did in remarkable fashion. Whereas alternatively, at RetailCo, the senior executives chose to interfere in the details of the project to try and micromanage the scope, resources, and target and thereby failed to maintain rigorous project discipline and best practices—compounded by those offering their opinions having no knowledge, experience, or expertise to do so—resulting in what can only be described as a colossal failure.

ADSAI strategy, like business strategy, is about the *who, what, when*, and *why*, but not the *how*. Albeit, it is about the *how much*, because resources need to be allocated and initiatives need to be funded. Once the target is identified, the approach is agreed upon, and resources are allocated, senior executives need to trust ADSAI leaders to execute the mission, course correct if necessary, and deliver the promised results.

In short, the ELT at RetailCo suffered from the ubiquitous affliction that when *everyone* is in charge of an ADSAI initiative, or any initiative for that matter, then *no one* is in charge. There is a need for collaboration and mutual understanding, but departmental leaders must also learn to stay in their lane and not stray too far into domains that they really know nothing about. ADSAI leaders need to spend an inordinate amount of time and energy communicating, clarifying, and making sure that everyone is on the same page regarding all the salient elements of the project. Additionally, they must also be given an unfettered opportunity to maneuver, operate, and execute the mission at hand. When ADSAI leaders can do this effectively, upper management truly buys in. This is not just passive support for ADSAI projects. And by doing so, upper management will be able to keep—instead of losing—their top leaders with AI capabilities, like Ben.

But even if Ben had managed to push through the strategic challenges facing him, what would have happened next? Once an organization has solved its strategic challenges, knows its strategic direction, and understands its vision, it encounters the next big hurdle of creating the proper internal processes to ensure success. We all know processes are important, but just how important are they to ADSAI project success? Surely, we can cut corners when needed or let each department do things its own way, like the IT team did at RetailCo? We'll find out.

Critical Thinking: How Not to Fail

- What role did the RetailCo ELT play in the failure of the personalization analytics project? What adverse behaviors did the ELT members exhibit? What else could Ben have done to try and prevent the undesired outcome?
- What were the three primary challenges AADT encountered in transporting AA's world-class revenue/yield management methodology to the passenger railroad company?
- How can a discrepancy arise between what the frontline data scientist considers a success and what the management or executive team considers a success? What could cause this? Which party should ultimately decide what counts as a success?
- What was the primary cause of WayBlazer's failure as an AI startup company despite their development of innovative, breakthrough AI NLP technology for the leisure travel industry?
- Utilize the Key Business Questions matrix to characterize a group of ADSAI projects at your company. Utilize the Project Scoring spreadsheet template to rank order the projects based on business value potential, complexity, and cost. See the chapter notes for details.
- Based on the AI adoption decision economic value heuristic rubric in Figure 2.3, did Mike (the Australian Outback farmer) make the right decision? Did Zolgensma (see chapter notes[15])?

	A	B	C	D	E	F	G	H
1	**Projects**	**Bus Value$**	**BusValScore**	**Complexity**	**CmplxScore**	**Resources**	**Res Score**	**Score**
2								
3	Project 8	$ 11,000,000	6	LOW	8	$ 2,500,000	5	240
4	Project 2	$ 8,000,000	4	LOW	7	$ 1,800,000	7	196
5	Project 9	$ 5,000,000	2	VERY LOW	10	$ 1,000,000	9	180
6	Project 5	$ 7,000,000	3	LOW	7	$ 1,750,000	8	168
7	Project 4	$ 12,000,000	7	MEDIUM	5	$ 3,500,000	4	140
8	Project 1	$ 10,000,000	5	MEDIUM	4	$ 2,000,000	6	120
9	Project 10	$ 4,000,000	1	VERY LOW	10	$ 500,000	10	100
10	Project 6	$ 14,000,000	8	HIGH	3	$ 4,000,000	3	72
11	Project 7	$ 16,000,000	9	VERY HIGH	2	$ 4,500,000	2	36
12	Project 3	$ 20,000,000	10	VERY HIGH	1	$ 5,000,000	1	10

FIGURE 2.5
Example calculation to rank project importance.

Notes

1. Rosman, K. (2013, August 14). Weather Channel Now Also Forecasts What You'll Buy: Company's Data Helps Fine-Tune When and Where Advertisers Should Place Spots. *Wall Street Journal Online Edition*. https://www.wsj.com/articles/SB10001424127887323639704579012674092402660.

2. In addition to our own research on this topic, the books Davenport, T., & Harris, J. (2017). *Competing on Analytics*. Harvard Business Review Press and Davenport, T. (2023). *All in on AI*. Harvard Business Review Press provide some good overviews. Davenport's D-E-L-T-T-A-A model from his best-selling book *Competing on Analytics* (2017) provides an excellent framework for establishing a strategy, i.e., data, enterprise view, leadership (engagement and buy-in), targets (KPI, business value, economic impact), technologies, analytics techniques, and analysts. His book *All in on AI* (2023) provides a similar framework of required elements for enterprises seeking to engage in applying AI in their respective businesses.

3. Smith, B., Leimkuhler, J., & Darrow, R. (1992). Yield Management at American Airlines. *Interfaces*, 22(1), 8-31.

4. How American Airlines Weaponised Data. (2020, August 3). The Flying Moose. https://www.theflyingmoose.net/articles/how-american-airlines-weaponised-data.

5. CAE concludes acquisition of Sabre's Airline Operations (AirCentre) portfolio. (2022). CAE.com. https://www.cae.com/news-events/press-releases/cae-concludes-acquisition-of-sabres-airline-operations-aircentre-portfolio/.

6. Davenport, T., & Harris, J. (2017). *Competing on Analytics*. Harvard Business Review Press. P. 88.

7. Snowden, D. J. (2015, December 7). A leader's framework for decision making. *Harvard Business Review*. https://hbr.org/2007/11/a-leaders-framework-for-decision-making.

8. Wikipedia contributors. (2024, March 14). 2019–20 Australian bushfire season. In *Wikipedia, The Free Encyclopedia*. Retrieved 02:13, March 16, 2024, from https://en.wikipedia.org/w/index.php?title=2019%E2%80%9320_Australian_bushfire_season&oldid=1213596041.

9. CBS. (2021, February 9). How do we use our land? - The Netherlands in Numbers 2020. https://longreads.cbs.nl/the-netherlands-in-numbers-2020/how-do-we-use-our-land.

10. Ashton, D., Martin, P., Frilay, J., Litchfield, F., Weragoda, A., & Coelli, R. (2021). Farm performance: broadacre and dairy farms, 2018–19 to 2020–21, ABARES research report, Canberra, March, DOI: https://doi.org/10.25814/ycy6-3p65. CC BY 4.0.

11. Davenport, T. (2023). *All in on AI*. Harvard Business Review Press. We refer the reader to Tom Davenport's book, *All in on AI* (2023), for a blueprint of how to prepare for, then execute, and reap the tremendous rewards from AI embedded into your company's products and services.

12. Sullivan, J. & Zuvatern, A. (2017). *The Mathematical Corporation*. New York: Public Affairs.

13. Robbins, L. (1932). *Essay on the Nature and Significance of Economic Science*. London: MacMillan.
14. Agarwal, A., Gans, J., & Goldfarb, A. (2018). *Prediction Machines: The Simple Economics of Artificial Intelligence*. Harvard Business Review Press. Here, we build on the work of Joshua Gans who has pioneered the economic analysis of AI systems with a series of papers, and a summarizing book *Prediction Machines: The Simple Economics of Artificial Intelligence*.
15. Another interesting and poignant example comes from medicine. In May 2019, the US Food and Drug Administration (FDA) made a decision that created international headlines by approving the world's most expensive drug treatment to date, Zolgensma[24]. This medicine treats spinal muscular atrophy in infants, replacing annual lifelong treatments with a once-off cure. The minimum price is (only!) $2 million (USD) for a single treatment. To many, this price point makes no sense; however, when we apply our economic heuristic, we can better understand why pharmaceutical company Novartis chose this fee.

    Zolgensma is part of a new wave of drugs that promise to usher in a revolutionary era of personalized medicine using AI to leverage big data and discover treatments bespoke to individual genetic profiles. Zolgensma works by replacing the defective SMN1 gene that expresses itself in infant spinal muscular atrophy with a normal copy. To discover this technology for bespoke genetic medicine, Novartis had to mine terabytes of genomic data to find the right compound that, when delivered, would introduce a highly specific change to a highly specific point in highly specific individual genomes.

    Does this AI-enabled technology make economic sense? Let's apply our heuristic. In this case, the direct benefit of the technology is to save (quality-adjusted) statistical lives by improving the quality of life for infants debilitated by spinal muscular atrophy. The value of a statistical life (used by governments and corporations across the world in daily policymaking) is typically between $4 million and $10 million (USD). Novartis' AI-enabled drug costs around $2 million (USD). Given that we are talking about infants with an expected life of up to 80 years, there are a wide range of statistical lives that could be saved by the drug that would justify adoption. The marginal benefit (statistical lives saved) is greater than the marginal cost of adoption, and the profit is greater than the opportunity cost of doing nothing or inventing other drugs. This calculus may sound cold-hearted until we remember that opportunity cost may also very well be the value of allocating funds to research infant oncology.
16. Troyanos, K. (2020). Use Data to Answer Your Key Business Questions. *Harvard Business Review*. https://hbr.org/2020/02/use-data-to-answer-your-key-business-questions.
17. This project efficacy scoring, evaluation, and analysis approach can easily be done in MSExcel—one of the few times we will recommend that a data scientist use MSExcel (see Figure 2.5 for an example):
    A. Start with a list of projects by name in Column A, one project per row.
    B. In Column B, estimate the *business value potential* in dollars that each project will generate:
        a. On a scale of 1–10 (in which 10 is the highest business value potential), for each project, put a business value potential score in Column C.

C. In Column D, assess each project's *complexity* as VERY HIGH, HIGH, MEDIUM, LOW, or VERY LOW (if it helps, think as if you were doing Planning Poker estimating Story Difficulty Level with Fibonacci numbers in Agile Scrum) [9].

    a. On a scale of 1–10 (in which 10 is lowest complexity), for each project, put a complexity potential score in Column E.

D. In Column F, estimate each project's total resources in dollars, i.e., labor time, materials, computing.

    a. On a scale of 1–10 (in which 10 is the lowest cost), for each project, put a total resources score in Column G.

E. In Column H, multiply the scores for each project in Columns C, E, and G.

    a. The *maximum* score is 10*10*10 = 1,000 (indicating a project with highest relative business value potential, lowest relative complexity, and lowest relative cost).

    b. The *minimum* score is 1*1*1 = 1 (indicating a project with lowest relative business value potential, highest relative complexity, and highest relative cost).

    c. Each project now has a score from 1–1,000.

F. Sort the project rows from highest to lowest (score) on Column H.

G. The result is a prioritized list of data science projects, using an objective, quantitative scoring mechanism.

The primary takeaway from this exercise is that the multiplicative scoring approach ensures that not just high business value projects bubble to the top of the list, rather, the magnitude of business value is tempered by a combined effect of complexity and cost. Complexity, in effect, is an important surrogate measure for risk; i.e., the more complex a project is, the more likely it is that you will run into difficulties that end up manifesting themselves in timeline delays and budget overruns and jeopardize the whole project. In the chart, we see the highest scoring projects are those that have low-to-medium relative business value moderated by (very) low complexity and low-to-moderate costs. The highest value projects, in this example, happen to have the highest risks and costs, which result in lower scores. This is actually a fairly commonly encountered set of circumstances, i.e., high risk/cost, high reward.

In the context of the later WayBlazer story, based on comments from the executives about high value offset by high integration complexity and costs, the innovative travel AI NLP itinerary engine might have looked something like **Project 6, 7**, or **3** with the lowest overall scores at the bottom of the list.

18. Sorrells, M., & Biesiada, J. (2018, July 26). WayBlazer shutting down. *Travel Weekly.* https://www.travelweekly.com/Travel-News/Travel-Technology/WayBlazer-shutting-down.

19. Weissmann, A. (2018, August 21). WayBlazer postmortem: Why did travel's highest-profile AI company fail? *PhocusWire.* https://www.phocuswire.com/Wayblazer-postmortem.

20. Sorrells, M. (2018, July 26). WayBlazer closes shop, cites lack of funds and time. *PhocusWire.* https://www.phocuswire.com/Wayblazer-shutting-down.

21. Crunchbase. (n.d.). WayBlazer. https://www.crunchbase.com/organization/wayblazer.

22. Full disclosure: Doug actually worked for Terry Jones as his founding head of technology at Travelocity from July 1995 to July 1997 (in effect, as his CTO and "one throat to choke," as Terry jokingly put it, for all software, hardware, and network issues). In Doug's opinion, Terry is as brilliant as he is innovative, as well as driven, and articulate, and the outcome at WayBlazer is in no way a negative reflection on his accomplishments and contributions to the travel distribution industry. If anything, what he, Manoj, and Noreen created was ahead of its time, and just a bit too early to be substantively monetized by big travel companies. Startups have short runways and high-risk profiles, something both co-authors are all too familiar with as veterans of numerous tech startup ventures. Doug also worked alongside Noreen when they were both directors at Sabre, and she has emerged as a highly sought-after, top-notch travel industry CEO.

    In fact, Doug's R&D lab at Travelocity experimented with an early version of this type of AI technology in the mid-1990s. Known as *AITA* (the *Automated Intelligent Travel Agent* pronounced *Aye-EE-tuh*), the prototype system converted customer-entered free-form natural language browser queries about travel destinations into prospective travel itineraries that could then be booked using Travelocity. Unfortunately, AITA never made it out of the lab because there was just too long a list of other higher priority, revenue-generating project opportunities, in addition to airline bookings, to be built into Travelocity, including rental cars, hotels, cruise lines, tours, etc., to warrant the investment in AI. Maybe someone will eventually make money where AITA and WayBlazer could not.

23. Brijj. (2022, March 21). 5 easy to implement routines to always deliver actionable insights. *Medium*. https://medium.com/@brijj.io/5-easy-to-implement-routines-to-always-deliver-actionable-insights-f37466e4bdc9. The majority (66%) of respondents (data scientists) indicated that their projects were a success at least most of the time, and 11% saying all of the time, demonstrating the point that the failure rate is likely higher.

24. Novartis presents new data on safety and efficacy of Zolgensma, including maintained and improved motor milestones in older and heavier children with SMA. (n.d.). *Novartis*. https://www.novartis.com/news/media-releases/novartis-presents-new-data-safety-and-efficacy-zolgensma-including-maintained-and-improved-motor-milestones-older-and-heavier-children-sma.

3

Process

"We don't have the data!"

Said almost every client with whom I have consulted, and many students I have taught, when confronted with the prospect of doing a real-word data science project.

"If your data is everywhere, then it is nowhere."

—**Doug Gray**

As companies scale up, so do their security challenges. Frustrated, unhappy, or even malicious employees might take advantage of the larger so-called attack surface (the different points where a hacker can compromise data or services). Valuable company secrets from this attack are often anonymously sold for millions on the dark web, followed by dreaded ransomware locking down the entire enterprise using the leaked passwords.

What should a company do in a situation like this? Implement draconian processes and policies that make it almost impossible to do business? Just because of the possibility of a few bad actors? Intrusively monitoring employees 24/7 will lead to bureaucratic dystopia. Where can we turn for a practical solution?

Enter the AI savior.

In the field of cybersecurity, one of data science's core strengths is leveraging distributions of past behavior to predict what will happen next. Anomalous behavior can be identified by flagging data points that don't fit the standard behavioral distribution. For example, ADSAI techniques can uncover unexpected downloads, file sharing to personal e-mail addresses, or unusual USB usage. Detecting such behavior could allow a powerful enough system to prevent cyber theft. At least, this is what an overzealous consulting company thought should be possible.

Our first story begins with an organization that decided to develop an innovative AI tool to help solve precisely these kinds of problems: those leading to criminal investigations. The project focus was technology fraud in a corporate IT environment, such as flagging when a departing employee may have tried to download and steal company secrets. In theory, this was a good idea, but in the hands of this company, not so. Unfortunately, this consulting company is one of the most analytically immature organizations we'll meet in this book and the execution of the project deeply reflected this.

DOI: 10.1201/9781032661360-4

Despite its low analytical maturity, the consulting company did have domain expertise because it had previously worked closely with a fraud investigations team from a large enterprise. This investigations team was created to scrutinize employees who appeared to steal information when leaving the enterprise. The consultants acquired the knowledge from them to recognize what right or wrong looked like at that company. They wanted to be proactive to prevent this for other clients before it happened and believed that AI could help. Their vision was a system that would automatically raise concerns in real time as soon as something suspicious occurred.

Their idea was to start mapping all employee behaviors and create profiles of usual behaviors, which would become their frame of reference for discovering behavioral anomalies. For example, a typical employee logs in every weekday at 7 or 8 a.m. and logs off around 5 or 6 p.m., so if an employee logs in at midnight, that would be a red flag. Similarly, with company data, if an employee uploads or downloads an abnormal number of files to or from the company's cloud storage, that would be another red flag. Such abnormal behaviors would trigger a review from IT. It was anticipated that the technology would provide a powerful defense against theft of information but also a significant new revenue stream.

Excited by the prospect, the consulting company started talking to a number of vendors, but could not find a suitable one. Frustrated by their failed search, and convinced they could do it themselves, they launched an internal project, which quickly and ignominiously failed.

Realizing that their internal capability was lacking, a senior staff member brought in two computer-literate friends and introduced them to the executive management committee. It is not clear whether the pair truly had AI skills, but it didn't matter because the executive team was relieved to finally have a path forward, and immediately, they eagerly launched the project (procurement's due diligence process went out the window at this point).

The two contractors did a great job of selling the company's ambition back to them, and before they even began the project, the executives were congratulating themselves on the expected boost to their bottom line. The firm's partners had clearly fallen headfirst into the AI hype.

Unfortunately, they landed hard.

That project marked the last time data science was welcome in their organization; the CEO/managing partner could not even bear to hear the words "artificial intelligence" for years (actually, not until the recent large language model hype). Back then, mentioning it in his office resulted in an unceremonious eviction, and even talking about this project inside corporate walls is still forbidden.

The project launched in 2020, guided by talk and fantasies about all the amazing new things clients would be able to do with the AI platform. The accounts team locked in their sales plans, flogging the AI solution to clients while hunting lofty new sales targets and bonuses. The two contractors fueled the hype by promising things such as full automation, i.e., no need for human involvement, leading to dreams of a veritable money-printing machine. Everyone was thinking about the size of their rewards, but unfortunately not about the necessary integrations or required functionality—it's not even clear whether there was a requirements document. If you doggedly tried to find out what this new *deus ex machina* would do, you were very likely directed to the sales pitch's PowerPoint slides. For a project that would require a $2 million investment and about two years' build time, this was not a good way to start.

Our two digital musketeers started developing the solution, which of course took *way longer* than anticipated. The project leaders were never short on reasons why delays occurred, but for those who hadn't bought into the AI hype, these excuses simply didn't make sense. No one was prepared to admit the truth. A steady stream of "unanticipated problems" protected the project from scrutiny and the inevitable difficult decisions.

As the launch deadline neared, the two consultants got to work on the best part of the whole project—their amazing launch presentation containing flashy videos as part of a professional unveiling event costing tens of thousands of dollars. However, because the entire project lacked any proper form of structure, the firm didn't know it wasn't working or that it was about to be a black hole in their profit and loss statement. What's worse, the contractors who built it probably didn't know it wasn't working either—at this point, they "drank too much of their own Kool-Aid" and must not have even bothered to test their AI tool in the situations in which it was expected to work.

Because the executives took the whole AI story on faith, they thought that this would be the company's ticket to double-digit growth and needed to protect it. When presenting their *pièce de résistance* to employees, the two consultants were required to make it extremely confidential (even internally) and ensure the entire organization understood its secret nature. This built even greater expectations across the company, overexciting an already giddy workforce.

The launch date was set for the following week. In the meantime, someone decided on a quick, pro forma internal test to show employees how it would work in each of their environments. But when they tried to implement it internally, the wheels began to fall off.

The first failure was the promise of a fully automated, 24/7 system. The users realized that someone would need to constantly monitor the red flags, i.e., it was clearly a human-in-the-loop tool requiring human intervention at all times.

Another (worse) failure was that the tool wasn't built to adapt to the purchasing client's infrastructure (including the handful of clients to whom it had already been sold!). Their tool barely hobbled through the consulting company's test environment; somehow, unbelievably, they never even took into account that this solution would have to be implemented in completely different customer IT environments—for those purchasing the platform.

As part of the testing, when the consultants tried to trial deploy it to one very close and trusted client, it couldn't even connect to their data. The solution was developed in an old SQL development database, and when they tried to run it on something a bit more modern, like a new Oracle database, it simply didn't work. They hadn't factored in the need to adapt the code base for other IT environments.

Fixing this error would require redoing months of work, but surprisingly, there was no need to because all of a sudden, everything disappeared. No attempt was made to fix the failure. The executive team lost all patience and threw everything into the trash. Suffering deep embarrassment, the company tried to recover their money from the two consultants through legal action. They didn't succeed because they technically got what they asked for.

There were so many things that went wrong during this project, that it provides us with one of the best possible introductions to this chapter.

The problems for the consulting company began with senior management that could not properly articulate what they wanted. Even if they had, the requirements would have been from a business/forensic point of view with no connection to the technology. The only technical awareness senior management had was of the current AI hype. They couldn't explain to the developers what they needed and how they would use it, because most of it had no connection to reality. They were completely lacking any knowledge as to what the final solution should look like, where and how it would be used, and whether the project was truly even necessary. The commercial expectations weren't reasonable. There was a failure to communicate exactly how it would be used, even within their own organization. They tried to build the entire AI in one attempt and didn't properly focus on the end user's use case. Somehow, they managed to fail on just about every process challenge that we discovered in the literature and will review here. A true masterclass on how *not* to run an ADSAI project.

If there is one redeeming aspect to this story at all, it is that our overall number two reason for analytics project failure—data issues—didn't materialize. So, let's start with that and then dig into the myriad other failures seen in the consulting company's ADSAI project.

Data Quality and Reliability Issues

Of all the reasons why ADSAI projects fail, the one that comes in as a clear number two, and almost as often as failing to have a proper business case, is issues with data. In fact, what kicked off part of the desire to write this book was a routine call that Evan made to an existing client in the logistics industry about their usage of a bespoke AI tool to resolve their supply chain challenges.

In the late 2000s, a large national supplier of delivery goods to producers spread across the country decided there had to be a better way to organize the shipments of its delivery goods. At that point in time, to solve its logistics challenge, a large team of humans manually allocated collections and deliveries one after the other to each customer. After years of inefficiencies, they rightly decided that this problem could be better solved with an analytics engine. It was a standard network flow problem, one that was well suited to existing optimization techniques.

After working with the client, gathering requirements, aligning the business case, and ensuring the need, an optimization engine was created that would allocate the delivery of goods to the right places at the right time. The tool was built on-time and on-budget and rolled out to the logistics company to the satisfaction of all parties involved. Because it seemed to be working well and there were no known adoption challenges, the tool developers naturally moved on to other projects and left the end users in the logistics company to solve their delivery challenges with their new analytics software.

Now back to that routine phone call some years later.

Evan had initially contacted the client with what he believed to be a few simple questions to better understand some nuances of the software's usage. His questions were posed to help him understand how the network would react to specific weather circumstances, but the responses just didn't add up. He persisted inquiring until, finally, the user stated:

> Sure, I use the optimization functionality. The first thing I do is connect the data, adjust the parameters, and then run the optimization. After the calculations are complete, I then delete the optimal solution and make up a new one on my own.

After a moment of silence to regain his composure, Evan politely protested that the whole point of the tool *was its optimization engine*. The rest of it was simply a digital layer to help utilize the "smart" results. Not using the optimal solution made no sense whatsoever. After an indifferent response from the client, Evan asked the critical question: Why don't you use the optimized deliveries?

It was at this point that the data issues emerged.

The client told him that the tool was unable to know key future parameters about the delivery goods that impacted how quickly they could be prepared for the next customer. This information was actually unknowable until the day of delivery, so future planning (i.e., short term optimization) was of no use in the current iteration. In addition, because the data inputs also changed so often, the engine's outputs would change too much for the users between optimization runs (even though this was part of the design). Practically, the planning team couldn't keep sending drastic changes for the operations teams to carry out. It is worth noting that during the design and implementation phases, this data issue did not exist, probably due to the existence of comprehensive historical data to backtest the model, which, for a given day, likely included the key future parameters. Finally, the opening stock on-hand calculations couldn't be trusted due to the timing of when the data reached the engine; it would come at different times and the engine would often end up computing with the wrong data, leading to nonsensical results.

What should have been years of streamlined operations and a significant ROI turned out to be additional effort for the planning team encumbered with a pointless optimization tool that created even more work than it had intended to save. Although the tool was still being used and did have a number of other benefits, the core reason for its usage (an AI engine) ended up being the least valuable part because of data issues.

Unfortunately, this is not an isolated case.

Given the importance of, and challenges with, this foundational issue, we are going to spend a bit of time unpacking the data issues that organizations face, beginning with some fascinating research from a team at Google. The research was presented at a computer–human interface conference in 2021 in Japan.

The global search organization's team ruffled some feathers with a provocative presentation entitled, "Everyone wants to do the model work, not the data work."[1] They argued that as AI models are applied in high-stakes domains, such as health and conservation, data quality becomes the defining factor because it determines the quality of predictions in applications such as cancer detection, wildlife poaching, and loan allocations. Therefore, the data should receive more attention than anything else. However, paradoxically, in spite of data being the foundation for high-quality algorithmic performance, the team from Google argued that data is the most undervalued and least exciting aspect. Even worse, it seems to receive the least attention and budget in such critical projects.

To come to this conclusion, the researchers talked to more than 50 AI practitioners across the globe to define, identify, and present empirical evidence on cascades of compounding events—negative, downstream effects when an application is used—arising from data issues. They showed that these adverse events are triggered by conventional AI/ML practices that undervalue the importance of data quality.

The authors claimed that failure cascades caused by low-quality data occur 90+% of the time, are invisible, and insidiously delayed. However, the worst part is that data-related failures are often avoidable. The Google presentation sums up the situation well:

> An overall lack of recognition for the invisible, arduous, and taken-for-granted data work in AI led to poor data practices, resulting in the data cascades below. Care of, and improvements to data are not easily 'tracked' or rewarded, as opposed to models. Models were reported to be the means for prestige and upward mobility in the field … with ML publications that generated citations, making practitioners competitive for AI/ML jobs and residencies.

One interviewee eloquently summarized it in what subsequently became the presentation title, *"Everyone wants to do the model work, not the data work."*

The team at Google continued:

> Many practitioners described data work as time-consuming, invisible to track, and often done under pressures to move fast due to margins—investment, constraints, and deadlines often came in the way of focusing on improving data quality. Additionally, it was difficult to get buy-in from clients and funders to invest in good quality data collection and annotation work.

To help facilitate this paradigm shift in recognizing the importance of data, the team at Google recommended a number of practical courses of action that organizations could adopt to help improve their data practices:

- *Move from goodness-of-fit to goodness-of-data*: Have a better understanding of the context of the data and its relationship to quality results, rather than just tweaking a model to achieve better performance.
- *Incentives for data excellence*: Bring more attention to the key activities of data documentation, provenance, and ethics, by rewarding people for good management.
- *Real-world data literacy in AI education* (a topic we will pick up in a later chapter, with an emphasis on "real-world").
- *Better visibility in the AI data lifecycle*: Establish better feedback loops that expose the data lifecycle to all, which probably requires the lowest level of analytics capability—the ability to create dashboards.

Because people don't want to do the data work, companies continually face the same repeating data issues that Doug discovered in AADT's passenger railroad Revenue Management (RM) system case study mentioned in the Strategy chapter. A dearth of historical enterprise passenger demand data, and the infrastructure to collect, organize, store, and manage the data, was a major contributing factor as to why the project took roughly six times as long as originally planned.

However, understanding the important role of data can be seen in more than just high-stakes domains. The way an application uses data can put enormous demands on the requisite quality and quantity of it.[2] For example, the more often you need to use a tool and/or the more accurate the tool needs to be, the higher the demand for the data to match, in currency and/or accuracy. On the other hand, if people don't have the right background or training, they may not even be able to utilize the results that arise from this more accurate and higher volume of data-generated decisions. Not knowing if what you are looking at is random noise or an important signal that must be recalled in future decisions, becomes harder as a system more rapidly generates recommendations.

Doug had the privilege of taking a marketing research course from an endowed professor and highly successful marketing industry executive/consultant, Dr. William ("Bill") Dillon, at Southern Methodist University (SMU) while in his Executive MBA (EMBA) program. Professor Dillon would famously say, "If you don't have any data to analyze, then you have two choices: you can start collecting the data, or you can go to lunch." As a data scientist, you need to resist the urge to go to lunch and instead, figure out how you are going to programmatically find and collect, or even purchase, the relevant data you need—at the quality, frequency, and volume required by your algorithms.

In the business analytics course that Doug taught in the EMBA program at SMU, he required all students to complete a project that applied the principles studied in class. This project, which would make up the majority of the final course grade, requires each team to frame an actual real-world business problem, collect and analyze the data, build one or more models to predict and/or optimize an outcome, interpret the findings and results, form conclusions, propose recommendations, estimate the business value and economic impact, and, lastly, present the upshot in the form of a TED Talk (roughly 18 minutes including Q&A) in front of the class cohort.

In more than five years of teaching that course to roughly 120 students, amazingly, *only one team* failed to collect the data required to complete their project. Surprisingly, they worked for a very large, very well-known global brand-name chain of convenience store/gas stations.

This team initially set out to analyze the consumables product portfolio of SKU (Stock Keeping Unit) inventory items at their stores that were in relatively close proximity to college campuses to see how sales compared to their other stores *not* located near college campuses. Their theory, not surprisingly, was that certain items, for example, snacks, prepared food such as microwaveable meals and salads, energy drinks, beer, hard seltzers, etc., would be markedly more popular in stores near college campuses. They planned to use the information and insights garnered from their analysis to better inform future merchandising and product mix decision-making to increase revenue at stores located near colleges. Shockingly, at least to the professor anyway, *they could not obtain the data for their project*. There was no clear reason provided, but seeing as this group worked in merchandising, one would assume that this sort of data would be available (perhaps it was a permissions/data confidentiality issue). Unexpectedly, even large, global brand-name companies suffer from data issues in areas critical to their operations.

Let the Data Hunt Begin

Sometimes the data you are presented with doesn't tell the whole story and you need to broaden the data aperture to see the whole picture and find the real data. How to do this is revealed in the next story from Doug's consulting company, which isn't so much about an outright abject failure because the project ultimately did result in a positive outcome.

Despite the favorable end result, the analytics consulting team did hit a major roadblock in the middle of the project that, at the time, seemed to be a dead end. They were ready to call it quits and advise the client to end the project as they had discovered no insightful result nor identified any tangible business value. In energy exploration, specifically oil well drilling, this is called a "dry hole"—no oil or natural gas! It happens often in ADSAI projects, despite the availability, quantity, and quality of legitimately good data, coupled with a valiant analytical modeling effort on the part of a highly talented team. Sometimes a project hits a dead end and you move on—no harm, no foul.

Our story begins around 2008–2009, when Doug's consulting company was asked to carry out an analytical project for a large (multi-billion dollar revenue) US healthcare organization's HR department. The organization has enterprise-scale operations spanning dozens of facilities, including general and specialty hospitals, outpatient surgery, clinics, treatment facilities, and imaging centers, located in the western United States.

At the time, the HR department was grappling with a perplexing wave of "no notice" voluntary self-terminations of nursing and radiological technician staff at several different facilities. Upon initial review, there did not appear to be any discernible pattern to the terminations; otherwise seemingly generally satisfied staff members simply didn't show up to work one day—no call, no show. When HR tried to reach out to the staff who quit, it was as if they had disappeared; they were just gone—unanswered phone calls, empty residences, and silence. Weird.

Employee turnover, albeit normal at a certain level for any enterprise, is one of the most difficult and expensive problems faced by HR and operational departments, given the inordinate expense of attracting, recruiting, hiring, onboarding, training, and retaining highly skilled labor. Employees can leave a company for any number of reasons, for example, better working conditions, better compensation, better management, etc. The problem is particularly acute in the healthcare industry given the shortage of nurses (i.e., registered nurses (RNs), licensed practical nurses (LPNs), and other licensed staff such as medical assistants) and other skilled, licensed technicians (e.g., radiological technicians (RTs), physical therapists (PTs), etc.).

The HR director, having reached his wits' end trying to figure out why these voluntary no-notice terminations were occurring in such large numbers, had heard from a mutual colleague about the analytical consulting services provided by Doug and his team, and decided to reach out for help in solving the mystery of the disappearing nurses and RTs.

The HR director offered up a large quantity of high-quality, highly relevant, easily accessible data as a starting point for the analysis and detective work. The hospital collected seven years of quarterly employee satisfaction survey data, i.e., roughly 28 surveys including dozens of questions designed to measure engagement and satisfaction across the entire skilled employee base and spanning the spectrum of employee work life. The surveys were anonymized to HR and management to encourage and help ensure candid responses, but were ultimately traceable back to each individual employee respondent by the HR director's IT team (using unique workstation login credentials and employee ID number—long story, don't ask).

The healthcare organization also offered anonymized (to the analytics team) employee job performance evaluations that were identifiable by employee ID number. Lastly, a record of all employee terminations, both voluntary and involuntary (i.e., for cause or performance reasons), were provided by employee ID number. So, net-net, all three data sources were able to be linked to a specific employee by ID number (not employee name): employee job satisfaction survey results, employee job performance evaluation results, and employee termination records.

Although there were crystal clear, easily discernible patterns in the data for involuntary terminations (i.e., employee had chronically, systemically poor job performance, drug theft, attendance issues, etc.) and most of the voluntary terminations (i.e., employee hated their job, their boss and/or co-workers, the working conditions, etc.), the voluntary no-notice termination employee data was favorable, if not pristine, in most cases (i.e., no red flags in any of the employee's satisfaction survey responses and solid employee job performance evaluations). The only data point that deviated from the favorable pattern was the voluntary no-notice self-termination event. Despite a reasonably high level of employee job satisfaction, and satisfactory or exemplary employee job performance, the nurse or radiological technician simply did not show up for work, without any kind of notification whatsoever.

Doug and his team were stumped. They had run into a roadblock (more like a brick wall).

Doug informed the client HR director that, based on all the data observed and analyzed, there was no readily apparent reason or discernible pattern in any of the voluntary no-notice termination cases that would indicate or provide any material or significant insight as to why these employees quit.

Doug, not wanting to run the risk of a major project failure due to an unsatisfactory outcome, conservatively advised the client that it would probably be best to cut their losses and terminate the project at this point—there was no economic impact or business value to be had. There was no sense in the client throwing good money after bad to continue to drill the dry hole. The voluntary no-notice terminations remained a mystery.

Understandably, the HR director refused to take no for an answer. He was stymied and he still had a serious problem with nurse and RT turnover that he could not explain to senior management, and for which he had no viable solution. The problem was costing his company a lot of money and could potentially adversely impact patient quality of care and outcomes. He implored Doug to go back to the drawing board and try to find the answer! He was not willing to stop the project or accept failure.

Doug, sympathetic to the client's predicament and heightened sense of urgency, and wanting to do a better job of helping him (and also being a capitalist/small business owner, certainly not wanting to turn down additional consulting revenue when it was being offered), decided to take a step back and have another look. Doug huddled with his project data scientist, Rob Williams, and brainstormed ideas on what else they could consider. What other factors, beyond the observed data, could be causing such a high number of these voluntary no-notice terminations?

Could the termination problem be isolated to specific facilities, for example, certain hospitals, specific departments within facilities (e.g., emergency department), or types of facilities (e.g., outpatient treatment centers)? Could the problem be isolated to specific geographic regions or subregions within the company's western US service area, for example, Southern, Central, or Northern California? Perhaps, could there be unique economic conditions or labor market conditions in certain regions causing changes to employment situations (e.g., higher paying competitive healthcare providers)?

Fortunately for the client, Rob is a brilliant and very creative data scientist who has a real knack for finding, leveraging, and analyzing a wide range of data sources using a variety of data visualization and predictive/probabilistic modeling tools.

Based on a joint brainstorming session, Rob started collecting macroeconomic data from a wide variety of publicly available government and third-party data sources, all of which were free and easily accessible, including employment patterns, wages, housing, etc. He then cross-referenced that data to the client's operating regions and subregions and healthcare facilities within those areas.

The voluntary no-notice terminations were highly concentrated in three subregions, specifically cities (and their respective adjacent surrounding suburbs) in which the company had a large number of facilities. However, the terminations were not linked to any specific company facilities or types of facilities within those regions. The cities were:

- Riverside, CA
- Phoenix, AZ
- Las Vegas, NV

Then, Eureka! Rob immediately found a statistically significant pattern across the range of datasets, validated with visualization, which linked a higher-than-expected number of mortgage defaults and foreclosures to these three cities and their respective suburbs.

To add some important historical macroeconomic context, 2008–2009 was the height of the global financial crisis that was precipitated by the collapse of the US housing market (bubble).[3] Just prior to 2008, mortgage companies were aggressively marketing adjustable-rate mortgages with low, teaser interest rates that would automatically reset to higher interest rates in 1–2 years. Home buyers were encouraged—by mortgage sales brokers incentivized by big commissions and spurred on by Wall Street mortgage securities brokers—to purchase homes with mortgages that were beyond what they could realistically afford, even with two incomes. In some cases, well beyond what would normally be considered financially prudent or fiscally responsible.

The horribly flawed assumption in the home mortgage markets was that when the teaser mortgage rates reset to higher rates, the homeowners would simply refinance the loan. Instead, what actually happened was that a large swath of homeowners simply walked away from their homes and financial obligations and defaulted on the loans, leaving the banks holding an unpaid mortgage and flooding the market with unoccupied homes and condominiums now worth a fraction of the originally mortgaged value.

Riverside, Phoenix, and Las Vegas were the three cities, *out of the entire US housing market*, which were most severely affected by the fallout of the mortgage foreclosure crisis.

Subsequently, following the mortgage foreclosure crisis, the US economy collapsed in a downward spiral of fiscal credit crises and degraded corporate performance, which resulted in extensive, widespread job losses, thereby further compounding the problem. Families faced foreclosure on their primary residence if one partner lost their job and the other partner's income alone was not sufficient to cover the bloated mortgage payment, after the interest rate reset.

With these fresh, critical insights arrived at by overlaying the company's facilities footprint geographically on the subregions most severely impacted by the double whammy of mortgage foreclosures and financial crises, the mystery of the voluntary no-notice terminations finally unraveled. The HR department began diligently researching, contacting, and tracking down any former employee they could locate in an attempt to find out why they left with no notice. As suspected, many of the nurses and RTs had fallen prey to the teaser mortgage rates, bought properties that were practically beyond their means, and were foreclosed upon when the low interest rates reset. Others were affected in the economic meltdown aftermath when a spouse lost their job and income, which also led to foreclosure. In every instance that was identified, the individuals were so mortified by the resulting outcomes of their poor financial decisions that they packed up, left town, and sought refuge with family or friends elsewhere, in order to escape the ignominy of facing friends, colleagues, and employers.

With the mystery solved and the client satisfied, primarily thanks to Rob's diligence and skills, the project was successfully completed. However, the project had come very close to failure because the originally provided data yielded no insights, clues, or impacts. The key learning for the data science team was that, oftentimes, the answer to the question or solution to the problem lies beyond the data the client presents to you (and is sometimes well hidden from view). Data scientists must broaden the data aperture and vigilantly seek the rest of the truth elsewhere. It's a lot like detective work, or even medical condition diagnostics, and requires a great deal of tenacity and perseverance—leave no stone unturned. Every problem presents itself in a different context of time, extenuating circumstances, and conditions of the surrounding environment(s). In this case, geographical subregions, macroeconomics, and human behavior all played a significant role in causing a painful business problem and initiating the resulting solution.

The healthcare company made several significant process changes because of the project's findings. Frontline managers, for example, nursing shift, department, and floor supervisors, were mandated to have regular, candid check-ins with nursing, technicians, and other highly skilled staff, to increase transparency and help leaders become aware of what is going on in an employee's personal life that may adversely affect their employment situation. Retraining and job placement programs, at the hospital or in the local vicinity, were created to help spouses who lost their jobs find and secure gainful employment. Meaningful temporary financial assistance was made available to help employees bridge the transition period so they could stay in their jobs and homes until they got back on their feet.

The total cost of the new programs *paled* in comparison to the inordinate cost associated with turnover and having to attract, recruit, hire, train, develop, and retain new highly paid, highly skilled, licensed healthcare professionals. A win-win-win for the employer and employees, as well as the patients who seek and desperately need healthcare.

This example illustrates well the number two reason why data science projects fail. One of the most common sub-issues we found in this theme is simply a lack of suitable data or, at least, not being clear on the necessary data and where to find it.

In fact, missing data is the first complaint we usually hear from clients when asking how to do analytics in their enterprise, and from students when confronted with the reality of having to do a real-world data science project. *"We don't have the data!"*

Many companies, especially small- to medium-sized businesses, are either bereft of (automated) data altogether, or are lacking clean, accurate, consistent, high-quality, and high-integrity data.

More often, what people really mean is that the data is *not all in one place*. This is a common data affliction of many enterprises. Data is literally scattered among dozens, or even hundreds (no exaggeration), of enterprise applications, legacy systems, databases, CSV files, data warehouses, data marts, now data lakes in cloud accounts, third-party systems, and, yes, the ubiquitous Excel spreadsheets.

A data scientist alone, in most enterprise instances, is not going to be able to solve the lack of data problem. They need to collaborate with the IT team, database administrators, data architects, cloud data engineers, or the chief data officer's data engineering team (if you are lucky enough to come across one).

Don't try to "boil the ocean" and solve *all* of the enterprise's data issues (because you will figuratively "drown"). Stay laser-focused on organizing the project's data, which will be challenging enough. Practically, to avoid the circumstance of not being able to find or interpret the data, focusing on two big issues enables the data science project to succeed:

- Data Integration
- Data Governance

Fortunately, both of these are becoming simpler with technological advances. Historically, the database, data warehouse, or data mart were the most common enterprise data stores. Recently, these have been superseded by the data *lake* (usually unstructured, raw data landing zones) and now, yes, the data *lakehouse*, which combines attributes of the warehouse and lake into one entity (e.g., the ability to crawl largely unstructured data landing zones and automatically create schemas that then allow querying and access to the data, like in a traditional data warehouse). Regardless of the exact data platform, getting all the data cleaned, organized, and integrated into a single physical or virtual (accessible) workspace or view is critical to enabling a data science project to get out of the gate.

Some companies, such as large retailers, airlines, telecommunications, and financial services, are blessed (and cursed) with enormous amounts of data (i.e., duplicates and sheer voluminous amounts of unmanaged data). This is a good problem to have from a data richness perspective, but can present problems of storage and management.

Data governance, including metadata, data lineage, and data stewards, is a hot topic and an absolute necessity to ensure one version of the truth, and consistent data definitions and usage patterns. Once again, the data scientist will not solve this problem alone, but will need to partner with the data governance team, or at least data owners and stewards (official or unofficial), who control access to and governance of some or all enterprise data.

On the whole, both co-authors have been greatly blessed when it comes to data, having worked for companies that were rich in data resources, relatively mature in the way data was managed, and that were legitimately data-driven and analytically inclined, including American Airlines, Sabre, Volvo, Mercedes-Benz, Marathon Petroleum, Blue Cross and Blue Shield of Kansas City, and Walmart.

Data issues manifest themselves in myriad ways, as varied as there are companies attempting to manage and analyze their data.[4] Simply having access to the data is probably the most important first step to any ADSAI project. The next critical step is to ensure that people understand what is possible with the data they do have.

(Un)reasonable Expectations

"Under Promise, Over Deliver."

—**Tom Peters**[5]

One of the critically important lessons that we have personally learned the hard way early in our careers involved setting (un)realistic expectations. It is easy to cave in to the pressure of a busy enterprise executive, whose expertise is not in AI, demanding an unreasonable delivery timeline. When trying to moderate their expectations, both co-authors have been on the receiving end of surprised and frustrated glances when informing decision-makers that our complex, enterprise-scale AI project will take more than two months.

There are two primary domains impacting expectation setting that plague both IT and data science professionals:

1. Project-related variables, namely scope, timing, resources, and budget
2. Business value and economic impact

For the first domain, numerous books have been written with regard to the use of techniques to help data scientists, such as Agile Scrum and Kanban estimation. Much of estimation is an art (but also some science) that is learned over time from lots of practical experience. We won't delve into this here, apart from recommending leaning toward conservatism rather than big stretch goals. Clearly, it is always better to be a bit early (relative to the promised deadline) and on budget with the desired deliverables in hand, even if more could have been achieved.

In the business value and economic impact domain, balancing conservatism with stretch goals is also advisable. Figure 3.1 displays an important visual way to establish this *expectation-setting continuum*.

FIGURE 3.1
Establishing an expectation-setting continuum.

When we set the bar for benefits too *low*, we sail over the bar too easily and blow away our target (the far-right of the spectrum). This approach, known as "sandbagging," tends to lose customers' confidence because they will perceive the project team as not being aggressive enough in targeting potential business value.

At the other end of the spectrum, we see what happens when we set the bar for benefits too *high* and fail to deliver the promised business value. This approach, known as "overcommitting" or an "epic fail" as GenZ might say, can get you into really big trouble with customers (and their bosses/executives) because they were expecting you to deliver a monumental economic impact and you came up way, way short.

An example of sandbagging and overcommitting is if you were to achieve a $100 million verifiable cost avoidance, but either had promised $10 million (sandbagging) or a billion dollars (overcommitting), respectively. With sandbagging, you blew away your target by 10X, and with overcommitting, you missed the mark by 10X. Neither end of the spectrum is a good place to be, but overcommitting can be politically irredeemable and career jeopardizing, which may be why we see sandbagging so often in large, political organizations.

In business school, MBA students are taught to always analyze (at least) three case outcomes in any analysis or projection modeling scenario:

1. *Best Case* (everything goes right)
2. *Worst Case* (everything goes wrong)
3. *Expected or Average Case* (some things go right, some things go wrong, and balance out)

The process of estimating benefits is similar, and the last case is in the *middle* of the spectrum, in which we try to balance our (and the customer's) optimism and pessimism, and use an *expected or average case* to set a target we can hit or even exceed, without being too far off in either direction. We call this approach the "Target Zone." For example, we would estimate an $80 million benefit and deliver $100 million. The upper end of the Target Zone, and just beyond, is sometimes referred to as **BHAGs** or **B**ig **H**airy **A**udacious **G**oals.[6] These may also be referred to as "stretch goals."

This midzone of the expectation-setting spectrum would look like this: Set a Target Zone goal of an $80 million benefit *and* a BHAG of $120 million, and deliver a $100 million benefit. Although risky, there are some benefits in aiming a bit higher and pushing for the larger opportunity, regardless of whether you achieve the BHAG. Even if you don't achieve the BHAG, you don't fall as short as overcommitting wildly with the billion-dollar benefit. Setting a BHAG can show ambition and drive that may be worth more professionally in the long-term than the single failure of possibly missing the target.

The examples above are of course contrived because we have the benefit of hindsight (perfect information) and achieved a healthy business value outcome of $100 million. That doesn't always happen in reality. Sometimes the benefit is $0, or something close. Other times, we get lucky and hit the jackpot.

Some of the greatest achievements in the history of data science (operations research, analytics, and AI) at Fortune 50 companies were *9-figure annualized business value improvements*:

- It was independently verified that American Airlines' Yield Management System (DINAMO) generated $1.4 billion in incremental revenue over a three-year period (and was expected to deliver roughly $500 million in incremental revenue annually in the future) using its same fleet and airline schedule.[7]

- UPS' On-Road Integrated Optimization and Navigation System (ORION) avoids $300 million to $400 million annually in fuel and driver costs.[8]

- Walmart applied operations research to enhance retail truck routing and load planning using advanced optimization models and build a transformation roadmap for long-term supply chain capital investments, as well as an application supporting daily decisions of truck routing and loading. The application avoided 72 million pounds of CO_2 and resulted in a savings of $75 million during fiscal year 2023.[9]

Although there have been examples of even larger annual business value benefits of data science and analytics projects, the 9-figure dollar range provides a realistic upper bound on the highest possible practical expectations for the large majority of enterprises. So how do we find such opportunities in a company?

A good place to start is with the firm's financial statements in order to understand financial performance and estimate benefits. Next, examine a given department's contributions to the firm's financial results, for example, marketing, manufacturing, etc.

Some key business areas for economic opportunity include:

- *Labor*, for example, through AI-based robotics in warehouses, factories, and future driverless vehicles, including cars and large trucks, and optimization-based labor planning systems
- *Inventory*, for example, better matching product demand to supply to balance shortage and holding costs
- *Assets* (including facilities) allocation and utilization, for example, aircraft (hangars), optimal facility location, railroad engines and rolling stock, and truck trailers
- *Manufacturing*, for example, product mix, process controls and task allocation, and statistical quality control
- *Pricing*, for example, optimal markdowns (Walmart was a 2020 INFORMS Franz Edelman Award finalist with the predictive (demand forecasting)-prescriptive markdowns optimization solution, which balanced discounting goods too much or too little, too early or too late, to maximize sales revenue)
- *Yield or Revenue Management*, which originated in airlines and is now utilized in hotels, cruise lines, rental car companies, and even self-storage facilities

When estimating benefits, first calculate the maximum potential benefit (at 100% realization) and then perform a rigorous analysis based on the firm's actual economic data, to evaluate how much business value and economic impact is realistically possible to achieve with data science.

The estimated business value may very well be only 10%–25% of the maximum potential benefit. (Real life always gets in the way, whether lower than hoped for end-user usage, data issues, or too many edge cases leading to exceptional cases not being handled by the system.) You may decide to set a **Target Zone** goal at 5%–10% of the maximum benefit to avoid **sandbagging** or **overcommitting** (in both co-authors' experience this is a common outcome, although exceptions do exist). Rarely, if ever, will you achieve the maximum potential benefit, but multiplying 5%–10% by a very, very big cost or revenue dollar figure can still be a significant result.

Another aspect to remember when calculating the expected returns is the in-kind employee effort that will be required to manage the AI tool. Project leaders should be transparent in what happens next, lest the fantasy depicted by the movie industry set a manager's expectations of a fully automated, sentient program making continuously optimal decisions. Both co-authors can count on a single hand the number of projects in their careers in which the final solution was a fully automated AI tool with no human involvement (apart from just robotic process automation). It seems that invariably in all the systems we have built, humans want to adjust outputs, fix data inputs, simulate and evaluate multiple different scenarios, play with solutions, and more, before they accept an AI generated answer. This approach is known as *augmentation*, where the human's capability is augmented and enhanced, usually significantly, by the ADSAI solution rather than being 100% automated out of the process.

What we also notice is that in medium- to high-stakes decision-making, people rarely seem to want to fully rely on automated systems. Whereas, repetitive low-risk decisions that are simply too hard for humans to do well, such as pricing the long tail of tens of thousands of uncommon products and services for markdown, have a chance of being 100% automated. These predictable, tedious, mundane, or sometimes even dangerous tasks can often be fully handed over to AI (or even better, robotic automation), as happened with welding in the automotive industry. However, even in the first few *years* of such products, much human oversight is normally needed. The guiding principle should be, never set the expectation that the system you build will be fully automated anytime in the near future. The human-out-of-the-loop goal is just not a realistic assumption for any new ADSAI project.

So, given these caveats, where should we look for suitable projects?

In any organization, to see where data science can provide the greatest leverage, find the largest potential business value opportunities in which there is significant room for improvement in economic efficiency. Identify economically impactful problems that are currently being solved essentially manually in Excel with rules of thumb or simple heuristics that do not capture the fullness of the problem, the value of the solution opportunity, or adequately address the problem's underlying complexity. We gave a list before of the key business areas for economic opportunity within the organization where managers can direct the attention of the data science team.

In the airline industry (American, Delta, etc.), the largest opportunities were found in seat inventory pricing and yield management. These solutions directly impacted revenue. A close second was network planning/flight scheduling, followed by flight/cabin crew scheduling and fuel inventory management, which are an airline's two largest operating expense categories. The third was spare part inventory and aircraft maintenance management.

In the package delivery industry, the largest opportunities for companies like UPS were found in optimizing one of their greatest costs: fleet operations of 55,000+ delivery trucks and drivers (e.g., the oft cited rule of not making left-hand turns in the United States is allegedly because you burn more fuel waiting for a stop light to turn green or the traffic to clear so you can turn left).

In summary, the size of the business, in scope and scale, measured in terms of sales, revenue, costs, assets, labor force, and profits, matters greatly in how much business value can realistically be achieved in general, and in any one project. If an executive expects a big outcome, then they need to have picked a big problem and provided a commensurately big budget and long timeline.

Setting realistic business value, and economic impact targets and expectations, will depend heavily on how well data scientists understand the economics, operations, and financials of the company, as well as how rigorously they analyze the impact that data science can potentially have by utilizing the preferred Target Zone and BHAGs framework from the expectation-setting continuum. This is a recurring theme throughout the book: The full picture—extending beyond pure technical capability—will give you a much better chance of avoiding failure, than simply being a data science guru.

Houston, We Have a Communication Problem

In addition to not setting realistic expectations, the consulting company described at the start of this chapter also chose to keep secret the development of their revolutionary anomalous behavior detection tool. From a competitive advantage perspective, this made sense; from a risk-minimization strategy, it was a disaster. This stymieing of organizational communication meant that very few people had input in the development process. In turn, this increased the chances that the developed tool would not be fit for purpose and is *exactly* what happened.

In general, clear, concise communication, i.e., verbal, written, nonverbal, or lack thereof, represents a significant challenge in business. It is something we all strive to improve. In the field of data science, the communication challenge is even more acute for several reasons, not least of which is that business people and data scientists rarely speak the same "language."

Data scientists, who speak a language of mathematical models, symbols, and programming, must endeavor to understand the business domain and problem space, which is defined by terminology that is inherently foreign to data scientists. On the other hand, business managers, whose daily language is one of KPIs, jargon, and acronyms, must endeavor to understand how a complex, sophisticated mathematical model automated on a computer is going to solve their business problem. Data scientists need to be intellectually curious and dig deep to understand the business problem and context. Managers, who are very likely not mathematicians themselves, need to "trust but verify" through rigorous experimentation, verification, and validation that the model and solution (inside the "black box") is functioning appropriately to solve the problem at hand.

It can be human nature to abhor change and fear what one cannot understand. Famed operations researcher Gene Woolsey said, *"A manager would rather live with a problem they cannot solve than accept a solution they cannot understand."* The communication challenge requires the data scientist and the manager to create a conceptual and practical intersection between their two worlds in which they can communicate and understand each other.

Of all the habits in Stephen Covey's "Habits of Highly Effective People," Doug's favorite in the communication realm is Habit 5: *Seek first to understand, then to be understood*. This habit compels us to listen before we speak. The old adage, *"We have two ears and one mouth, so use them proportionately,"* provides an excellent heuristic for a data scientist to govern their communication approach. Throughout the project, and especially in the early stages, the data scientist should be listening two-thirds of the time and speaking one-third of the time. When they are speaking, they should be *asking exploratory and clarifying questions*. This ratio will tend to change toward the end of the project, closer to 50-50 listening and speaking, as the data scientist explains how the model and system works, presents findings, conclusions, and recommendations, and answers what will no doubt reflect a myriad of questions from the stakeholder or business manager.

In every data science project, it is critical to consider the context and audience in each situation and adapt the communication approach and content accordingly. Is the data scientist talking to another data scientist on their team or to the business side? Are they talking to the manager on the business side, or their upline executive, such as a director, VP, or higher, perhaps giving a demonstration or presentation of the model and solution? Maybe the data scientist is communicating with a business analyst equipped with an engineering degree or a quantitative MBA who would have a much better understanding of data science models, computers, and software applications than their manager. Knowing the audience allows both sides to prepare and communicate accordingly.

It is important to bear in mind that the success of communication does not come at the end of the project, it is established before, during, and after the project:

- *Before* the project to mutually set expectations on scope, timing, budget, critical success factors, and criteria, and achieve a mutual clarity of the problem at hand and the solution approach.
- *During* the project to ensure tight feedback loops because modeling is by nature and necessity *iterative*, and not necessarily strictly "linear." In addition, to provide updates on status and negotiate changes in direction or approach as new information and discoveries come to light.
- *After* the project to communicate and act on the findings, results, conclusions, recommendations, and most importantly, quantify the business value and economic impact of the model.

Once the model and solution are accepted, then comes the substantive communication phase, which is used to implement the model as part of the business process.

One piece of advice on communication media: *Avoid e-mail if at all possible*, especially on critical, sensitive topics. E-mail is a lousy communication vehicle for nuanced, complex information sharing. Data science project communication involves the utmost nuanced, complex information sharing, and e-mail avails myriad opportunities for misinterpretation and misunderstanding. There is no substitute for face-to-face communication, whenever possible, even via video conference in the post-COVID-19 age of remote work.

This important piece of advice builds the foundation for the next most important item in communication based on our research: presentation of the message.

Presenting the Message

In the opinion of the co-authors, the most effective data scientists are *storytellers*. They tell a story of what life was like *before* the model was developed and implemented, and how life changed (hopefully for the better) *afterwards*. They start presentations by grabbing the attention of the audience, in particular, executives who are prone to scanning their mobile device during business meetings. The most effective data science communicators ask provocative rhetorical questions such as, *"What if I told you that we could increase sales (or decrease inventory costs) and make (or save) the company an extra $X gazillion using data and data science?"* Now that's a way to get everyone's attention! The *key* is to communicate in the language of the audience, i.e., managers, executives, domain experts—not data science speak.

Building on this, for any data science project to move forward, you will inevitably have to address and adequately answer the age-old question: *"What's in it for me, my team, my department, the company?"* As the late NBC Sports Television executive Don Ohlmeyer once said, *"The answer to all of your questions is 'money.'"* In a business context, this can be a useful guide.

The answer may be operating expense or capital expenditure savings or avoidance, increased revenue, increased customer satisfaction, or increased resource utilization, all of which may lead to some economic improvement for the people involved (like a bonus, raise, or promotion!) or the company at large (higher stock price, increased dividend, increased profit sharing, etc.). Everyone wants to understand how they, and their stakeholders and constituents, are going to benefit by undergoing this cataclysmic change in their business processes.

If this information can then be presented in a story format, demonstrating a past scenario without the data science solution and then the new future with all its benefits engendered by data science, that's a powerful way to win over the audience and solve another communication challenge—but not the last challenge yet.

Breaking Down Silos

Demonstrating financial benefits applies to most ADSAI projects, but is clearest in the finance industry because at its core is the most numeric of data—money—and, synonymously for credit providers, risk. By reducing risk, credit providers can increase their returns, especially on products sold in large volumes, like home loans. However, what may appear technically simple, given the voluminous amounts of data, can lead to well-trusted technical approaches (even when combined with high levels of analytic maturity) surprisingly failing due to something much less complex and less foreign—poor communication.

For example, take a project—relayed to one of the co-authors by a peer—to build an AI engine to predict defaults on home loans at a local, mid-sized financial institution. The finance company decided to engage an external AI consultant with experience in this domain. Machine learning models that can predict the chances of a person defaulting on a loan are well known, so it was no surprise that within a three-month proof-of-concept period, a functioning model was developed that could proactively engage customers and help them with financial hardship issues before their situation deteriorated. The initial testing showed that the model was effective and would return value to the company in the most critical way—the bottom line.

However, as you might already suspect from a book like this, the project was not that simple. There were two main problems that the consulting team conjectured would cause serious issues later on—and they were right.

The first problem was that the organization already had an actuarial team, who wasn't actively involved in the project. Over the years, this team had built for-purpose functioning statistical models that they understood and trusted, and were already incorporated into mission-critical systems (which allocated an appropriate risk profile across the lending portfolio). Recall Gene Woolsey's opinion on replacing understood models with black boxes—this was definitely the case here for the actuaries. From day one, the actuarial team was suspicious of the machine learning approach and didn't understand why a replacement was necessary. Such a replacement would also mean the team could no longer independently maintain the model without further training or additional hires.

The second problem was working and communicating with the IT team. This is not to criticize IT teams; they have their own schedules, their own challenges, and their own projects, and don't need an uninvited external team putting demands on their time.

Throughout the project, IT continued to follow their familiar and well-proven security protocols, and in the process, inadvertently slowed down the external data science team's access to environments, data, and most importantly, approvals to use cloud environments. That occurred because the data scientists had put together a plan without consulting the IT team first. This tends to happen.

This issue initially pushed out timelines by a few days, then by a few weeks, and finally by months. This deceleration across the project was constant and consistent, for example, the data science team would request the security rules and IT would agree but, due to their own priorities, not prioritize the delivery of the requirements, or the delivered rules and policies would render the project impossible. In the end, the data science team resorted to bringing in a physical server located on-site to allow the project to move forward, hence avoiding the need to provision new cloud environments.

Another problem is that in many companies, IT is a cost center that provides services to the entire organization and their activities are usually driven by the business's needs. In this case, instead of remaining the background service provider, IT decided that they not only had the AI knowledge necessary to contribute to the project, but in fact felt proprietorial toward it. Unfortunately, their AI knowledge was not up to the task, and ultimately, the data scientists should have been left to operate independently across the business. It was now a case of "too many cooks spoil the broth." IT had "many other dishes to prepare" but still wanted to make sure that "every meal included their flavor" of technical input.

This situation became untenable for the data scientists. If a company has a team that wants to solve problems across the business, they shouldn't be in a single silo. Rather, the team should have their own capabilities and associated privileges as well as their own work and development environment, for example, cloud-based sandbox. This would have resolved many of the consultants' IT problems.

In fact, what was tragic about this scenario was that the CIO was really keen—she was a very capable executive and had the right vision. As a key stakeholder, she wanted to get it done. But her involvement presented two further challenges:

1. She probably had too many projects to manage.
2. She left the company at the end of the proof-of-concept period and prior to kicking off the next stage that would get the tool into production and deliver value for the business.

In spite of all this, the credit default risk project still showed some promise, but it wasn't what it could have been. In fact, from a comprehensibility perspective, the data scientists used a standard explainable ML model—the actuaries could have upskilled and learned about it if they wanted to. The model showed the ability to predict with decent accuracy and precision, but not at the expense of recall, which is important. (All three terms have a technical meaning: *accuracy* answers the question, out of 100 examples, how many did we predict correctly? *Precision* asks, of those that you thought were correct, what percentage truly were? *Recall* asks, out of all the cases that were correct, what percentage did you end up saying were correct? In machine learning it is important not just to focus on accuracy.)

To try to get stakeholder buy-in, the external consultants showcased the model to anyone who would listen, including other relevant stakeholders. However, the CIO successor was not eager for innovation—an immediate concern for the now struggling data science team. Their final defense fell when the CEO moved to a new job. At this point in the project, all key champions were gone. As the dominoes began to fall, the data science team lost the support of the rest of the company; in particular, the actuaries who weren't really on board, had joined only a handful of the weekly showcases along the way and had zero interest in the new approach replacing their existing models. From here, the opportunity to increase profitability and give customers a better experience ultimately died with a final whimper as the company went back to business as usual ... to the quiet satisfaction of the actuarial staff.

Starting Small and Simple

> Brooks's Law: "Adding manpower to a late software project makes it later." [10]
>
> "Ramp-up" time: The time it takes for new engineers to become fully productive.
>
> Limited task divisibility: "Nine women cannot have a baby in one month."

Sometimes, doing the easy thing can be difficult, even if it involves simply picking the easier of two options (e.g., picking a small problem instead of a big one). The trouble with this advice is that starting small and simple is not often straightforward (or even a guarantee of success, as we'll see in an example in this section).

The culture of a company typically affects whether they start small and simple, regardless of whether it's the right thing to do. Although small and simple may seem to make sense (from a risk minimization perspective), in an organization that has always done things big and complex (likely because they believe only those types of projects will lead to payoffs big enough to be worth their time), the small and simple may not be so simple after all.

The fascinating thing with this approach is that it not only reduces risk, but in many scenarios, simpler models have been shown to perform better than more complex ones (likely due to less overfitting). In fact, the greater the problem complexity, the simpler the model should become; this appears to make a great deal of practical sense.

Numerous publications have shown for a variety of domains, from healthcare to management,[11] that the simpler the model, the more reliable the performance outside of the training set. In fact, one successful sepsis prediction model from Dascena used a simpler set of variables than Epic's model (remember that rocky analytics journey from the Introduction?) and the news outlet STAT's own internal testing showed that the performance of such a model didn't decrease as much over time when compared with the more complex model.[12]

Even if you do use a simple model, at some point you need to face the unavoidable complexity that will arise when you integrate your simple (or complex) model into the organization's IT infrastructure. Here further challenges await you.

The Standish Group has published the **CHAOS** (**C**omprehensive **H**uman **A**ppraisal for **O**riginating **S**oftware) Report for nearly 40 years. In it, they have chronicled the failure of many IT projects to be delivered on time, within budget, and with all promised functionality (scope). According to "CHAOS 2020: Beyond Infinity," only 19% of all IT projects achieve this lofty goal[13] (on time, within budget, and with all scope). This just might be the worst statistic in the last 40 years of CHAOS Reports. Many projects will of course achieve a combination of some subset of these goals (e.g., timing and quality, but not scope and budget), but very few achieve all.

Is this statistic even relevant in the context of data science project failures? Especially since we haven't been following these strict criteria in the book?

The answer is yes, because, beyond the data analysis and modeling phases, i.e., the "fun part," successful data science modeling projects ultimately evolve to become problems involving software, hardware, networks, data infrastructure, and systems engineering and integration. We recall Tom Davenport's version of Stephen Covey's second habit—begin with the end in mind—*"Models make the enterprise smarter; models embedded in systems and business processes make the enterprise more economically efficient."*[14]

Having been involved in software and ADSAI in large corporations, software product companies, and many technology-based startups for as long as we have (combined almost 50 years), we have utilized most of the major system development methodologies, from Waterfall to Rapid Application Development (RAD), Extreme Programming (XP), and Agile Scrum/Kanban/SAFe. (At Sabre, Doug was on the team that created their own *homegrown* methodology to qualify, compete for and win large-scale projects for other Fortune 500/Global 2000 companies.)

Agile/MVP (minimum viable product), and its precursors XP and RAD, have provided a marked improvement over Waterfall in creating a more flexible, more realistic framework for software and system engineering projects. In fact, according to "CHAOS 2020: Beyond Infinity," software projects using Agile methods *succeed 3x more often than Waterfall* (60% vs. 20%).[15]

A large company at which one of the co-authors previously worked, decided to make a complete transition to Agile, using Scrum, and then to Scaled Agile Framework (SAFe). Whilst that co-author is trained in and a proponent of Agile/Lean/MVP methods, both co-authors believe that Agile Kanban is more suitable to the iterative, investigative, exploratory, discovery R&D nature of ADSAI modeling, model development, and model-based systems development (both co-authors recognize the importance of Agile Scrum in software development). This is because modeling is inherently more *reactive*, i.e., learning more and more about the nuanced business process as you go, uncovering more variables and features, objectives and constraints, new data sources with which to integrate, and *far more* difficult to envision *a priori* than building GUI screens or more structured business logic that is governed by well-defined, strict rules. This preference is in full awareness of the half-dozen different approaches described earlier in the book, including the above, and also of methodologies that partially achieve what we described here, such as Cognitive Project Management for AI (CPMAI).

At first in this large company, the analytics teams (who were building analytical models in the form of microservices connected via Application Programming Interfaces (APIs)) were *forced* by the program leadership in charge of the larger system project to utilize Agile Scrum, which was operating on 2-, 3-, or 4-week sprints, depending on the project and the teams involved. Early on in data science projects, there are far more unknowns than knowns, and even the knowns are far more complex and difficult to estimate, despite using approaches like Planning Poker (i.e., Fibonacci numbers).

This misalignment meant that the analytics team kept missing its sprint timeline milestones and deadlines. Progress was being made, and a lot of productive work was being done, but the team was *failing* as far as the program leadership was concerned due to chronic lateness, and was jeopardizing the macro project delivery schedule. The data scientists finally sat down with program leadership and explained why Agile Scrum was not working on the analytics side of the house, and explained why they thought Agile Kanban was more suitable for the nature of the work. Everyone came to an agreement that Agile Kanban would be used for model development and testing, as long as the analytics team could complete its work within a 4-week window.

This is an excellent example of IT and ADSAI teams compromising and collaborating to align different approaches to system development—Scrum with (typically) shorter sprints for software systems, and Kanban with longer sprints for model-based software and microservices. Using Kanban with 4-week sprints, the analytics team had more time for iterative exploration, experimentation, and discovery, and a sufficiently long-time window to complete their activities without disrupting the macro project delivery schedule. The working relationship and morale of both teams improved considerably, and the project continued toward a successful conclusion.

Project Management for ADSAI

Project management for ADSAI projects is important. There must be structure and discipline. As stated before, Agile Kanban, in the co-authors' experience, is more suitable for ADSAI projects than Scrum. Kanban enables you to start small and simple, and build from there. That said, data scientists will oftentimes be required to fit an ADSAI project management framework inside that of a much larger system project, so the choice of delivery may not always be an available luxury.

Building a turnkey production system-based version of a model that supports an enterprise business process of more than modest importance will entail:

- building APIs to multiple data sources,
- architecting a microservice application around the model,
- implementing data and model drift detection,
- model refitting,
- model assumption revalidation,
- error handling,
- fault tolerance,
- high-availability and high-reliability robustness, and
- failover capabilities

to get to 99+% uptime (mission-critical systems required the elusive "five nines" or 99.999% uptime). Executing this endeavor successfully is a complex undertaking. Both co-authors have been through this process many, many times and strong project management practices, processes, skills, discipline, and judgment are critical to successfully achieve scope, timing, budget, and quality goals, or at the very least, not the empty set of the intersection of these four measures.

Project management for ADSAI modeling initiatives (regardless of whether they reach production) should be somewhat more relaxed in that they should be understood to be a "research project," an application of the scientific method, a voyage of discovery, almost as prone to "puffs of smoke over the lab bench" as Edison inventing the lightbulb. The four dimensions of the inviolate Project Management (PM) "box" in Figure 3.2 (formerly an 'iron' triangle until "Quality" was added) are each as important in setting realistic estimates and expectations for stakeholders as to how long the project will take to complete (note that we have collapsed four dimensions into two, i.e. the two dimensional square, indicating that all four can vary but are all interconnected and not independent of each other, hence the two dimensions rather than four).

FIGURE 3.2
Dimensions of Project Management.

The co-authors have worked on projects that began ill-defined (such as trying to recreate an expert's decision-making process), which required multiple iterations based on end-user feedback (in such cases, the number of iterations will likely be unknown upfront). The timeline must accommodate this uncertainty. Similar to the notion of MVP, *minimum viable model* (MVM) is most appropriate for emphasizing the importance of stakeholder confidence to get a basic model up and running by functionally providing some insightful output as soon as possible (although, as we'll see in the steel industry example below, even this simple approach can lead to challenges). The real goal is to receive user feedback and align expectations as early as possible.

Once the model is deemed successful and too important to live without, and a budget is approved to convert it into a production system (mission critical or not, planning or real-time), data scientists become part of a *much* larger team consisting of data engineers, software engineers, MLEng, MLOps, cloud system engineers, test and QA engineers, project managers, business analysts, etc. Most likely, the data scientist will no longer be in control of the project.

As mentioned earlier, once this stage of the project is reached, teams will typically employ Agile Scrum for systems development and SAFe for enterprise-scale systems development. We highly recommend ambitious data scientists to train in both to reduce project management risk and become a more valuable team member in such projects.

In spite of these frameworks, there is a set of "the usual suspects" on the IT project management side contributing to project failures, which have formed the basis of many books such as the fantastic *Project Recovery* by Harold Kerzner. These include:

- Underestimating scope
- Overcommitting on scope
- Underestimating complexity, for example, technological, architectural, change management, system integration
- Overestimating team capacity and capabilities, especially new staff or newly formed teams (there is always a ramp-up, learning curve period)
- Over prioritizing too many features, i.e., every feature cannot be a P1 for R1 (Priority Level 1 for Release 1)
- Unrealistic timeline to address scope and no slack in the timeline for contingencies and unforeseen circumstances
- Artificial deadline/timeline set by someone in "upper management," independent of and regardless of actual scope, resources, and complexity
- Insufficient quantity of (adequately skilled) resources to address scope
- The project manager's ability to manage through adversity and make decisions to course correct when things go awry (which they ultimately will)

These failures still occur because project management is part science and part art form.[16] It is based on experience, instinct, judgment, and most importantly, knowing key people, processes, technology, and the business problem domain. The fewer unknowns and "new stuff" on a project, the higher the probability of success.

As in most endeavors, such as learning to play an instrument or sport, project management skills are developed through the *experience of doing project management*, including making mistakes and learning from them, not just reading about it in a book or taking a course. *Studying* project management may be necessary but is by no means *sufficient* for developing and honing skills to become a good project manager. There is no substitute for project management experience and learning from other, more experienced project managers. In our observation, it takes *years* of hands-on intensive experience managing projects of larger and larger scope and greater and greater complexity to develop ample enterprise-grade expertise.

The best advice we can provide is to always err on the side of conservatism when making project commitments on scope, timeline, resources, budget, quality, and complexity (recall earlier section on sandbagging and BHAGs). When in doubt, seek advice from a more experienced project manager.

Always be transparent with team members, stakeholders, and constituents, and report bad news and offer solutions as soon as an adverse situation occurs. *Bad news does not get better with age!*

This is a deep and rich topic and we felt compelled to discuss it here. Not only is project management in ADSAI projects different from IT and other projects, sometimes the usual successful approaches in the latter can fail miserably in the former, as we'll see next.

Asking the Right Questions

Many of the project failure reasons revealed by our research were not surprising—but perhaps the biggest surprise was why so many of these issues keep arising. One of the most salient issues is making sure the problem being solved matches what the customer wants—and not just at the beginning of the project but all the way through. (It is possible for a customer's understanding, scope requirements or priorities to change throughout a project.) This is a subtle challenge and can be very complicated. This section will show an example of how starting small and simple can also lead to failure despite this being a generally good principle.

Sometimes in the problem discovery phase, all questions get clear answers and the data science team builds a very good understanding. However, if you have asked the *wrong questions*, then those right answers don't matter much. The team may design a technically brilliant solution that quickly and accurately solves the problem, but if it doesn't match the user's workflow, then they won't adopt it. Our next story involves what is in fact a best practice approach to developing a data science tool—build an MVP, iterate, and de-risk the project. However, following this best practice still ended in an unexpected failure.

This story begins with steel manufacturing, which is a challenging task to execute well at scale. Once a secure job provider supporting the American way of life, it evolved into a highly competitive sector with many headline insolvencies. Integrated steel companies dominated the steel industry worldwide, until a cheaper alternative emerged: the mini mill. These compact mills melt metal scrap in electric furnaces. In the late 20th century, they began offering a significant cost advantage compared to integrated mills, producing low-quality steel such as the rebar used in strengthening concrete. This approach succeeded because rebar has minimal specifications, and once encased in concrete, its quality becomes even less important. It was the perfect market for a lower quality product and the cheaper mini mills.

As the mini mills targeted the rebar market, integrated mills gladly relinquished their stake in this fiercely competitive commodity. Why defend the least profitable aspect of their business when they could focus on more lucrative areas, such as angle iron and thicker bar and rod? By shedding the lowest-margin product lines, integrated mills bolstered their gross-margin profitability.

As famously chronicled in Clayton Christensen's book, *The Innovator's Dilemma*, this innovative drive that initially seemed like a windfall to integrated mills actually caused nearly all integrated mills to face bankruptcy by the end of the 20th century, culminating in large, major integrated producers, for example, National Steel Corporation, becoming bankrupt and joining a queue of 40 other steel majors, which closed down between the 1990s and early 2000s.

These struggles forced integrated steelmakers everywhere to look for any opportunity to improve their operations, and with the hype surrounding data and analytics, companies sought its magic touch. In the steel industry, not all companies have a proper understanding of what data science entails, but that doesn't stop the allure of AI emboldening companies to try their luck at running the analytics gauntlet. One of those companies, with which one of the co-authors worked, is a global, vertically integrated steel and mining company with tens of thousands of employees in hundreds of locations.

For this integrated provider (like many of its now insolvent American peers), production began with the creation of liquid steel made from raw and recycled materials and finished with high-value precision-engineered steels and associated services sold to customers around the world.

The company even supplied raw materials to its integrated supply chain as well as to external customers from its own iron ore mining business and coking coal mines. A truly giant conglomerate and one that definitely stood to benefit from improving operational efficiencies at scale—exactly the type of thing AI can provide.

This particular steel company embarked upon a journey to build a value chain optimization tool. The tool was designed to examine the existing value chain and find ways to optimize it via adjusting connections, inputs, process timings, and much more. With it, the company would produce high-level budgets and financial analyses of the new configurations of the production network with the goal of finding the most profitable configuration.

With high hopes, the project kicked off by building the tool that was expected to disrupt an industry. The company signed up for a two-year project having anticipated what the final tool would look like, but still, they sensibly staged the project by first launching an MVP (or MVM!) as recommended earlier. Unexpectedly, the problems began there.

After developing the first iteration, the data science team discovered that an optimization engine in its MVP form simply wasn't useful for this client. Without significant investment, such an iteration could never get to the level of detail required to keep the nontechnical end users happy. When the MVP was completed, the corporate team gave each other a pat on the back for finishing the first step, but it was the planners who then unexpectedly out-right rejected the tool due to the level of detail. The horrible truth dawned on the data science team that the planners would never be satisfied until the full product was built. But the developers were now caught in a Catch-22 because the executives weren't prepared to finance the full product until the planners verified the value of the MVP.

This dilemma reveals a common challenge for data science projects. There can technically be three "bosses":

1. The executive sponsoring (and funding) the project.
2. The manager responsible for overseeing its implementation.
3. The frontline staff who will be using the tool.

Unfortunately, pleasing all three is difficult but necessary. Even though the frontline staff appear to have the least corporate clout, their buy-in is just as important.

At the MVP stage, the optimization engine producing the optimized pro-duction configuration was not easily explainable. There were some instances in which the tool (based on a mixed-integer programming formulation) would make certain decisions that the subject matter experts couldn't under-stand. The problem could be a missing constraint from the optimization model (that the experts failed to reveal during scoping) or simply that a constraint was incorrectly stated. Furthermore, even if the proposed solution was valid (feasible), it simply may not be something the planners would do in real life, leading them to reject it. Every time such problems arose, the data science team had to go through a root cause analysis and report on results. Each time, unfortunately, it eroded the planner's faith in the optimization engine.

The analytics team realized they were never going to be able to bridge this comprehension gap (and simultaneously hit their performance targets)—the end users weren't ready or willing to trust a "black box," even if it had been thoroughly validated. Every time something didn't make sense to them, the data scientists needed to get to the bottom of it. Finally, the perceived (or real) lack of confidence on the part of the planners led to the decision to stop the project altogether. The MVP and its adjustments would simply never be rich enough—each iteration had the developers adding a new constraint that was planned to be added in a later project phase. (This is actually a quite common occurrence in complex mathematical optimization modeling.)

In this case, if the data science team could have rigorously captured all the constraints, the optimization engine would have provided a lot of value and the project would have yielded a favorable outcome. But the team chose another approach instead: They captured 80% of the requirements to model *most* of the problem. However, the missing 20% of the problem formulation was critical enough that missing it meant the engine fell short of providing the planners with a sufficiently robust solution they could trust. That was the death knell for the project.

The key observation from this story is one we have presented many times—data science projects are complex. We said to start small and simple, but we've also shown that for certain data science projects, an MVP may not be the best approach because presenting end users with an intermediate solution (i.e., something they perceive as "half-baked") may dissuade them from fully engaging and adopting it. Hence, they aren't going to be ready to consider going further unless it solves the problem completely, without question or incident.

This sense of discomfort and distrust that can be caused by an MVP may lead stakeholders to turn off the AI engine and go back to their *status quo* process, as we saw earlier in the national logistics example. Data scientists really must either address what the customer wants and needs, even if it means breaking away from proven frameworks in certain situations, or alternatively, data scientists must work even more diligently at explaining and getting the user to understand and embrace the *iterative, multiphase* MVP approach (vs. a "one and done").

However, there is an even better solution to having process upon process to ensure success at addressing every conceivable challenge, and that is simply having great people with the right skills together with the right amount of process. In our research, this was shown to be one of the greatest problems facing an organization—how to find, attract, hire, and retain the right people. But what happens if you don't have the right people on board? What could possibly go wrong?

Critical Thinking: How Not to Fail

- Why don't companies typically collect large quantities of high-quality data? What would be the pros and cons of simply collecting data on everything? Under what circumstances would you recommend it?

- Why do data silos arise and how can enterprises bridge these silos to gain more value from their data?

- If you worked for a company that faced data quality, access or availability issues, what first step would you take to rectify the issue depending on its cause?

- If unknown data quality issues exist, what downstream problems will arise in the organization as a result of decisions that rely on this data?

- What is a challenge to setting clear and reasonable expectations in ADSAI projects in companies today?

- Why is organizational communication so important in ADSAI projects?
- When communicating results, you need to tailor them to your audience. How would the message you deliver to an executive differ from what you would deliver to your technical team?
- When working on a project, what issues can arise from not working closely with the end users and customers?
- Why do you think adding more data scientists and developers to an already late project would simply delay it more?
- From a career perspective, which option seems worse: slightly underpromising and overdelivering on an underwhelming result, or slightly overpromising and underdelivering on an ambitious result? Why?
- When looking at the failure reasons for IT projects presented in the "Starting Small and Simple" section, what new issues arise for ADSAI projects that may not be present in IT projects?
- What benefits exist when starting small and simple? What pitfalls exist?
- Under what circumstances is it a bad idea to follow an iterative project approach and start with an MVP?

Notes

1. Sambasivan, N., Kapania, S., Highfill, H., Akrong, D., Paritosh, P., & Aroyo, L. (2021). "Everyone wants to do the model work, not the data work": Data Cascades in High-Stakes AI. *Proceedings of the 2021 CHI Conference on Human Factors in Computing Systems*, Art. no. 39, 1-15. https://doi.org/10.1145/3411764.3445518.
2. For example, with forecasting engines, the rule of thumb that many data scientists, including the authors, prefer to use whenever possible a *minimum of three years'* worth of data to adequately capture the most recent salient patterns and trends in the time series data (i.e., you need one year to get the seasonal trends, two years to track yearly trends, and the third year to give yourself some confidence in those trends). In the late 1980s and 1990s, the standard approach to RM passenger demand forecasting was to utilize Holt-Winters triple exponential smoothing, i.e., if you've heard of a moving average then this is a more robust version that allows you to add to it a linear trend (i.e., slope) and seasonality. At that time, mainframe computing power still came at a premium price point, and Holt-Winters provided a computationally efficient yet highly accurate method for forecasting passenger demand patterns based on historical data. It also has the benefit of not overfitting the data due to its limited number of parameters, a benefit we will discuss later in the book.

3. The reader is strongly encouraged to read Michael Lewis' book, or see the Academy Award-winning movie *The Big Short* for a rigorous, yet darkly entertaining, account of this period and its aftershock effects on consumers.

4. Davenport, T. (2014). *bigdata@work*. Harvard Business Review Press. (The book provides a great resource in the big data domain.)

5. Peters, T. (1987). Under promise, over deliver. TPG Communications. https://tompeters.com/columns/under-promise-over-deliver/.

6. Collins, J., & Porras, J. (1994). *Built to Last: Successful Habits of Visionary Companies*. William Collins. (The book provides detailed elaboration on BHAGs.)

7. Smith, B., Leimkuhler, J., & Darrow, R. (1992). Yield Management at American Airlines. *Interfaces*, 22(1), 8-31. (1991 INFORMS Franz Edelman Award Winner).

8. Konrad, A. (2013, November 1). Meet ORION, Software That Will Save UPS Millions By Improving Drivers' Routes. *Forbes*.

9. Smith, A. (2023, April 17). Operations Research Enhances Retail Truck Routing and Load Planning: Walmart Awarded the 2023 INFORMS Edelman Award. INFORMS. https://www.informs.org/News-Room/INFORMS-Releases/Awards-Releases/Operations-Research-Enhances-Retail-Truck-Routing-and-Load-Planning-Walmart-Awarded-the-2023-INFORMS-Edelman-Award.

10. Brooks, F. (1975). *The Mythical Man-Month: Essays on Software Engineering*. Addison-Wesley.

11. The reader may refer to the following articles (Gerd Gigerenzer and the ABC research team have published numerous findings on this topic, too):
    - Dawes, R. M. (1979). The robust beauty of improper linear models in decision making. *American Psychologist*, 34(7), 571–582.
    - Kleinberg, J. (2018). Human Decisions and Machine Predictions. *Quarterly Journal of Economics*, 133(1), 237–293.
    - Holte, R. C. (1993). Very simple classification rules perform well on most commonly used datasets. *Machine Learning*, 11(1), 63–90.
    - Einhorn, H. J. (1972). Expert measurement and mechanical calculation. *Organizational Behavior and Human Performance*, 7, 86–106.

12. Ross, C. (2023, July 31). AI gone astray: How subtle shifts in patient data send popular algorithms reeling, undermining patient safety. *STAT*. https://www.statnews.com/2022/02/28/sepsis-hospital-algorithms-data-shift/.

13. Portman, H. (2021, January 6). Review Standish Group – CHAOS 2020: Beyond Infinity. Henny Portman's Blog. https://hennyportman.wordpress.com/2021/01/06/review-standish-group-chaos-2020-beyond-infinity/.

14. Quote attributed to Thomas Davenport's Keynote Speech at the International Institute for Analytics (IIA) Analytics Symposium. October 11, 2017. Chicago, IL.

15. The Standish Group. (n.d.). *The Standish Group*. https://standishgroup.myshopify.com/.

16. Refer to Project Management Institute (Project Management Professional (PMP) Certification) and the many tools and techniques available for managing software projects).

4

People

Both co-authors agree that placing the People chapter this late in the book initially felt wrong. As we were planning the structure and the ideas we wanted to cover, we were both sure that the first and most important chapter for us to address would be this one. However, when we reviewed the research data, superficially, it told us a different story. Because we are both scientifically minded, we went with what our research told us, but we knew it wasn't the whole story.

Strategy, processes, and even technology are all *people-led*. Although our categorization put such things as lacking the right resources in the people category, we could see that many of our earlier chapter choices could also have been classified as *people* issues. For example, when analyzing the root causes of the strategic and process challenges, it was also clear that the underlying issues involved people. So, in deciding how to categorize failures as "people" ones, we placed all failures caused by issues with knowledge, attitudes, skills, and behaviors into the people bucket. What surprised us was the small number of very common people challenges that arose from this.

We have both lived these challenges throughout our careers and supplemented a lot of our technical education with management and business operations edification. For example, one of Doug's favorite quotes is by Ralph Waldo Emerson, who famously said, *"All history is biography."* Business, like history, is all about *people*.

In 1999, Doug worked as a CTO for an e-commerce technology company whose CEO—a highly successful, award-winning former CIO—told him that in large companies, the CIO is really more of a *people* leader and less of a *technical* leader. The CIO has lots of specialists on their team, so their job is to motivate, communicate, mentor, guide, measure, and get the *maximum value* from the team who, quite frankly, know more "nuts and bolts" of the IT than the CIO.

There are many great resources to help people find and nurture the right team. But sometimes this people management advice can lead us astray, as we'll see in our first example in this chapter. In his book *Good to Great*, James Collins espouses the notion that team building is all about "getting the right people on the bus, and the wrong people off the bus." Billionaire founder/CEO of Electronic Data Systems (EDS), and later Perot Systems, Ross Perot once described his most important job as "surrounding himself with the very brightest, best, most talented people he could find." However, what

DOI: 10.1201/9781032661360-5

this can lead to is some leaders hiring only "their kind of people" who fit their mold and behavior patterns. When given the opportunity, those leaders end up kicking people "off the bus" who really were useful "on the bus." Those same leaders define who is the best and brightest based on intangibles like tenure, loyalty, and going along to get along. Compliant employees who don't rock the boat, but row the boat, are more valued and advance faster than those who bring in new ideas about different, more efficient, more effective approaches.

One of the co-authors professionally knows two highly experienced, expert analytics leaders who encountered similar people challenges when they were hired to lead the Advanced Analytics function at a multibillion-dollar company—let's call them ReliableCo. (The two experts served consecutively in this leadership role.) Despite building a dedicated, award-winning group of a dozen brilliant, passionate, and highly effective OR analysts and data scientists who delivered world-class optimization-based solutions in capital asset, human resource planning and scheduling, and inventory management optimization, the CIO and senior executive leadership at ReliableCo had no interest in further leveraging or growing this invaluable capability. They saw Advanced Analytics as a department-level "cog in the (Technology Department) wheel," only good for solving *niche complex problems* that IT alone could not solve with software applications, or the business could not solve with Excel.

The culture and leadership of ReliableCo always espoused *teamwork* far and above technology, let alone *mathematics*. Though admirable, especially when it was a scrappy underdog startup, and even later as a historically highly successful company that was consistently profitable for decades, such a strategy ultimately had its limitations when ReliableCo evolved to become a large, operationally complex Fortune 200 company, one of a handful of top companies in its industry. After being in business for decades, the culture at ReliableCo was described in research and press reports as "insular" and "close-minded to new ideas from the outside" that "don't align with the ReliableCo way of doing things."

The shortcomings of this approach have been evidenced by ReliableCo's multiple technology system failures in recent years. Their system challenges, which led to significant business and customer service disruptions and ended up costing ReliableCo several hundred million dollars, are attributed to insufficient investment in upgraded technology systems and fully integrated operations-oriented analytics solutions. The sheer scale of ReliableCo's operations outstripped the capacity of their manual business processes and human-centric decision-making, and clearly warranted more scalable, streamlined, automated, and optimization-based solutions.

Despite the Advanced Analytics team at ReliableCo winning multiple industry awards for data and analytics excellence from multiple reputable companies and noteworthy industry organizations, as well as delivering over $100 million annually in cost avoidance, the Advanced Analytics team never grew beyond a staff of two dozen. Their proposals for greater investment in much needed fully integrated operations-oriented analytics solutions were deprioritized. After the two consecutive leaders departed, the team was subsequently split up and the remnant elements were merged with counterpart domain IT organizations.

The situation at ReliableCo demonstrates that delivering world-class departmental solutions that optimize resources and operations and consistently generate substantial business value and economic impact, in addition to having an extraordinarily capable analytics team and leadership, does not necessarily result in opportunities for growth, expansion, or even favorable recognition and support from senior executives. Senior executives must make a conscious choice to recognize, invest in, double down, and support Advanced Analytics programs, projects, and initiatives, as well as data-driven and model-based culture, attitudes, and behaviors, for them to effectively proliferate across the enterprise, creating ever greater business impact (i.e., a top down approach is necessary).

What caused the outcome at ReliableCo?

Funding for additional analytics initiatives was never prioritized commensurately with pure IT initiatives, despite relatively low project costs and inordinately large ROI. Oftentimes, the Advanced Analytics team completed departmental analytics efforts in key business areas "under the radar" as self-funded side projects because IT leadership was more concerned about and interested in big budget, large IT system upgrades, and replacement projects. These low cost, low risk, high value "after school, off book" advanced analytics projects were actually *publicly frowned upon and discouraged* by the CIO because they fell outside their pure IT project portfolio; also perhaps (politically) because they were too efficient, too effective, and just a bit too popular with the business stakeholders who greatly appreciated the alacrity with which they were completed and the substantial ROI that was realized. ReliableCo is an example in which *ADSAI projects succeeded,* but the *culture, leadership, and the organization as a whole failed to capitalize and double down on the ADSAI success generated by the Advanced Analytics team.*

As we've discovered by now, data science failure comes in many forms. This is also true with people factors—ReliableCo's failures resulted in both economic and opportunity costs, a consequence of failing to embrace and build upon the successes of the Advanced Analytics team. Although our story contains strategic elements and could belong in the Strategy chapter, we include it here due to the failure in attitude and skills of the upper echelons of the business. We will focus on these types of failures—caused by the people and culture of an organization—in this chapter. We'll start with the most common people-related failure that our research uncovered: lacking the right resources for the job.

Lacking the Right Resources

Although COVID-19 was the worst of times for some companies, others were able to discover a silver lining in the calamity. The shock and economic turmoil were experienced by all organizations, but in the disruption, not all companies were equally affected.

A large clothing retailer (known to one of the co-authors) that began its data journey long before 2020 by acquiring key technologies missed its greatest opportunity by not leveraging the digital assets it had built up prior to the pandemic. Unfortunately, when COVID-19 arrived, the retailer chose to return to the old way of making decisions because they felt they had more control, i.e., manual approaches. Mismanaging supply chains and making slow manual decisions cost the business millions in sales while its competitors thrived during lockdown by pivoting online and leveraging nascent trends to predict sales and capitalize on the working-(and exercising)-from-home trend.

Another company that Evan worked closely with—also employing thousands of people and operating in the agribusiness sector—committed to using AI to intelligently redirect goods as entire countries locked down, making fast decisions to locate new customers and markets. This company resisted the temptation to return to its old ways, even if it was initially uncomfortable, and thereby generated higher-than-usual profits by serving short-term clients at higher prices. The company was aware of—and exploited—the power of data.

Each company was already digitally empowered, had up-to-date AI technologies, and encountered a problem that could easily leverage those technologies. So, what was the difference between these two companies?

The people.

More specifically, the *right* people with the *right* skills and resources.

The New Digital Divide

As the COVID-19 pandemic raged on, companies were forced to rapidly accelerate their digital journey in order to thrive. This was the recommended path forward to avoid failure.

Countless digital coronavirus survivors leveraged data and analytical tools (e.g., AI) to make better decisions in what became high-pressure environments. They ran more scenarios, optimized more possibilities, and predicted more future states—in essence, they more effectively managed the uncertainty.

On the other side were those adversely impacted by the pandemic that may have had digital capabilities but lacked the right people, quality data, or confidence to leverage these capabilities (including AI tools to make data-driven, model-based decisions in those challenging times).

To get a better understanding of the factors causing these differences in outcomes, in addition to augmenting the research carried out for this book, Evan reached out to his network of companies and clients from over the years and asked both successful and unsuccessful companies a few questions: How do you manage uncertainty? How do your teams use and interact with data and AI tools? How do you identify suitable problems? What do you do when things go wrong with your AI tools?

A clear set of factors emerged from this impromptu survey, which separated the companies successfully leveraging AI tools from those that struggled. The analysis showed that the "people challenge" seemed most difficult to fix. What were the human factors Evan discovered that separated the analytical successes from the failures?

A key factor in many of the successful companies that was missing in the unsuccessful companies Evan talked to, including the aforementioned agribusiness company, was the existence of an "Analytics translator" (or AI translator),[1] and the strategic placement of such a person amid the other operational people in their business. Such a person typically has analytical skills, but works on the *operational side* of the business.

For the world to successfully leverage the power of AI, we will need more people with these skills, i.e., people who understand both the business domain *and* the AI methodologies and technologies, and can simultaneously communicate equally effectively with both business and AI team members. The absence of this resource in a company may lead to failure, even with a great analytics team and brilliant business units. The disconnect can be a gap too difficult to bridge. Let's dig a bit more into what this role entails.

Analytics (or AI) Translators

As mentioned, an important trend separating the AI survivors from the AI failures in Evan's impromptu survey was the existence of team members who were domain experts and dedicated users of AI tools—in other words, they had both the domain knowledge *and* analytical skills that a company wants and needs to be successful.

Silos are common in large organizations (see Figure 4.1), for example, HR teams and finance teams. In many companies, AI teams are facing a similar fate. This can lead to the trap of creating a centralized analytics function (like an IT team) that advises other parts of the organization, even if they don't properly understand how things work in that division or silo.

As we flagged earlier, siloing AI functional capability, when applied without thought, can cause serious issues for a company.

For example, another company Evan worked with, which successfully outperformed their peers during COVID-19, had deep analytical skills embedded in a functional silo. They operated in the retail sector and continued to price their goods as per the outputs of their AI engine without losing faith in its recommendations. In fact, during this critical time, they leveraged the AI to run

FIGURE 4.1
Some typical organizational silos in large companies.

more scenarios and reduce uncertainty, giving them even more confidence than during their business-as-usual periods. It was a lot of work and required constantly retraining models with the latest data, but the key to success was that Analytics (or AI) translators in this company reported to their functional silo but also maintained collaboration with the analytics professionals in the organization (their so-called chapter). This level of communication and coordination helped to ensure a consistent set of best practices and sharing of critical knowledge about data and models, especially important during those difficult times.

This approach is not new and has been described by a number of authors over the years, so setting people up for success and using such a federated model of analytics capability does not need to be reinvented (see Figure 4.2).[2] However, no one model suits all scenarios (e.g., a federated model in a

FIGURE 4.2
A federated (or agile) model of analytics capability.

startup probably makes no sense if the startup is small) but being aware of the options will ensure better outcomes from ADSAI teams.

Where Do You Find Analytics Translators?

The challenge for organizations now is to find AI translators and insert them into relevant teams. On the recruitment side, there are a number of ways to find them. We suggest looking for people with:

1. Analytical skills and the ability to work in a functional team (e.g., supply chain), or
2. Domain knowledge and trained in AI technologies (e.g., it is a personal interest and they might be doing side projects in their own time).

We've seen both types of people in organizations successfully leveraging AI.

Take the example of a clinical data analyst, as of writing a new job title that is becoming more common in large hospitals. This role typically includes someone trained in mathematics and computer science, but who also has completed training in medicine or a related undergraduate degree. They work with functional teams to improve results, such as theater scheduling, emergency department patient flow modeling, optimizing patient coding, or efficient staff rostering.

Critically, these Analytics translators play key roles in troubleshooting the inevitable problems that arise with AI engines because they understand how such systems work and where to look for issues. They are also better able to interact with vendors on requirements and problems, if solutions are provided by vendors.

How can we ensure that more AI translators are present in the workforce? A good place to start is at universities, which are beginning to recognize the need for degrees (sometimes called things like Business Analytics) that will train analytics translators who can then fill this critical gap. Without such trained people in the volumes required, ideally an organization will fill an AI translator role with a specifically trained person as described above.

This leads us to ask: How *are* universities addressing these challenges? Specifically, are they doing anything to tackle the trends we have presented in this book?

Strengthening ADSAI Curricula

We have the utmost respect for the university system teaching analytics, data science, and AI, and the underlying fields of mathematics and computer science. We are both products of the university system (Doug in the US and Evan in Australia and Europe), and we are both still active participants, teaching undergraduate and graduate-level courses to students, executives, and practitioners in degree programs (bachelor's, MBA, MS), as well as teaching continuing, professional, and executive education certificate courses in analytics, data science, and AI.

US and Australian universities, and in particular, graduate schools in science and engineering, are world-renowned and students come from all over the world to study and obtain advanced degrees in mathematics, computer science, data science, analytics, and other engineering disciplines. We can both say with certainty that we would not have had the same career trajectory and success were it not for our university education and degrees. These programs are designed to provide a solid, robust *technical* foundation on which to build real-world learning and experience.

That said, we believe that when it comes to being aware of potential pitfalls in ADSAI initiatives, and holistically understanding the pillars of data science success beyond the technical, there is indeed a void that needs to be addressed by university education. There is a clear and present opportunity to enhance and extend the ADSAI curriculum and learning experience to more directly address the types of problems that we identify in this book.

How can we claim this? With data.

To back up our claims, we examined the curriculum of more than 40 of the top US graduate-level MS programs in data science from two well-known industry lists. (The undergraduate-level programs reviewed in this dataset showed the same characteristics.)

1. The first list we looked at was *Fortune's* Top Information Technology & Data Schools in 2023, a well-respected annual ranked list of the best master's programs in data science.[3]
2. The second was MastersInDataScience.org,[4] founded by Harvard and MIT in 2012 and produced by the online education learning giant edX (2U, Inc) to make the world's best education available to everyone. The Best 20+ Schools with Data Science Master's Programs list was produced in 2023.

All MS programs surveyed in these lists are in the neighborhood of 30 credit hours and consist of 10–12 technical courses that are essentially exclusively focused on ADSAI topics, methods, and techniques in their prerequisites, core, and elective coursework. These topics, methods, and techniques include, but are not limited to:

- Programming in Python, R, or other similar languages
- Probability and Distributions
- Statistical Theory: Distributions and Inference

- Statistical Analysis and Modeling
- Forecasting Models
- Machine Learning Models
- Artificial Intelligence
- Data Mining
- Data Structures and Database Management Systems
- Visualization
- Applications (in particular sub-domains, e.g., biostatistics)
- Cloud Computing
- Related Fields (such as operations research and mathematical optimization)

The results were not surprising, but in reflecting on the themes raised here, we saw a huge gap. University curricula tend to have predominantly, if not exclusively, a *deeply technical* focus, which is a problem. There are probably several reasons for this, including:

1. Most importantly, most necessarily, and most obviously, a *foundational understanding and competence* in the theory and application of ADSAI methods, models, algorithms, techniques, and programming for development and deployment of model-based solutions is a *mandatory prerequisite* for credibility and being hired into real-world corporate settings, and professionals literally and figuratively must be able to "do the math" to function effectively in this field of endeavor.

2. Most full-time university faculty are *not real-world practitioners* involved in the messy details of implementing ADSAI models, but rather, extraordinarily intelligent, highly trained, and educated (i.e., PhD or other doctoral degree) researchers with *deep technical expertise* in a few relatively narrow fields. These faculty are on a career path that is geared and focused on obtaining *tenure* (literally tenure-track). Achieving tenure is primarily governed by the paradigm of *"publish or perish"* in which faculty must regularly and frequently publish their research in a number of sufficiently notable refereed journals, and in addition, publish textbooks or chapters that are then referenced by others in their field, as well as teaching (i.e., course load) and contributing to other department/university service-related activities. Net-net professors *teach the material they know best*—mostly technical material.[5]

3. The technical courses are arguably the most fun, interesting, and enjoyable to teach and learn (especially for those who love math

and programming), and most apt for grading and measuring discrete learning outcomes (i.e., quizzes, exams, homework, and project assignments) in the span of a semester-long course.

4. Implementation details are viewed by many in academia as too mundane, too messy, or lacking in rigor to be taught in a university classroom, and are often marginalized by telling students that "you'll learn about all of that when you get into the real-world" or during "on-the-job training" (both co-authors were told this during their university education).

5. In spite of mathematics having been around for decades, even centuries, and myriad textbooks amply covering these topics, the fields of operations research and AI (including machine learning) have only been around since the 1940s–1950s, and came to relevance practically in corporations in the 1960s–1980s. The ADSAI application *explosion* has only occurred in the past 10–15 years, thanks to the availability of a lot more data and computing power, but *no books* (that we know of to-date) have been written on the *pragmatic realities of why data science projects fail* (one of the primary reasons we decided to write this book). Hence, it is no surprise that the topics we address here are not appearing in university curricula.

A final point on curricula. Things have not changed a whole lot in ~40 years. For example, since Doug earned his BS in Mathematical Sciences in 1986, and MS in Operations Research (MSOR) in 1987, from Georgia Tech's School of Industrial & Systems Engineering (ISyE).

Doug's bachelor's degree consisted of 132 credits, half of which were liberal arts core and elective courses, and the other half were courses in mathematics (7), physics, statistics (4), operations research (2), mathematical modeling, mathematical economics, and computer science (4).

There was no formal training or education on communication, change management, project management, expectation setting, deploying systems into production, etc. Students worked on some real-world problem datasets and completed projects using MINITAB, MATLAB, and FORTRAN, and had to interpret and present the results, but that was about as close as they got to the "real-world" of ADSAI.[6] Doug completed two internships that then landed him a part-time job as a programmer/analyst at the same company during his junior and senior years, so that experience provided some real-world exposure while still an undergraduate student.

Notwithstanding the superior reputation of Georgia Tech ISyE,[7] the curriculum was still missing some critical ADSAI training. Doug's MSOR degree consisted of 48 credits, including 16 3-credit courses in: mathematical programming (4), probability theory and models (2), queueing theory and models, decision theory, regression analysis, time series analysis, simulation analysis, production/inventory/distribution systems analysis (3), and engineering economics (2). Doug's research assistantship consisted of conducting theoretical statistical research experiments using simulation analysis which involved extensive programming. There was a mandatory Seminar Series that consisted of visiting professors presenting their research on extremely technical topics, i.e., essentially a mathematics lecture with bagels.

Doug did have several *programming* assignments. The *Simulation Analysis* class was the closest he got to modeling and solving real-world types of problems, for example, simulating and analyzing bank branch queues and port cranes unloading cargo ships. In the *Nonlinear Programming* class, he coded algorithms to see how they performed on specific problems. Although technically demanding, nothing remotely addressed why data science projects fail or how to execute and lead ADSAI projects in the real world, including all the parts that go wrong.

Fortunately, things have evolved somewhat in ADSAI education since the late 1980s and early 2000s when Evan completed his undergraduate studies. Practically every university program curriculum we surveyed included, and required, some combination of one or more practical, real-world learning experiences, including:

- Capstone Course
- Practicum Course
- Internship Course
- Colloquium Course

The first three courses involve (to varying degrees) students working on a real-world challenge for a partner company using real-life data, and building and implementing one or more models to analyze and solve a problem, support decision-making, answer a question, or assess an opportunity to provide insight, understanding, and hopefully identify, if not deliver, a tangible business value or economic impact. They conclude with a detailed presentation of results to constituent stakeholders at the partner company.[8] The Colloquium Course is similar to a Seminar Series in which students hear from real-world practitioners on the realities of developing and implementing ADSAI models.

These types of experiences are without a doubt *invaluable* to students, especially those with limited or no relevant real-world work experience. However, they are limited in scope and scale, with a typical duration of three to six months. Students must figure out the right analytical modeling approach to solve the problem at hand, as well as manage their project and deal with real-world data challenges. Fortunately, the students do get some exposure to the "soft skills" of communication when they present their project results, conclusions, and recommendations.

Students typically do not *implement* their solution into production or leave behind a working system ready for use by nontechnical users. Therefore, they don't have to deal with the myriad IT system/application/data pipeline integration challenges. They also do not have to deal with change management as decision-making moves from human beings, who are used to total control over their environment, to a model-based system. Additionally, students don't have to worry about obtaining funding, budgeting, or executive leadership support because the project costs are either $0 or limited (e.g., $10,000–$15,000 to cover faculty time and materials, such as cloud costs, as students are earning credits), and their faculty advisor/sponsor already sold the project to the partner company.

However, worst of all, we rarely see students being trained in everything else that is critical for an ADSAI project, beyond the technical, that we discuss in this book. Students are put into a situation in which their technical training only covers a fraction of required skills to successfully deliver their capstone project.

Some of the top university MS programs indicate *some* awareness of the challenges and are augmenting their curriculum with practical learning opportunities aimed at increasing awareness of real-world project dimensions. We present some recent examples of such universities (as of 2023) in Table 4.1.

As of writing, Drexel University (LeBow School of Business) is an institution with an excellent MS in Business Analytics that offers "co-op" programs (co-operative education on-the-job for pay) in which students work at a corporation for periods of up to 6–12 months at a time to gain real-world experience while they are completing their degree. Drexel LeBow also sponsors an annual competition for the best real-world corporate applications of analytics known as the *Analytics 50*. Students are exposed to the competition entrants' case studies and have the opportunity to meet with the winners at an awards dinner held on campus in Philadelphia, Pennsylvania.

In addition to a Capstone Project, Southern Methodist University (where Doug currently teaches in the EMBA and MS in Data Science programs—at the time of writing) offers a Business Analytics course that includes Doug's lectures on "The Top 10 Analytics Leadership Skills" and "The Top 10 Reasons Data Science Projects Fail," which provided part of the genesis of this book.

At the University of Queensland, where Evan teaches (at the time of writing), a Capstone and Business Strategy course are offered as part of a business analytics major. Additionally, students are clearly exposed to the ideas from this book via his lectures.

In addition to the outstanding technical curricula, and real-world capstone, practicum, internship, and colloquium courses offered by MS programs at universities, both co-authors strongly advocate for and recommend including the research and lessons learned in this book in a standalone seminar course or incorporated into one of the other practicum courses taught by industry professionals, or clinical professors of practice, who can provide *their own examples* of how and why data science projects fail. We believe these key learnings provide an invaluable perspective on the pitfalls of executing

TABLE 4.1

An Example of Universities Offering Education Beyond Just Technical Skills

Institution	Program	Relevant Program Elements
University of Michigan	MS in Data Science	• STATS 504: Principles and Practices in Effective Statistical Consulting • EECS 409: Data Science Colloquium
Stanford University	MS in Data Science	• DATASCI 198: Practical Training • DATASCI 197: Datathon Independent Study
University of San Francisco	MS in Data Science	• Practicum Course, in conjunction with an industry partner-sponsored Internship supervised by a faculty member in an apprenticeship style of learning
Georgetown University	MS in Data Science	• Digital Storytelling, which emphasizes communication styles based on data visualization to explain analyses
Fordham University	MS in Data Science	• Data Ethics, Communication, and Research
Duke University	MS in Data Science	• Capstone Course and a course in Data Science Dialogues with real-world professionals who describe the challenges and opportunities with data science in corporations
Syracuse University	MS in Data Science	• Internship Course and a course in Managing Data Science Projects
Drexel University	MS in Business Analytics	• Co-operative ("Co-op") Education programs working in industry while completing the degree

real-world ADSAI projects at scale, and how to avoid them. In addition, the research we cite in the introduction shows that learning from others' failures is highly effective.

A final element that all courses would benefit from is less focus on the models and more focus on the *data*. Similarly, for reasons previously stated, many university curricula lack the single most important course for building models—*working with data*. (Although, this type of course is actually more common than the much-needed focus on the softer side of analytics, i.e., non-modeling.) This is an endemic problem not just in applied mathematics degrees but also in computer science. In the Process chapter, we introduced the paper "Everyone wants to do the model work, not the data work,"[9] which summarizes the situation well:

> Lack of adequate training on AI data quality, collection, and ethics led to practitioner under-preparedness in dealing with the complexity of

creating datasets in high-stakes domains. AI courses focused on toy datasets with clean values (e.g., UCI Census, Kaggle datasets), but AI in practice required the creation of data pipelines, often from scratch, going from ground truth to model maintenance.

The article quotes two practitioners, who say:

In real life, we never see clean data. Courses and training focus on models and tools to use but rarely teach about data cleaning and pipeline gaps […] we in CS are never trained, nor [are we] thinking actively about data collection.

The authors of the article go on to say that:

Computer Science curricula did not include training for practical data aspects such as dealing with domain-specific 'dirty data', dealing with live data, defining and documenting datasets, designing data collection, training raters, or creating labeling task designs.

This is not just an opinion that the co-authors share; high-level research also shows a misalignment with the hype surrounding modeling versus the need for data management, engineering, and architecting. According to work published by ex-Amazon and RideOS data scientist Mihail Eric, there are 70% more open advertisements at companies for data engineering roles than data scientist roles.[10] This is another area that requires more attention at the university level and perhaps even earlier to attract students to this commercially critical area.

For both co-authors, the problem with the historic university focus is particularly acute if we recall the statistics quoted in the chapter on Analytically Immature Organizations. The Kaggle survey we cited there showed that consistently around 60% of respondents have less than two years of experience. It is a fair assumption to say that most of them had only recently graduated, hence, ensuring they have the right skills is critically important. By doing so, we'll help solve the final common people problem—poor analytics culture within an organization.

Analytically driven Leadership

Doug was fortunate to start his career in the Operations Research (OR) Department of American Airlines (AA) in 1987, where he was able to learn from the very best. Arguably one of the most successful analytics organizations in history, quickly growing from 40 to more than 500 staff from 1987 to

1992 and led by Dr. Thomas M. Cook, the analytics team helped transform AA in the post-US airline industry deregulation environment into the most technologically advanced airline in the industry.

By applying data from Sabre (an airline booking system developer) and other foundational information systems, AA's OR team built a wide variety of sophisticated analytics solutions for nearly every department in the company, and leveraged OR and analytics as a *strategic competitive advantage* to reduce costs, increase revenue, and improve resource and asset allocation. (In case you skipped it, more details about the incredible work done by the AA OR team can be found in the Strategy chapter.)

So what made the AA OR team so successful when other airline OR groups and analytics groups in other industries were less so?

According to folklore either Apple co-founder/CEO Steve Jobs or GE CEO Jack Welch allegedly said that "culture eats strategy for breakfast." This was never truer than at AA in the 1980s. Led by CEO Robert Crandall, a Wharton MBA, and CFO Donald Carty, a Harvard MBA, AA was one of the first truly fact-based, data-driven, and analytical decision model-oriented Fortune 500 corporate cultures, in general, and certainly in the airline industry known to the authors.

Crandall realized that in order to survive (and then thrive) in the post-deregulation US airline industry, characterized by rapid growth and expansion, new entrant low-cost competitors, and bloody fare wars, AA would need to *optimize* its route network, flight schedules, pricing, seat inventory allocation, and utilization of capital-intensive assets, such as planes, gates, spare part inventory, and hangars, as well as efficiently manage operating expense-heavy resources, such as jet fuel and unionized flight crews and maintenance crews. He discerned early on that to operate at scale, humans alone could not process the data, deal with the uncertainty and stochasticity, and analyze the myriad objectives, constraints, and variables that characterize airline operations decision-making. Computers, software, and mathematics of far more than modest rigor would be required for this sort of complex analysis and sophisticated decision-making. This kind of visionary leadership led Crandall to hire an OR professor from the University of Tulsa who had an MBA and a PhD in Operations Research. This professor had also written a textbook on management science and had experience working as a consultant. He would help Crandall to further explore ways in which data, computers, and mathematics could be used to improve "yield" or revenue-per-passenger-mile, a key metric for airlines. That professor was Dr. Thomas M. Cook.

Crandall asked Dr. Cook to transform a small, 12-person OR group into a more impactful, substantive capability. As with all great leaders, they surround themselves with people who know more than they do in specific domains. As Crandall had hired Cook, Tom Cook hired Barry Smith from MIT Sloan as the point person for designing, developing, and implementing a systematized approach to yield management based on OR (i.e., a large, complex, stochastic, dynamic, integer programming problem). As the previously noted accolades attest, the rest, as they say, is history. AA CEO Crandall, CFO Donald Carty, and Cook formed a formidable partnership that transformed the airline industry and markedly influenced other transportation, travel, and hospitality industries, in particular with pricing, yield, and revenue management methodology and technology.

Interestingly, culture and leadership, in and of themselves, have little in common with OR and analytics. One might say that they are at opposite ends of a spectrum ranging from intangible human traits to tangible mathematics and computer/software/data technology. However, having the awareness and insight to make that choice to create, develop, and rigorously enforce a *corporate culture* based on facts and data, and make complex decisions using super-sophisticated mathematical models, is what made all the difference.

Being a true *leader*, in this context, is having:

1. The foresight and humility—as a CEO of a Fortune 50 company—to recognize that you are not an expert in the field, so you need to hire someone who is; and

2. The mental acuity (brains) and fortitude (guts) to *invest heavily*, to the tune of hundreds of millions and into the billions of dollars, over *decades*, to analyze and solve the most difficult strategic, tactical, and operational problems, and create the industry's foremost analytics infrastructure to enable a competitive and executable strategy.

THAT is analytically driven leadership!

Most of the major US airlines created at least a modest form of OR organizational capability, including Continental, TWA, and USAir. Continental, in conjunction with CALEB Technologies, won the 2002 INFORMS Edelman Award for its Crew Recovery Optimizer (CrewSolver). Others, like United and Delta, created formidable internal OR organizations, including their own commercial organizations offering services to other airlines, similar to AADT. Delta's manifestation of yield management, led by Robert Cross, author of *Revenue Management: Hard Core Tactics for Market Domination*, was developed in parallel to Barry Smith's (and his team's) work at AA. Other airlines, like Northwest, tried to expand their own OR department by *hiring away* people from AA's Yield Management Department.[11] However, until now, in the opinion of both co-authors, no US airline has ever achieved the level of success, scope, and scale of AA OR and AADT. It went beyond AA/Sabre to deliver its solutions to airlines, rental car companies, cruise lines, and railroads worldwide. AA's unique culture and insightful, capable, strategic leadership made all of the difference.

The step-by-step approach taken by Crandall and the dedication of his team belong to the top 1% of organizations. So, what can the other 99% of organizations do to maximize their chances of success when they launch ADSAI programs?

High-quality change management.

Change Management

> There is nothing permanent except change. All is flux, nothing stays still.
>
> **—Heraclitus**

> It is not the strongest or most intelligent who will survive, but those who can best manage change.
>
> **—Charles Darwin**

Despite the unassailable veracity of these age-old adages, most people, in general, don't appear to be getting any more adept at or comfortable with accepting, embracing, or effectively dealing with change.

Technology, in particular over the past 50 years, has dramatically accelerated the pace of change in business. From robots building cars, to conducting meetings via video conference, to AI-based systems streamlining, automating, and optimizing large-scale complex decision-making, we are solving problems better, faster, and more effectively than any human ever could and the change is daunting for many people. The fear that jobs and livelihoods will be eliminated can be damaging to the psyche.

The simple fact is that data science is disruptive.

The sheer volume of data and the dynamism and complexity of business decision-making and problem-solving mandate the use of automation and mathematical logic and intelligence. However, when we "let the data speak," inconvenient truths are revealed. Gut instinct and heuristic rule of thumb planning, decision-making, and problem-solving processes that sufficed for decades are now challenged and often outmoded by new-and-improved fact-based, data-driven, and model-based solutions. Solution-embedded models, be it in a robot or business system, radically change the way we work, make decisions, and solve problems. This in no uncertain terms *threatens* the human beings who are used to doing things "their way, the way they have always done it for 30 years with their 150-tab Excel spreadsheet" (no exaggeration, this is an actual example from a project Doug worked on, and Evan has worked with clients with a combined total of much more than 150 tabs of Excel sheets for individual projects).

Change management is without a doubt one of the key dimensions of successfully executing a data science project, and it often comes most critically at the point when the AI team thinks it can relax. The data scientist must gently, diplomatically, and ever so delicately *win the hearts and minds* of the business people who will be instrumental in first approving, funding, then designing, developing, testing, validating, approving, deploying, and ultimately using the new system. If the business side won't come along for the journey—and their support is imperative—then the ADSAI project will fail with 100% certainty. Period.

It is not enough to *say* that the black box, mathe-magical computer system is better, faster, and more economical than the old way. Data scientists need to *show*, step by step, from beginning to end, and case-by-case, by making the client (business leaders) an *integral part of the process*, not the *recipient*, or even worse, the *victim*, of it. Change can be a daunting and sometimes painful process as business people move through the full range of emotions and reactions to the new solution, including (not unlike the five stages of grief) denial, anger, bargaining, depression, and acceptance (hopefully). Throw in the well-documented "not invented here syndrome," which can lead to outright rejection of the new solution in favor of the incumbent.

One of Doug's favorite quotes on this topic sums it up best with the wisdom of a political sage from five centuries ago:

> It must be remembered that there is nothing more difficult to plan, more doubtful of success, nor more dangerous to manage than the creation of a new system. For the initiator has the enmity of all those who would profit by the preservation of the old institution and merely lukewarm defenders in those who would gain by the new one.

—Niccolo Machiavelli, The Prince (1532)

So what can we do to stop failure at this critical juncture of the project?

One of the first principles in change management is *empathy*. Have awareness of the position of the business people who are your stakeholders and constituents. Your tone, body language, mannerisms, and communication style all need to soften the sharp edges of the pure rationality and logic of the data, math, and code.

Put yourself in the position of management to see the situation from their perspective. We'll delve into this more later in the Analytically Mature chapter.

How to do this goes back to *communication—first seek to understand, then be understood*. The data scientist should position and present themselves as a *colleague* on the same team, not the intruder trying to disrupt processes. Data science is intended to make things better, more economically beneficial for all parties, not just be more change for change's sake.

It is an important reminder that data science, analytics, and AI/ML are more about *augmentation* than *replacement* (for the foreseeable future anyway). The human-in-the-loop working interactively and iteratively with the model, not being replaced by it.[12]

Doug learned first-hand all about change management in 1990 on his first project to build a new decision-support system from scratch for American Airlines. The system was intended to schedule all aircraft heavy maintenance checks and plan hangar capacity for a five-year planning window.

Historically, the airline, comprising 200 aircraft, created its long-range five-year heavy maintenance and hangar plan on large sheets of paper using colored pencils, driven by calculator computations of when aircraft would be due for their respective checks. When the fleet rapidly grew to 600 aircraft, the paper-pencil-calculator solution became unwieldy and untenable, so the analysts (two at the time, later a total of three) switched to Excel macros. Unfortunately, the macros sometimes took as long as *10 hours* to run to completion for the larger sub-fleets using an Apple Macintosh IIcx desktop computer, and many times "errored out" prior to completion. Senior management quickly grew impatient and also very, very concerned as only uncertainty loomed as to when a new hangar might need to be built, and check yields (see notes for a definition of check yields)[13] were bleeding down to a suboptimal 80%, increasing heavy maintenance costs.

An industrial engineer at the AA maintenance base did an analysis that demonstrated a system could be built to *automate* the maintenance check, hangar planning and scheduling process, and *optimize* the schedule to maximize the check yields to ~100%. (Two heavy maintenance checks, $1 million each, could be avoided for each of the 227 wide-body aircraft over the lifespan of that sub-fleet, amounting to a staggering cost avoidance of $454 million!)

A project was authorized to build the system as described, and Doug was assigned as the project manager/OR analyst to build the scheduling model and algorithm (a *greedy heuristic* based on job scheduling on parallel machines with firm due dates written from scratch in C), along with a software engineer who built a color-coded Gantt-chart GUI for the analysts' Macintosh computers that emulated their wall-hanging paper schedule charts of old.

As one might imagine, the analysts were skeptical about the ability of a computer to generate higher yield, more efficient five-year maintenance check schedules and hangar schedule plans better than they could. Their skepticism turned first to incredulity and then quickly to unmitigated fear and dread when Doug and his partner delivered an early version of the software within a few months that, with the right input parameters (running on a Mac IIcx desktop computer), could generate a five-year 600 aircraft fleet heavy maintenance and hangar plan schedule with optimized ~100% check yields in about *18 minutes*! (It used to take *weeks* for 2–3 people to generate one feasible plan with 80% check yields.)

At that point, the analysts took Doug aside and said something to the effect of, "You are going to put the three of us out of work with that computer program of yours!" Doug assured them that not only was that *not* the case, but he also predicted (and bet them a steak dinner) that they would all get *promoted* as a result of their ability to use the new system to create more efficient, cost-effective maintenance plans in a far more timely manner than before.

As Doug predicted, the new system was very much more a case of (AI) *augmentation* rather than *replacement*. The system employed a design framework (conceived at Georgia Tech in the late 1980s where Doug earned his MS degree) known as *interactive optimization.*

The approach combines prescriptive optimization-based techniques, including heuristics when appropriate, and an evaluative simulation-based approach to quickly generate optimized schedules interactively with a "human-in-the-loop" iteratively providing the necessary inputs and feedback to *guide and push* the algorithm in the right direction toward an optimized solution. Therefore, the human and system work *together*, leveraging their respective strengths to quickly generate better solutions that neither would be able to deliver on their own. It is much easier for a human being to *inspect* a graphical Gantt-chart representation of the schedule and *see* where hangar capacity needs to be added, or excess capacity taken away, to optimize check yields. On the other hand, a computer can instantaneously add and subtract, and store information, and an algorithm can be programmed to automatically generate maintenance plans and schedules the same way a human could, but far faster.

Suffice it to say, the project was a success. The software engineer and Doug, both working full time, delivered the first production version of the system in about six elapsed months (12 labor-months) and demonstrated how AA would achieve the originally targeted benefits over time, i.e., $454 million *(in 1990 dollars)* in maintenance cost avoidance through increased wide-body aircraft check yields, along with multiple additional unforeseen benefits.

By optimizing yields and, in effect, pushing aircraft maintenance events further out in time, but still within the FAA's legal limits, the analysts used the model to open up additional hangar space, which allowed:

1. Maintenance work that had been contracted out to a third party, due to a perceived lack of in-house hangar capacity, to be brought back in-house, avoiding incremental costs.
2. American Airlines to bring in maintenance work from *other* airlines that didn't have ample hangar capacity to service their fleets (and that work was done at a profit).
3. One narrow-body aircraft to be returned to the fleet for revenue-generating service for a period of one year after an entire maintenance line was deemed superfluous and then shut down (i.e., an 8-figure annualized revenue impact).

The analysts not only received promotions, but they also became a valued, trusted resource to the executives, including the SVP, as a result of their ability to "see into the future" with greater confidence and increased accuracy, and evaluate all manner of various planning scenarios with the new model/ system in a way they never could have dreamed of doing before.[14]

What were the key change management factors for the project's success?

There were clear goals, objectives, and a well-defined project scope, including a tangible business value target. To start, Doug spent the first six weeks of the project *literally sitting and working side-by-side* with the analysts at the maintenance base in Tulsa, Oklahoma, learning about and understanding the art and science of scheduling aircraft maintenance and hangar facilities, the data, and decision-making until he could do the job himself. He listened two-thirds of the time and asked questions the other third.

The team had regular status and update meetings every time they hit a noteworthy milestone and deliverable (what today we would call Agile-MVP) during each stage of development of the model, algorithm, and schedule GUI. There was ample two-way communication, i.e., demonstrating in detail what had been done, and the analysts provided constructive feedback and guidance to validate the model's performance and results. Doug continually reassured the analysts that the system was not designed to operate "completely autonomously," but rather for *them* to operate it and "drive it" iteratively and interactively, much like a driver directs an automobile with inputs from the gear shift, accelerator and brake pedals, and steering wheel to reach their destination.

The changeover from a cumbersome, manual spreadsheet-based process to a streamlined, automated, and interactively optimized process was orchestrated to reduce fear of and instill confidence in the new solution. The team endeavored to make the transition to the new system as seamless and stress-free as possible by reusing all of the same data, terminology, scheduling logic, KPIs, report formats, and familiar visualization tools in software GUI, even using the Gantt-chart format from the historical paper-based maintenance activity and hangar schedules. That way, the learning curve on the new system was actually not very steep at all.

The interactive optimization approach, based on the analysts' own step-by-step processes, also made the analysts feel much more comfortable with the solution, instead of it being a "black box" that they didn't understand. One of the analysts even sanguinely referred to the new system as "a big calculator" that could register the analyst-provided input data, and output an optimized five-year maintenance schedule and hangar plan. A great metaphor indeed![15]

Justification for Change

The best way to "grease the skids" of change management is to deliver significant, tangible, measurable business value that can be categorically attributed to the new model/solution, and demonstrated by before-and-after experiments (or even better, randomized controlled trials, see the Technology chapter for more on this). The AA aircraft maintenance case did that, and the after scenario delivered *far* more and better solutions faster than the analysts could have ever imagined. This made for a very effective justification for change. It's rarely that easy, but sometimes it can be. (Promotions, raises, and escalation of one's status in the organization goes a long way toward acceptance!)

Doug went on to use this same identical end-to-end approach multiple times during his career, including once at another airline to build a new jet fuel supply chain purchasing and inventory management optimization system. As with the maintenance scheduling scenario, the science and technology were sophisticated and substantive, leveraged augmentation versus replacement, and got the job done. That said, it was the use of "soft skills" that really made the difference.

The jet fuel supply chain business team were quite attached to their 150-tab Excel spreadsheet that they had been using for 30 years, and did not necessarily want to trade it in for a new-and-improved data-driven, analytically based forecasting, purchasing, and inventory optimization model suite. In fact, they initially put up quite a fight. However, when the results of a head-to-head bake off between the spreadsheet and the new models were validated, the supporting case for the new models/system was made... *an 8-figure annual cost avoidance opportunity generated by the models in a matter of minutes, versus days and weeks by the status quo process!* That makes it tough to continue to argue in favor of the status quo.

The outcome was quite similar with significant business value and economic impact, and satisfied business stakeholders who benefitted from continuous close engagement with Doug's team from the start of the project. A smooth, seamless transition facilitated by a change management process focused on large doses of communication, mutual understanding, and empathy, with iterative testing and validation, made all the difference.

What this example powerfully revealed to Doug was that many human touch points exist across a project. From selecting the right team with the right skills, to engaging with stakeholders throughout the project, and finally, ensuring that the change management at the end of the project was effective, allowing data scientists to focus on the part for which they train—the technology. We turn to this final *raison d'échec* as the final reason why analytically immature organizations fail.

Critical Thinking: How Not to Fail

- A lack of resources is not something unique to ADSAI, however, due to the hype surrounding AI, it leads to those who may have read an article on analytics having more confidence than is warranted just because everyone is talking about it. What simple things can management do from the top down to prevent unprepared people from launching disastrous AI projects?

- When crises hit, people sometimes naturally revert to what they know best. What attitude should a company have so that if a crisis occurs, the ADSAI tools aren't abandoned? What should management demand from its employees when making decisions?[16]

- What do you expect to occur in companies that lack an analytics translator? What additional difficulties arise?

- Without changing entire university curricula across countries, what simple things could students do to bridge some of the key people and business skill gaps they will face after graduation?

- Why do you think universities, in general, don't integrate more soft skill learning into highly technical degrees? Many universities will offer these courses in other departments.

- What key aspects of change management do you think are important to ensure successful adoption of ADSAI tools?

- What is one big mistake a technical team could make when handing over a newly developed tool to its end user, which would result in the client refusing to use it? How can this be mitigated?

Notes

1. Shellshear, E. (2023, May 10). Only 15% of AI investments succeed. An AI translator could help the other 85%. *Sydney Business Insights (SBI)*. https://sbi.sydney.edu.au/only-15-of-ai-investments-succeed-an-ai-translator-could-help-the-other-85/.
2. Davenport, T., Harris, J. G., & Morison, R. (2018). *Analytics at Work: Smarter Decisions, Better Results*. Harvard Business Press, pp. 104-108.
3. Fortune Education. (2024). Best Master's in Data Science for 2024. *Fortune*. https://fortune.com/education/information-technology/best-masters-in-data-science/.
4. edX. (2023). Best 20+ schools with Data Science Master's Programs. *Mastersin DataScience.org*. https://www.mastersindatascience.org/data-science/masters/.
5. A notable exception to this paradigm is that many universities are now hiring non-tenure track Clinical Professors or Professors of Practice, including Adjunct Professors like Evan and Doug, who do have extensive real-world experience and can bring that to the classroom; however, curricula are often governed by tenure-track department chairs and curriculum committees that are largely governed by career academics, not practitioners. Evan and Doug are both examples of these practice professors.

6. Doug was fortunate that two of his professors worked as part-time consultants for the US Social Security Administration, and did bring the mathematics of their projects, at least, into the classroom regarding predicting the likelihood of a person injured on the job returning to work using logistic regression for binary classification. Doug's internships and part-time job exposed him to mathematical modeling and analysis of military equipment vulnerability/survivability and scenario phenomena conducted by senior OR practitioners for the US Department of Defense: Army, Navy, Air Force.

7. Georgia Institute of Technology's Stewart School of Industrial & Systems Engineering is recognized for its elite undergraduate and graduate programs, which have been ranked #1 by *U.S. News & World Report* for 25 and 33 consecutive years, respectively, so their choice of subjects is well respected albeit predominantly technically concentrated.

8. Both co-authors have sponsored Internships and Capstone Projects at multiple employers and universities and can vouch for their efficacy as a valuable real-world learning endeavor.

9. Sambasivan, N., Kapania, S., Highfill, H., Akrong, D., Paritosh, P., & Aroyo, L. (2021). "Everyone wants to do the model work, not the data work": Data Cascades in High-Stakes AI. *Proceedings of the 2021 CHI Conference on Human Factors in Computing Systems*, 39. https://doi.org/10.1145/3411764.3445518.

10. Mihail, E. (2021, January). We don't need data scientists, we need data engineers. Mihail Eric Blog. https://www.mihaileric.com/posts/we-need-data-engineers-not-data-scientists/.

11. Northwest Airlines settled out of court with American Airlines (AA) in a lawsuit brought by CEO Robert L. Crandall for allegedly attempting to "re-use without permission" AA's unique yield management intellectual property—there's no higher form of flattery than when a major competitor tries to replicate, i.e., steal, your technology!

12. Davenport, T. (2018). *The AI Advantage: How to Put the Artificial Intelligence Revolution to Work*. The MIT Press. The book does a great job of explaining this concept.

13. Maintenance check "yield" is defined by the FAA as the percentage ratio of hours flown by an aircraft to hours legally allowed to be flown in between maintenance checks. An aircraft flying, say, 8,000 hours in between checks when 10,000 hours are allowed would have a yield of 80%, or 8,000/10,000. Over time, for example, 40,000 flight hours, an aircraft would have five checks performed when four would have sufficed at maximum yield. This is significant because each check costs $1 million (in 1990 US dollars). Achieving maximum check yield in this example would avoid $1 million in superfluous costs.

14. For example, airlines are continually increasing or decreasing aircraft utilization (flight hours per day), which will affect when checks are due relative to check limits (e.g., one heavy "C" check due every 10,000 flight hours). It is common for aircraft manufacturers, or the FAA, to issue Airworthiness Directives, Fleet Campaign Directives, or other myriad inspections and checks that all require aircraft (sub)fleets to be inspected for potential defects, which will take up a greater amount of hangar capacity than planned. A literal *multitude* of these types of "what if…" scenarios affecting when checks are due and impacting available hangar capacity kept the planners busier than ever, even with the automated optimization system.

15. Gray, D. (1992, December). Airworthy: Decision support for aircraft overhaul maintenance planning. *OR/MS Today, (Transportation Edition), 19*(6), 23-29.
16. To assist with this question is something W. Edwards Deming, PhD (Math/Physics), the father of statistical quality control & assurance, said, "In God we trust, all others must bring data.".

5

Technology

When applying ADSAI to solve a complex, industry-specific problem, there is a salient nexus between truly understanding the nature of the business problem at a fundamental, detailed level, and being fully aware of and knowledgeable about the various potential modeling approaches and their respective pros and cons to ensure that the best approach is applied. Failures often occur at this intersection of problem and solution for a variety of reasons, including not fully grasping the nature, size, and complexity of the business problem, and/or not being aware of the implications of the alternative technical modeling approaches and their respective application to the problem at hand.

In this chapter, we will dig into these reasons for failure and uncover the most common technical causes. In an interesting twist, the first story connects us back to our discussion of university education from the People chapter.

ADSAI professionals frequently have an inherent bias toward a particular technique or approach based on their education, training, and experience, and indiscriminately apply that approach to problems they encounter. As a result, to them, an approach intuitively *appears* to make sense, but actually doesn't work as well as intended in the practical application. A nice example of this arose in some of Doug's teaching.

In Southern Methodist University's EMBA Business Analytics class, Doug teaches a 3.5-hour lecture on ADSAI applications in the airline industry, which is rife with complex operational problems to solve and is based on his 15-year experience in the industry. He assigns a case study analysis that each student can understand, absorb, and appreciate. For example, conceptualizing a modeling approach for predicting the On-Time Performance (OTP) of a large, commercial airline for a particular day of the week at an airport- and system network-level, i.e., all scheduled airports combined.

US commercial scheduled airlines are monitored and measured by the US Federal Aviation Administration (FAA) on their flight schedule *On-Time Performance (OTP)*. OTP is measured as follows:

> A flight is judged to be "on time" if it departs the gate within 5 minutes of the published scheduled departure time, and arrives within 15 minutes of the published scheduled arrival time. So, for example, if Flight #123 is scheduled to depart the airport DFW at 0800 and actually departs DFW at 0803, then that flight is said to have departed/operated "on time,"

DOI: 10.1201/9781032661360-6

whereas had the flight departed at 0806, then that flight would have been judged as a late or not on-time departure. Similarly, if arriving Flight #789 is scheduled to arrive at airport BWI at 1205 and actually arrives at 1219, then that flight is said to have arrived/operated on time, whereas had the flight arrived at 1221, then that flight would have been judged as a late or not on-time arrival.

OTP is measured and tracked at three levels: (1) individual flight level, i.e., origin-destination-scheduled departure and arrival time; (2) airport level, for example, Dallas-Fort Worth International Airport (DFW) or Baltimore/Washington International Thurgood Marshall Airport (BWI); and (3) flight schedule network level, i.e., the aggregate OTP of every flight flown over a period of time, for example, day, month, quarter, year, or schedule period. At the airport or network level, OTP, as a *statistic*, is defined as the *percentage* of flights operating on time (departures and arrivals), i.e., (Total # of flights operating on-time)/(Total # of flights operating).

Doug's students, based on their own experiences as avid business and leisure travelers, are encouraged to think about and consider the *nature* of the underlying problem of analyzing and predicting OTP, as being characterized by:

1. Problem factors:
   - Weather patterns, i.e., cloud cover, thunder showers, and events, for example, a major winter snowstorm
   - Seasonality, for example, month of year (obviously correlated with weather)
   - Airline and airport operating characteristics, for example, day of week
   - OTP trends, specifically on recent prior days
   - Fullness of flights, i.e., Load Factor (defined as the percentage of seats filled/seats available by flight and overall on average)
   - Air traffic conditions and actions (managed as per Air Traffic Control, or ATC)
   - And so on

2. Problem conditions:
   - Deterministic
   - Stochastic
   - Hybrid

3. Which analytics model would best fit as a solution to and a model of this problem:

- Predictive, for example, probability or a future value
- Prescriptive

The primary deliverable of the case analysis write-up is to address these three topics and recommend one (or more) as the most applicable and viable model form to predict OTP at an airport and network level for the next day.

Using publicly available US airline data and OTP statistics to model and solve the problem, and create a benchmark answer by which to grade the case, Doug found the following:

1. The nature of the underlying problem is clearly *stochastic*, as well as *nonlinear* and *multivariate*.

2. A *predictive* model is most suitable, specifically one that estimates a future value (i.e., OTP as a *percentage*, not a probability).

3. The most statistically significant factors (*variables, features*) to predict OTP include:

   a. Month (to capture seasonality)

   b. Day of week (to capture differential airline operating characteristics)

   c. Weather patterns and events, including airport cloud ceiling, visibility, and storms

   d. Load factor (i.e., an indicator of how busy the airlines/airports are)

   e. Air Traffic Control (ATC) schedule impacts due to Traffic Management Initiatives (TMI), for example, delay programs, ground stops

   f. Yesterday's OTP, i.e., time series effect of consecutive days operating conditions

4. The *most effective* predictive models were Regression (LASSO) and Gradient Boosted Trees (XGBoost); both were quite accurate.[1]

5. Model predictive accuracy only dipped in the case of four major winter storms that dramatically reduced OTP across the network; in a later model version, categorical variables were used to identify the presence of a major winter storm to improve accuracy.

Fortunately, all but one of the student teams performed very credibly on the case analysis, achieved the objectives, and addressed the three topics. Most teams recommended some type of predictive model form, such as regression, time series, tree-based model, or neural network, all of which are potentially viable to address the stochastic nature of OTP.

One team, however, recommended a *logistic regression* model. This was a surprise to Doug. Both co-authors are frequent users of logistic regression, especially when one needs a *binary classifier* to determine the probability of whether someone:

- Is going to have a stroke or a heart attack,
- Will need to be readmitted to the hospital after surgery,
- Has cancer based on the result of some type of non-definitive diagnostic test, or
- Will buy a particular product.

Doug's curiosity got the better of him (also, for grading purposes, he wanted to see if the student team really understood what was going on in class), so he asked the lone group, "*Why would you use logistic regression to predict OTP?*" They responded, "*We thought you wanted the probability, or likelihood, that flights were going to be on time or not.*" Interesting. A very different approach than what was sought.

To their credit, they got the *stochastic* problem and *predictive* model part right, and they did list several appropriate *factors* impacting OTP.

Although we can empathize with and understand their interpretation of OTP, a *probability* of on-time performance in this context, while somewhat *informative*, it is most definitely *not* the manner in which the FAA, airlines, airline operators, and, typically, passengers interpret OTP at an airport or across a network over a specified period of time. OTP makes more sense contextually as a measure of *magnitude*, to say "*89% of the flights at Chicago's O'Hare International Airport will operate on time tomorrow (Tuesday).*" Whereas a probability *may* be an interesting measure for a *single flight* (e.g., Flight #123 departing O'Hare at 1200 will operate on time tomorrow with probability 0.89), but not for 300 flights per day at O'Hare, or for thousands of flights across an entire airline flight schedule on a given day (or over a month or year). In predicting OTP, airline operators really want to know just how good or bad the day is going to be, measured in terms of a *percentage* of flights operating on time.

There are a few key learnings we can glean from the story about Doug's rogue student group.

First, real-world problems are nuanced, layered, and complex. Case in point, OTP is a *definition* that determines whether a flight departs or arrives on time, but is also interpreted as a *statistic*, i.e., a percentage of flights that depart and arrive on time at an airport, or every airport in aggregate in the network for a period of time, such as a day, month, or year. The latter interpretation is of greatest practical interest to the FAA, airlines, and the traveling public.

Second, it is critically important to understand the problem at a detailed, granular level to ensure proper interpretation and context. This will allow ADSAI teams to adequately address the question at hand. "Predict OTP," in this context, means *the percentage of flights that will operate on time tomorrow at an airport or across the entire flight network.*

Lastly, once the problem is well-defined, terms and conditions are well-understood, and the target is clearly identified, there is a *far* less likelihood of misapplying a model (including selecting the wrong one). Many different model forms may be applicable and perform well, as we saw with LASSO and Gradient Boosted Trees, but some modeling approaches will be wrong for the problem at hand. In our research, we discovered that this was the most common reason for technical failure. We turn first to the technical problem of misapplying a model (whether incorrectly applying the right model or simply using the wrong model altogether).

Model Mishaps

Misapplying the (Right or Wrong) Model

> All happy families are alike; every unhappy family is unhappy in its own way.

> —Leo Tolstoy, *Anna Karenina*

One of Doug's favorite sayings, based on years of experience and observation, is:

> There are many ways to do something wrong, but often only one way to do something right.

Sometimes data scientists, especially ones with insufficient education, training, and practical experience, make the mistake of incorrectly applying a model to a problem. With so many ways to incorrectly implement a model, it is sometimes surprising that models are ever correctly deployed. To make this concrete, let's begin with an actual real-world example that one of the co-authors personally encountered.

A travel website merchandising manager wanted to test which of two landing page designs would capture the most customers interested in purchasing air travel, rental cars, hotels, and tours. This is a classic problem, and properly calls for the use of *A/B testing*, which anyone can run as an experiment using any number of tools available online.

Prospective customers are randomly shown one of two landing page designs, A or B, and either choose to click through to the travel offer content, or not. The results are tallied as a ratio of the number of customers who clicked through landing page A, divided by the number of total customers who were randomly shown page design A (whether they clicked through or not), and similarly for landing page design B. The ratio measures the success rate, or "hit rate," for each landing page as follows:

$$\text{Hit Rate A} = \frac{\text{Number of Customers That Clicked through Page A}}{\text{Total Number of Customers Shown Page A}}$$

$$\text{Hit Rate B} = \frac{\text{Number of Customers That Clicked through Page B}}{\text{Total Number of Customers Shown Page B}}$$

When testing a new design (e.g., webpage B), what we'd like to show is that it is better than page A, in the sense of Hit Rate B > Hit Rate A.

A/B testing is a standard and appropriate use of Pearson's Chi-squared test of independence[2] to determine if there is a *statistically significant difference* between the two hit-rate ratios, such that if a material difference does exist, it would indicate that one page is more effective than the other at attracting customers to view the offer.

The *misapplication* of A/B testing manifested when the travel website manager wanted to use the *exact same test* to determine which page would generate more *revenue*. Whereas hit rate is a simple ratio of page click-throughs to total page views, revenue is a far, far more complex, multivariate and multidimensional quantity. The myriad variables that determine the total revenue on a travel website transaction include, but are not limited to, the number of ticketed passengers on the itinerary, origin-destination market pair (e.g., BNE-SYD, SYD-DFW, DFW-PIT, PIT-LGA, etc.), fare class, fare price, purchase date relative to flight date, type of hotel room, number of room nights, and so on. You get the picture.

To statistically, accurately determine which landing page generates more revenue, you would need to rigorously design a *series of highly controlled experiments* to account for all of these variables that materially affect revenue to ensure an apples-to-apples comparison and not apples to oranges, bananas, or mangoes. A simple A/B test *may* arrive at the right answer for greatest revenue, but that would be sheer luck. The A/B test experimental design *would not* be sufficiently robust to work reliably in consistently and accurately predicting revenue capture.

In our experience as practicing statisticians applying our education and training, we find that a fundamental lack of understanding by professional and citizen data scientists of the *principles of experimental design*, as illustrated above, is one of the biggest gaps in solving these types of real-world problems, i.e., comparing two alternatives against a metric. We work in a world that is complex and multivariate with confounding effects, and we must account for all of that in data science projects if we want to have confidence in the results. Entire books have been written on the topic of experimental design and the practical applications of these techniques in industries as disparate as farming to pharmaceuticals, and all share the goal of legitimately, logically, and statistically accurate results, conclusions, and decision-making.

A classic example of experimental design is the testing of two fertilizers, A and B, to see which one generates greater crop yields (see Figure 5.1). If you have one field next to a running river rich with nutrients, you would not want to plant crops using fertilizer B alongside the river, and use fertilizer A on another field further inland. The *effect* of the river would *confound* the experiment by giving an unfair advantage to fertilizer B, i.e., more nutrient-rich soil. You need to *control* for the effect of the river to ensure that both fertilizers have equal access to river-enriched soil. Therefore, planting the two fertilized crops *adjacent* and *perpendicular* to the river would be the best option (even if not perfect).

Alternatively, an experiment to test for the efficacy of a new pharmaceutical drug, for example, a blood thinner, would need to be controlled for many variables, including (perhaps) gender, age, weight/BMI, cardiac disease history, blood pressure, pulse rate, overall health, and genetic makeup, among many others.

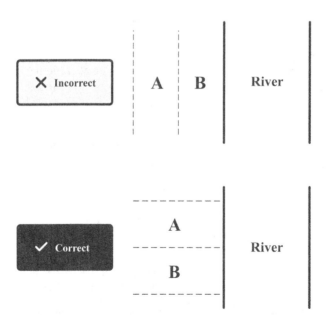

FIGURE 5.1
The correct and incorrect design to test two fertilizers A and B.

The point is that, for as many models that exist, there are many, many ways to misapply them. Experimental design is one of the easiest and most common traps that a data scientist or business person can fall into.

When undertaking predictive analytics modeling, overfitting (i.e., a model excessively tailors to training data, failing to generalize) and bias (i.e., a systematic deviation from true values, incorrectly pushing predictions in one direction) are also model characteristics to aggressively guard against to avoid erroneous results. As more complicated models with more parameters occur, it is becoming easier and easier to accidentally overfit a model. Data scientists must take great care to consider the problem's context to ensure a proper fit of the model's application with the problem at hand.

Sometimes there is more than one model form that may be legitimately applicable to a given problem's context. For example, to predict the likelihood of the presence of cancer in a patient based on radiological exam results data, a data scientist might use logistic regression, Bayesian inference, and/or an artificial neural network, but they would not use linear regression. With today's available cloud computing power, data scientists can easily fit all three models against the data and compare how they perform to determine which is best (and avoid overfitting at the model level).

Early on in an ADSAI project, it is always a good idea to consult with an experienced colleague—either a peer or former professor—as a sounding board on the best approach for model selection. The art of understanding the best model and experimental design for the problem at hand is as important, if not more so, than the science. The old carpenter adage, *"Measure twice, cut once,"* is apropos here.

Equally, by spending an inordinate amount of time indulging in the technical pros and cons of every conceivable model applicable to the problem at hand, we land at our next trap: excessive focus on the model, technique, or technology.

Keep It Simple: Overemphasizing the Model, Technique, or Technology

A model is a means to an end, not an end itself.

—Tom Kim, "Of Models and Modeling"[3]

I honestly do not understand all of the math, but I am convinced of the strategic competitive advantage, and significant, tangible, economic value that is created with Yield Management.

—Robert L. Crandall, Chairman, President & CEO of American Airlines (circa 1991)

Both co-authors have always been enamored with the power and beauty of mathematics. In 1959, Eugene Wigner adroitly expressed this sentiment in the title of his article, "The Unreasonable Effectiveness of Mathematics in the Natural Sciences."[4] Proclaimed by one of the greatest mathematicians to ever live Carl Friedrich Gauss to be the "queen of the sciences," mathematics provides the tools that enable other sciences, such as physics (providing much of the foundation for the engineering fields), economics, and computer science.

The beauty of mathematics is relatively abstract, and on the other end of the spectrum, we have the practical world of business. In capitalism, companies are in the business of making a profit and returning some of that profit to shareholders, while benefiting society along the way (a business's social license to operate in the long term). Although more idealistic considerations may guide some business thinking, it is recurring physical dollars in the bank that matter for many people—a very practical matter.

At the intersection of mathematics and business, fields like operations research, management science, statistics, and now analytics and data science are intended to contribute to the betterment of a corporation's economic and financial performance. *In business, mathematics and models are a means to an end, not an end themselves.*

It is not uncommon, especially among recent data science graduates, to become excessively focused and too infatuated with the model and the mathematics, algorithms, and technology. At the beginning of our careers, both co-authors fell victim to this attraction, so we know its appeal.

In *Project Recovery*, Harold Kerzner brilliantly illustrates how this focus can mislead us when considering the triple constraints of project management (cost, time, and scope):

> In the eyes of the typical engineer, each of the triple constraints did not carry equal importance. For many engineers, scope and especially technical achievement were significantly more important than time or cost. The DOD [Department of Defense] tried to reinforce the importance of time and cost, but as long as the DOD was willing to pay for the cost overruns and allow schedule slippages, project success was measured by how well performance was achieved regardless of the cost overruns, which could exceed several hundred percent. Even though the triple constraints were being promoted as the definition of success, performance actually became the single success criterion.[5]

The Pareto principle (80/20 rule) can be of interest and application here, i.e., getting 80% of the benefit for 20% of the effort (or cost). *Perfection is the enemy of doneness.* In business, most of the time, there is no need or willingness on the part of management to expend the remaining 80% effort to gain the last 20% of business value. The business needs an answer… and value delivered … *now.* It doesn't need to be perfect. It just needs to work and deliver against the economic impact objectives. Often, this is in the form of simply helping someone make a decision, or (sufficiently) answer a question, not providing an unequivocally correct answer (which likely doesn't exist).

As we saw earlier, the Agile principle of minimum viable product (MVP) (or model) is directionally correct and applicable as well. *Get to a version that builds, works, and generates value, ASAP.* Excessive tweaking, refinements, and feature additions or modifications, for little or no measurable incremental gain, is a waste of the company's time and resources.

For most businesses with which the co-authors have worked, the goal was *minimal elapsed time possible to value realization.* In fact, in status reports that are submitted to senior management, project update entries *must have a business value attached* or they are omitted forthwith. No technical jargon or detail is allowed. It is implicit and assumed that the correct model form was utilized, tested, and validated, as was the business value. Make sure business value information is upfront in the status reports.

Doug once had a team of Business Analytics course EMBA students whose final project was focused on improving the accuracy of (binary classification) models to predict mortgage loan default operating on a large volume of historical loan performance outcome data (a technique that would have come in handy circa 2008–2009). The students filled 20 PowerPoint slides with mind-bending mathematical models, arcane terminology, and symbols, and spent 19 of their 20 allotted presentation minutes talking about all of the different mathematical and statistical models that they had built (fast Fourier transforms, Bayesian inference, neural networks, etc.). In minute 20, now somewhat exasperated, Doug finally asked, "What was the *business outcome result* that you achieved?" They enthusiastically responded *"Oh, wow, we increased the accuracy of mortgage loan default prediction to over 93%! On their typical loan portfolio, the new and improved model demonstrated the potential to avoid tens of millions of dollars in bad loan default write-offs annually!"* Doug responded, *"That is fantastic! In the future, when presenting your projects, especially to executives, please start with that information."* In journalism, that is called "burying the lede" and reminds us of our earlier observations that the best data scientists also need to be good storytellers.

The moral of the story is the same when presenting to executives inside any company. *No one, except perhaps other mathematicians, cares about all of the technical details.* Save those results for the appendix. Instead, as suggested earlier, tell a story of what life was like *before* and *after* the model was implemented. Focus on the improved business solution and the incremental business value and economic impact that was achieved in terms of cost, revenue, asset utilization, customer satisfaction—what business executives understand in terms they use every day. Explain how much time and effort will be saved with a streamlined, automated, and optimized process. Refer to the controlled experiments that were run to prove the model's value, and mention the testing and validation to the business domain and finance folks. They'll want to know that you can "show your work" if required, but they don't need to hear about all of the math and code.

Nowadays for the practicing data scientist, there are so many impressive new AI technologies available, including intelligent robotics systems, computer vision, speech recognition, and natural language processing systems such as large language models, that restraining excitement and technical details can be hard. As analytics practitioners, we need to always remind ourselves of the importance of the significant, tangible, and measurable business value and economic impact that many of these technologies can generate in real-world applications in business and industry.

For example, Walmart Global Tech and Supply Chain teams are utilizing intelligent robotics to streamline, automate, and optimize their distribution centers for unloading, putting away, storing, retrieving, and loading goods onto store delivery tractor trailers. Intelligent automation reduces the amount of heavy lifting done by Walmart Associates, expedites product throughput, and further increases product availability in stores. The giant retailer is also leveraging computer vision in experiments with driverless delivery vehicles that transport goods between distribution centers and stores, and deliver grocery orders to consumers, where drivers are in short-supply. Walmart is utilizing natural language processing (i.e., LLMs, or large language models) to analyze verbal and written customer feedback when items are returned to determine the root cause issue(s) that motivated the return, with the objective of improving both supplier performance and the customer experience in the future.

All of these AI applications have well-established, rigorously proven business cases that are backed up by substantial business value and economic impact that lower operating costs, enhance working conditions, increase productivity and operational efficiency, and enhance the customer experience. This business analysis came before the technical work.

Both co-authors have, however, observed instances in which a data science team became excessively focused on a particular AI technology, without having a strong business case that would generate a dramatic improvement over the status quo incumbent solution to the problem at hand. An application of computer vision aimed at expediting passenger airline aircraft boarding comes to mind.

For passenger airlines, the boarding process presents a lengthy, time-consuming, and sometimes frustrating experience that can adversely affect a flight's on-time departure. Verifying passenger boarding passes, and getting passengers onto the plane and safely seated with all of their carry-on baggage properly stowed, is an FAA requirement that *must be completed* before the plane can leave the terminal gate. As is often the case on fully booked flights, the cabin overhead bins fill up and excess carry-on baggage must then be gate-checked and moved to the aircraft's cargo area underneath the cabin. The extra steps of tagging carry-on bags, moving them back out to the jet bridge, and sending them down the chute to the ground crew to load into the cargo hold can further delay the boarding process and departure.

Typically, in the *status quo analog scenario*, the responsibility resides with the cabin-stationed flight attendants who monitor the boarding process to guess-timate when the overhead bins will fill up and then notify the boarding door-stationed flight attendants to start gate-checking the remaining bags that are too large to fit underneath the seat. With experienced flight attendants, this process seems to function fairly efficiently in the co-authors' considerable airline travel experience (we both have traveled extensively on many domes-tic and foreign airlines).

Doug heard of a particular airline's data science team that decided to use video cameras located in the jet bridge, coupled with a computer vision algorithm, to *scan* the carry-on baggage, and *estimate* each bag's volume (L x W x H) to *predict* in real-time when the available cabin overhead bin space capacity would fill up, and gate-checking of the excess carry-on bag-gage would need to commence. The intent was to (hopefully significantly) expedite the boarding process by streamlining the excess carry-on baggage stowing procedure, relative to the status quo analog solution. Every second counts in achieving an on-time departure!

The computer vision algorithm, as one might expect, actually worked quite well at identifying the carry-on baggage items coming down the jet bridge, estimating their respective individual volume, and accumulating total carry-on baggage volume boarded, compared with the total (remaining available) overhead bin volume. The AI algorithm was trained to predict, based on the bags it could see on the jet bridge, when the overhead bin capacity would be exhausted. At that point, a message was sent to notify the gate agents and flight attendants to start gate-checking the excess carry-on baggage.

As per the primary thesis of this book, the issue in this case study is *not* with the computer vision algorithm technology itself, or even its application to the problem at hand. The technology worked as intended.

However, what are the costs of designing, engineering, developing, and deploying a new solution to generate *what types of and how much* incremental business value and operational and/or economic impact over and above the status quo incumbent solution? The reader will recall our recommendation in the Strategy chapter to do some basic economic calculations to ensure the project makes sense.

While the exact figures are not important, it is estimated that the airline spent *hundreds of thousands of dollars* in hardware, software, internal labor, and third-party consulting services to build and deploy a single POC prototype of the solution (not to mention the opportunity costs of more viable projects, consumed management bandwidth, etc.). When the airline data science team field-tested the solution at a few airports, they discovered that the time sav-ings in the boarding process was not all that significant when compared with the status quo incumbent solution, i.e., the flight attendants monitoring the boarding process and remaining overhead bin space available to determine when the remaining carry-on luggage should be gate-checked. At that point, the data science team determined that the total cost of deploying the solution at all airline network airports was not warranted, because the project would not generate an ample return on investment. Doug was able to confirm with a colleague who works at the airline that the solution was in fact not widely deployed.

The co-authors are the first to admit that data science R&D projects are not guaranteed to always result in production deployment and an economically viable result. After all, 80%+ of all ADSAI projects either fail to be implemented or deliver business value. That said, a bit more forethought and consideration prior to initiating a project as to just how much more benefit could be achieved with a sophisticated, expensive ADSAI digital solution over and above the *status quo incumbent analog* (or even a less sophisticated digital) solution is advisable. It certainly would have been useful in the carry-on baggage system—the required savings were simply impossible to attain no matter how good the system. As we saw in the Strategy chapter, letting the world of engineering possibilities guide the conversation may be suitable for a university but not for a business.

Excessive focus on a model, technique, and/or technology (i.e., "technology for technology's sake" because it's cool or interesting) without consideration of the true potential upside business value and economic or operational impact can waste valuable time and resources, something few companies can afford. This principle is closely related to topics we've covered earlier in the book:

- Understanding the business problem (and prospective solution approaches)
- Focusing on projects that are closely aligned with business priorities
- Properly setting expectations (of potential incremental business value)

Focusing too much on the technology can also mess up the whole minimum viable model to production-ready, deployed model process, by not focusing on what matters at the right point in time. We turn to this challenge next.

From Sandbox Model to Production System

In response to questions from business colleagues and students as to why ADSAI projects take so long, Doug's common refrain is,

> Building models is easy, you can do that in a day, with a few thousand dollars, especially now with tools like AutoML, Jupyter notebooks, and cloud computing instances, or in weeks with optimization suites. Building a model into an enterprise-grade production system is difficult,

can take years, and cost tens of millions of dollars (and in a few cases hundreds of millions of dollars), especially if it is mission-critical or utilized for real-time decision-making.

Evan's opinion is no different.

The next common question, and one that we discovered in our research underlies a common reason for failure, is: *How long does it take to transform a sandbox model to a production system?*

The answer, as usual, in business (and consulting) is: *it depends* (on many factors). It can take months or sometimes years for large-scale, sophisticated systems solving the most complex types of problems to be available, reliable, and able to access the requisite amounts of data across the enterprise. We've seen estimates from experts in earlier chapters that it can be from 10x to 100x more effort than the pilot and this seems about right.

Some significant factors to consider and gauge when determining whether the production system will be 10x or 100x more effort than the pilot are:

- *Dynamism*—Is the input data largely static, such as planning information, or continuously changing in real time? System complexity increases as you move toward real-time.

- *Integration*—Is the system relatively stand-alone or heavily reliant on integration with numerous other data sources and enterprise systems? System complexity increases with the number of integration points.

- *Mission Criticality*—If the system can fail and no one is more than moderately inconvenienced, then it's easier; if the entire company grinds to a halt, then multiple layers of error handling, fault tolerance, and failover capabilities and infrastructure must be built in to increase availability (e.g., "five 9s" or 99.999% uptime) and reliability, which becomes far, far more challenging.

- *Problem and Model Complexity*—How difficult is the underlying problem, and how sophisticated, mathematically and computationally, is the model generating the solution? The more sophistication, the more complexity and long-term risk that will arise often due to the many edge cases that refuse to fit the more stringent model assumptions.

The first project Doug worked on from the "ground floor" up was to build American Airlines' aircraft heavy maintenance check/hangar planning and scheduling system. This project took him and another software engineer working in parallel about six months to deliver version one of a fully system-tested, working MVP. Another three months were required to install and configure the software for the local environment, train the users, and work out some additional bugs and kinks discovered during a rigorous User Acceptance Test on all of the fleet scenarios. For example, it turned out, one of the three users was *colorblind* and needed a different GUI using uniquely distinguishable patterns to differentiate colored icons.

The system was intended for long-range (five-year) planning and scheduling purposes, not real-time decision-making on operational considerations. The main input data file, from which the system was driven and reported updated accumulated flight hours by aircraft tail number, was downloaded from a mainframe and uploaded into the application once a week. All of the other input files (about a dozen) were manually edited, kept up-to-date, and modified to run a variety of scenarios. Using these input files, the system generated a schedule in a matter of minutes, which was displayed on the computer in the form of a scrollable five-year Gantt chart.

Thus, the level of dynamism was low, the level of integration was low, the system was not mission-critical (worst-case requiring a PC reboot), and the problem and model complexity was low (a *greedy heuristic* algorithm solving a well-understood job scheduling on parallel machines with firm due dates problem for 600 aircraft divided into sub-fleets). Net-net, this was a relatively easy problem to solve, and an easy system to build and deploy in less than a year in an enterprise departmental context but still worth significant enterprise value. A great choice of problem to solve with analytics.

At the other end of the spectrum, consider some of the systems we mentioned earlier, including:

- UPS' ORION (delivery-truck routing)
- American Airlines' DINAMO (yield, pricing, and seat inventory management)

Both ORION and DINAMO have a high level of dynamism, high level of integration, high degree of mission-criticality, and high degree of problem complexity and solution sophistication.

UPS' ORION solves 55,000 (one for each delivery truck as of 2013) traveling salesman problems (each of which is NP-complete) based on package delivery information scheduled for the next day. The system took *more than 10 years to build and deploy* and *cost $250 million* but *saves $300 million to $400 million in costs annually.*

American Airlines' DINAMO performs tens of thousands of passenger flight demand forecasts nightly and dynamically optimizes seat inventory pricing using a mixed-integer linear programming model for 2,800 flights per day (circa 1991). The system took several years and cost hundreds of millions of dollars to build and deploy (billions if you count SABRE, the underlying computerized reservation system that provides the data for DINAMO) and generates an additional ~$500 million in revenue annually.

Along with colleagues Dr. Phil Beck and Dr. Mark Song, and domain expert Supervisor of Dispatch, Charles Cunningham, Doug helped lead the successful development and implementation of a real-time airline disruption recovery optimization system in 2015 at Southwest Airlines, which had high levels of dynamism and integration, and high degrees of mission-criticality, problem complexity, and solution sophistication.

Code-named *"The Baker"* (posthumously for Supervisor of Dispatch Mike Baker, the domain expert who originally conceived the concept), the system can take a real-time, data-based snapshot of the airline (i.e., aircraft, flights, passengers, maintenance events, airport weather and operating conditions, such as low ceilings, curfews, or ground stops, but not crew members) before, during, or after a major disruption, like a snowstorm, hurricane, FAA ATC ground stop, etc., and utilize a network optimization algorithm, with several side constraints, to recommend flight delay and cancellation decision alternatives with the intent to minimize passenger disruptions. Solutions could be generated in *5 or 30 minutes* for isolated or network-wide scenarios, respectively. Previously, such complex decisions made manually by Supervisors of Dispatch required *several hours*, by which time, conditions would have changed, further complicating decision-making.

Recognized at the time by senior airline operations executives, specifically the COO and VP Network Operations Control, as the single most impactful operations-oriented system delivered by the Technology organization at Southwest, the Baker took about *8 elapsed years* to complete from the initial conceptual model development in 2008 to the solution's initial delivery in 2015. The long project duration was primarily due to the problem's sheer multivariate technical complexity and both the quantity and real-time nature of the input data, which were obtained via pipelines integrated with another enterprise information system. The Baker cost millions of dollars, i.e., high 7-figures, to design, develop, rigorously test, and deploy. The solution dramatically improved the airline's On-Time Performance (OTP) in major winter storms by a factor of two and cancellations by a factor of two as well, and increased overall annualized airline OTP by 2.11 percentage points. The number of passengers delayed by two hours or more decreased by 95% when the Baker was fully implemented in 2016.[6]

This project succeeded, where many, many prior attempts by other airlines had failed to even remotely adequately solve this incredibly complex, real-time airline operations decision-making problem. That success is a testament to the hard work, partnership, commitment, perseverance, business domain knowledge and skill, and superior technical excellence of the IT and Analytics team members that made The Baker a reality.

For example, in 1990 at AA, OR staff had great success building and deploying limited day-of operations control analytics models into production, for example, Arrival Slot Allocation System (ASAS) (1990 INFORMS Edelman Award finalist), which optimized assignments of arriving AA aircraft to airport-specific FAA ATC arrival positions or time slots, according to the flights' *actual* vs. *scheduled* ETAs. However, when Doug and his colleague attempted to *expand* the scope of these models to *network-wide* flight delay and cancellation, and aircraft swap decision-making, they did not have all of the real-time, updated data, or the available computing power required to solve such large-scale problems in a timely manner. They wrote a very elegant mathematical model formulation,[7] but when they went to implement it, it failed due to a lack of streaming, real-time data, and computing power—the project never got beyond the prototype stage. *The sheer complexity of the real-world problem overwhelmed the solution approach.* The head of AA Systems Operations Control at the time also wasn't enthralled with the idea of turning over that level of real-time airline decision-making to a computer. *The change management hurdle to continue the project was simply way too high at the time.*

These examples help illustrate that there is a broad spectrum in the transformation from sandbox model to production system. Factors such as dynamism, integration, mission criticality, and problem and model complexity play a huge role in determining the time, effort, resources, and investment required to deliver an enterprise system, as well as the likelihood of the project's success or failure. Although we recommend starting small and simple, using Agile Kanban, we have to warn that large-scale enterprise systems can be *decade(s)-long* projects.

That said, smaller scale, relatively simple systems implemented with relatively little investment, can still deliver tremendous business value compared to incumbent solutions, if the economic potential is there. However, large (to extremely large) relative investments are required to reap the enormous rewards delivered by robust, larger scale, more sophisticated systems.

When launching into production, it is advisable to the keep the following in mind:

- As stated before, building production systems around and underneath models is 10x–100x more complex and resource-intensive than building the model itself.

- The model will need the support of the Data Organization, in particular, Data Engineering and Governance, to provide data pipelines that the model needs for access to timely, high-integrity data and their sources.

- The model will need support from the Technology Organization, in particular, software engineering, to facilitate the interfaces with other enterprise systems, cloud services to provide the compute, storage, and network services needed, and test/QA to verify, validate, and certify the model's application.

- If the company has a Change Management team (they may sometimes sit in the Project Management Office), we recommend enlisting their help with orchestrating the transition of all involved business constituent staff and management stakeholders from the old way of doing things to the new world order that the model is creating. Change management has become a new discipline and it can help with major changes in policies, processes, and procedures driven by the model.

- Aim for as much reusability as possible and build the model as a *microservice* that attaches via contract-programmed APIs rather than a stand-alone system; chances are, in most large enterprises, a model will be part of an *ecosystem* of many other systems rather than a stand-alone entity.

Truly understanding scope and complexity *prior* to delivering estimates or embarking on such a journey is *critical* to success. This ensures that people treat the tools the right way, understanding that numbers provide guardrails and users must add common sense and their own domain knowledge to the outputs—data scientists (or end users) can't 100% rely on an automated tool's suggestions and blindly trust the results. Confidence in models is built over time, upon relentless rigorous testing and validation on as many problems as practically possible. End users should be data informed, not data hypnotized (i.e., putting blind faith into the data)—it's imperative to know the limits of the data and the model. Doing so allows us to recognize that the tools we build aren't perfect.

Tools Make Mistakes

At the beginning of Evan's career, shortly after completing his PhD, his confidence in his technical capabilities was at an all-time high. That high was soon to crash because in the real world of applications, you cannot simply assume away problems (as in research papers) and will often discover that solving one problem simply creates a new one. However, with his PhD in hand, Evan had full confidence in his abilities to build sophisticated algorithms for the automobile industry.

His first assignment at his new employer was to speed up a virtual collision detection library, used by his employer to continue to grow their leadership in automotive path planning applications. Evan enthusiastically jumped headlong into the opportunity to demonstrate his technical prowess and within a short period of time, with all the technical discipline of his doctoral studies, created a complex solution using recursive, nested algorithms to execute geometric collision queries faster.

With the task now completed, the next step was to present his work to the rest of the group who were highly technical and experienced individuals. This is when Evan learned one of his most important lessons.

The mantra of Evan's employer was that all engineers had to bear in mind that their everyday software users were not mathematically sophisticated— even if they were sophisticated in their own domain knowledge and in their intuitive knowledge of how to do their job. Given this important principle, it was naturally disconcerting for Evan that when he presented the results of his work, he was barely understood by his technically minded colleagues. They found his work unnecessarily complex and completely opaque.

Even worse, when he demonstrated how it worked, the system failed because there was a bug hidden somewhere in the overly complex code base (due to its technical sophistication). He immediately realized that when things go wrong, people will feel frustrated unless they understand what has gone wrong and, if need be, how the tools work under the hood to diagnose the issue. Allowing end users to be hands-on in diagnosing and fixing their own problems saves time for both parties. In this case, this lesson was obvious with technically savvy users, so we can understand how much more important it must be with nontechnical end users.

Rectifying this embarrassing situation took Evan outside of his technical area of expertise to an area he knew nothing about, but was just as important as what he had been studying during his PhD: Good user interface design (in this case, documentation) to reduce usage mistakes (but also to ensure user acceptance).

What his new geometric acceleration structure presented was a poorly documented, difficult to understand, technically complex solution that even his technically sophisticated peers struggled to comprehend. This was certainly not the moment of glory that Evan had hoped to demonstrate his intellectual prowess. Instead, it was a moment in which he was able to learn humility and empathy, and a critical lesson in how technical tools can go wrong.

Fortunately, Evan's employer had the necessary tool infrastructure (a broad set of open source mathematical algorithms) to find a new approach to solve the original problem, but in his career he has discovered this isn't always the case. This reason for failure, presented next, is one that Evan has seen often at client organizations in his consulting career and was a common reason discovered in our research, and the issue doesn't seem to be going away.

The Final Hurdle: Proper Data and Tool Infrastructure

If you've made it to this point by maneuvering through the minefield of analytical requirements and haven't wiped out, well done. However, before you can cross the finish line and launch your successful analytics pilot, which has of course a clear business case using high-quality data, co-designed with end users, aligned with an executive vision having a reasonable set of expectations, and resourced with the right mix of talent, you face one final major hurdle according to our research. Do you have the right data and software infrastructure needed to deploy your carefully crafted work of art?

You might reasonably point to the cloud and state everything you need is there, but the trap is not the 95% of analytics infrastructure available in the cloud, rather, it is the 5% that is missing, as we saw earlier with ChemCo in the Analytically Immature Organizations chapter. If we turn back to that story, it was exactly because of the consulting team's lack of experience and knowledge that they built a set of basic scripts (an inappropriate technical approach for this problem and all that they had available) to solve a large-scale, business critical problem of optimizing the company's supply chain.

For the ChemCo team, at the point of deployment, instead of having the right data and tool infrastructure, which would include a testing (or staging) environment to test the solution before it went live, the plan was to deploy the script on the live (production) software and data infrastructure. In this case, it wasn't a missing 5%, more like a missing 80%, but the impact of *not* having this infrastructure (and not even knowing what infrastructure was required) meant that the project was never going to succeed, no matter how many of the other challenges they managed to sidestep.

The case with ChemCo was obvious, and the missing data and analytics infrastructure was clear, but in many other cases, what does "missing tools" even mean? There are nuances here that are worth unpacking, and it begins with the right technology for the problem.

If we take a step back and look at the types of problems solved with ADSAI, we see that they can be extremely broad and varied. From answering questions such as, what is the best allocation of vehicles to deliveries, to what are the predicted sales for this product next month, we can end up requiring completely different tools, skill sets, and frameworks.

For example, the problem of the best allocation of vehicles to deliveries to minimize costs is an optimization problem requiring tools that can solve so-called linear and mixed-integer programming problems (or even more complex stochastic and nonlinear versions). Predicting next month's sales is more of a statistical problem and can be approached with statistical or machine learning tools. Wanting to simulate the arrivals of passengers to a venue, or the distribution of profits, will probably require Monte Carlo simulation tools. In each case, the teams will possibly have different backgrounds, require different tools, and be able to provide very different answers. Not all problems need the same approach, so the company needs to understand the type of problem it faces and determine the approach required.

After finding the right tools, the next step is to ensure that the solution can provide an answer that is acceptable to the end users. This typically means emulating the decisions that a good decision-maker makes. In a project for an Australian healthcare provider, Evan was required to create a set of rosters to optimize the allocation of staff to medical shifts that obeyed all the enterprise agreement and fair work rules negotiated by the unions. The problem sounded simple: The roster rules were gathered, a network flow optimization algorithm was configured, and rosters were digitally created, until Evan was told it was all wrong.

For the decision-makers, it was clear that having staff swap between day and night shifts was not an acceptable outcome, but this was not a rule that the engine knew, nor one the team was told they had to follow. For the healthcare provider it was obvious, but to a mathematical engine (and the programmers who built it) it wasn't, and if it wasn't told to do it, it wouldn't. Both co-authors have been involved in too many projects in which stakeholders believe an analytical tool is a magic box wherein you push a button and it works perfectly. Having a stakeholder who understands ADSAI projects significantly increases the chances of success and mitigates many of our other reasons for failure (see our discussion around Analytics Translators earlier). In this roster case, when the decision-makers explained all of the unspoken (new) rules, which seemed obvious to them, the team realized that some of the new constraints would completely change the problem to a nonlinear one and the existing analytical infrastructure wouldn't be able to fully handle the entire problem. It was either back to the drawing board or compromising on a solution that solved 80% of the problem.

In some situations, data scientists can't even get as far as creating a roster that is usable straight out of the box. For example, for the healthcare provider, the team's suggested roster was always just supposed to be a good starting point. The mathematical consultants were clear that the final solution would still require tweaks by the local staff. However, due to the hype surrounding AI tools, end users often come with the expectation that the tools will magically create the perfect solution on the first go. As both co-authors have learned, data science tools typically create answers good enough to generate insights, but not always final solutions. If end users are aware of this, then they will have a lot more success and a better relationship with the outcomes.

Finally, in tool and software infrastructure development, we cannot forget the end user. How are they supposed to interact with the produced results? Will it be a web-based tool they log on to through a browser or something they have to install on their own device? Once tool access is clear, like Evan's story after completing his PhD, ensuring that the tool is designed so end users can solve their own problems will increase the chances of adoption.

It is not just a question of whether a person understands the technology, it's also a question of whether they can *use* the technology. The analytical engine needs to be delivered in a format that is appropriately easy to use. It may require the analytics team to upskill the end users, or to hide all the technical details, but all the while ensuring the end user can dig deeper if needed and understand why a result was produced (especially when things go wrong). Doing so may require software languages and tools that weren't anticipated by the analytics team if they are not experienced in doing this. (A strong partnership with IT/Software Engineering can greatly help to fill this particular void.)

So, if the solution is fit for purpose, built on a solid tool and data infrastructure, and has cleared all of the other hurdles, then you may *think* you are on the path to 100% success and the days of ADSAI failures are behind you. Unfortunately, this is not always the case. Our earlier back-of-the-envelope calculations in the Analytically Immature Organizations chapter showed that as many as 40% of all analytics projects fail even in analytically mature organizations. This still seems high, so why is it the case? What still causes analytically *mature* organizations to fail?

In the penultimate chapter, the co-authors will share the nuanced and rarely spoken about issues that trip up even the best of the best when it comes to ADSAI projects.

Critical Thinking: How Not to Fail

- What are four significant factors warranting serious consideration when moving a model from the "sandbox" to a production system?

- Having a "can-do" attitude in a company's management may end up forcing teams to take on problems they may not be able to solve. How can this lead to incorrect applications of models?

- Data scientists are probably naturally technical people, and with their technical hammer, many things can seem like technical nails to them. How can we balance this focus on technical solutions to problems with the necessary domain and people focus to ensure what we deliver is fit for purpose?

- What do you think are the main causes of the 10x–100x increase in difficulty in going from a pilot to an ADSAI tool deployed in production? Why are some of the main drivers making a solution 10x–100x harder rather than 2x–5x harder? What could cause a tool to be 100x harder rather than 10x?

- Having quality data and tool infrastructure is critical to success but not something you want to invest in up front in case you end up with the wrong tools. How do you suggest an organization approach this so they don't over-invest too early, but ensure they have the right tools at the right time?

Notes

1. For the technical reader, the LASSO model had a Root Mean Squared Error (RMSE) of 5.07.
2. Bartlett, J. (2014, May 31). A/B testing and Pearson's chi-squared test of independence. *The Stats Geek*, https://thestatsgeek.com/2013/07/22/ab-testing/.

3. Kim, T. (2013, March 11). Of models and modeling. SAP Community. https://blogs.sap.com/2013/03/11/of-models-and-modeling/

4. Wigner, E. (1960). The Unreasonable Effectiveness of Mathematics in the Natural Sciences. *Communications on Pure and Applied Mathematics*, Vol. XIII, 001-14.

5. Kerzner, H. (2014). *Project Recovery: Case Studies and Techniques for Overcoming Project Failure*. Wiley.

6. Hagel, J., Brown, J.S., Wooll, M., & De Maar, A. (2018). Southwest Airlines: Baker workgroup: Reducing disruption and delay to accelerate performance. *Deloitte Insights* (A Case Study in the Business Practice Redesign Series From the Deloitte Center for the Edge), 1-13.

7. Vasquez, A., Gray, D., Kirk, J., & Mirchandani, P. (1990, May). A Framework for Implementing Real-time Re-scheduling Systems. *Proceedings, Rensselaer's Second International Conference on Computer Integrated Manufacturing*.

6

Analytically Mature Organizations

We've spent the last few chapters examining some of the most common challenges encountered by analytically immature organizations. While these organizations might look up to their more mature counterparts as successful role models, life on the more capable side isn't perfect. Our earlier analysis estimated that around 40% of ADSAI projects fail, even for analytically *mature* companies that should know better.

One such example occurred at a large, global fast food retail chain that we'll call FastFoodCo. From an analytics perspective, this company has everything it needs: lots of high-quality data, a modern technology stack, scale of operations, and even the culture of a tech company. If it wasn't selling quick service food and beverages, FastFoodCo could very well have been a tech company.

Knowing the data science limits but wanting to push the boundary of data-driven decision-making, FastFoodCo engaged a local data science company to help scale up their capabilities to better manage orders. The choice of who to work with was easy: FastFoodCo rehired a data science company that had helped them deliver on previous ambitious analytics projects. It was not an inexperienced consulting outfit, as we saw in earlier stories, and a successful result was expected based on prior project outcomes.

The data science consultants took on the problem by first doing a pilot with a large sample of data, which represented about three years of order data across hundreds of stores. This was not a challenge for FastFoodCo because they had the luxury of a big data team that could extract such quantities of data with ease. The project also had a strong business case, so it seemed set up for success.

The analysis kicked off with the arrival of the dataset, and the consulting company quickly transformed it into useful features for a machine learning algorithm designed to make accurate forecasts about when a food order would progress through the order fulfillment stages. The model was complex with many rich attributes, such as aggregated sales and order volumes from different stores at different times of day, and their impact on the order fulfillment process. The fast food business was data-mature enough to provide the consultants with the necessary inputs as they digitally tracked all stages of the order preparation and delivery process.

The initial model was complete and produced good results when tested on unseen data; all parties were satisfied that the pilot showed it could indeed

  DOI: 10.1201/9781032661360-7

provide value to the business. The consultants pushed on, but soon after, things started to derail during the next step of the project.

Because the FastFoodCo executives and consultants were satisfied with the model's performance, the ultimate goal was now to put their work into production as soon as possible. The high-quality consultancy and analytically mature company both got to work with key stakeholders who brought in people from another internal data team to work on moving the model to production. The production system would be different from the pilot because FastFoodCo's original data team built historical batch processes to test the data but were now moving to real-time streaming data for the real-life system.

The consulting team put one of their senior engineers on the task. Although he wasn't the best at managing clients, he was still able to complete the necessary technical work because he had previously worked with FastFoodCo. During the six-week pilot, he had already prepared FastFoodCo's team to ensure they were aware that they'd need to prepare the pipelines for rollout to production. His plan was to take the pilot model and plug in real-time data (instead of the batched data) and then begin a final test run with the real-time data pipelines.

When the senior engineer began working on this step with FastFoodCo's team, he sensed something was amiss. There had now been two separate teams working on the data side—the team that did the batch processing for the pilot and the real-time data team for the production system. As the real-time team began building their pipelines, they had to reimplement the features that were built within the batch pipeline in order to make them available in the real-time production data storage systems (data coming from different systems have different scalability profiles, etc.). This section was where the wheels started to come off.

The first problem was that the real-time data team implemented the features with no communication with the original batch team and only based on feature definitions compiled by the consultant ML engineer. Because not all details are captured as part of a technical plan, there should have been at least one person working across both the batch and real-time data teams at FastFoodCo to bridge any possible communication gaps. The new team built the majority of the features quickly and made the data available by API within the allocated month. However, when the consultants connected their pilot engine to the new API, they realized the model wasn't quite right and the earlier promise of success started to evaporate.

After digging into the data, the consultants found that capturing a one-hour stream of real-time data didn't match the batch of one hour of data prepared earlier. The consultants quickly comprehended the problem, but the clock was ticking and their window of opportunity to fix it had closed. FastFoodCo was efficient with their data resources and had already reassigned their real-time data team to other mission critical tasks unrelated to this project, so they were no longer available to fix the problem.

The project had hit a major stumbling block before the finish line—the model was ready, the pipelines were built, but the *features* were wrong. The real-time data team misread the features, and the manner in which they were calculated wasn't precisely the same—the definitions were wrong. Because the real-time pipeline was written in a different code base and wasn't using the same pipelines as the batch processes, the split in the teams meant they didn't have the benefit of directly copying the code used in the batch pipeline. This problem wasn't discovered until the end of the project because it involved issues of eventual consistency and more nuanced consequences that were not completely obvious to the two FastFoodCo teams of data engineers operating independently. It was only at this final stage that the consultants realized the mistake, but the real-time data team had moved on.

The consultants were left scrambling to fix the issue. A team of four experts quickly gathered to work on the problem and burned an estimated $30,000 trying to fix it (not including the delay costs on other projects). For FastFoodCo, this amount of money was insignificant, but for the local data science consulting company, it was a major issue and threatened their financial viability at an inopportune moment. Moreover, the consultants had additional concerns: There might still be lingering issues in their fix, and it was entirely possible that new unforeseen issues could arise and balloon to disastrous proportions even after deployment of a solution. This debacle had the potential to not only ruin their finances, but their reputation too.

The consulting company and FastFoodCo both had significant experience and previously delivered many successful projects, separately and together. How did this particular project get to this point of failure? What went wrong? If both parties were able to understand the lessons from this project, it would be highly instructive for them and something they would unlikely repeat again.

On the surface, what looked like a technical problem cuts right to the core of why ADSAI projects at analytically mature companies can still fail. It is why, in spite of every framework, every approach, every methodology, and every capable employee, team, and partnership, we may never be able to reduce the failure rate to zero.

Let's start by unpacking some of the reasons for failure that the co-authors have observed in their networks to better understand why ADSAI project failure is something that might never be completely avoided.

(More) Real-life Failures

Once a model is built, data science teams are ready to realize the value of their hard work and deploy the completed model into production. Unfortunately, at FastFoodCo, this didn't go as planned. As an analytically mature organization, it would usually have completed the steps up until this point with ease. But the final step of deploying an AI model can trip up even the most experienced organization. This is an issue that has many layers, and lessons are still being learned by global analytics leaders. And of all the companies in the world, there are few that have analytics more deeply embedded than Booking.com.

In 2019, the machine learning/data science (ML/DS) team from Booking.com published a revealing and fascinating paper in which they summarized their learnings from 150 ML models and extrapolated the six major lessons harvested from this wealth of activity.[1] Although all six lessons were fascinating and edifying summaries from an analytically mature organization, there was one lesson that is relevant here—the challenge of successfully and sustainably deploying to production. This is a topic that we addressed in the Technology chapter but we are going to look at it from another important angle here.

The ML/DS team's learning focused on that critical transition phase from the offline pilot to the online deployed production system. Once companies have completed the difficult grind of iterating, testing, testing, and more testing, they (and management) can become anxious to get the model into production and start generating a return on the development investment.

In this phase, the analytics team may end up believing—by relying too much on the hard work of the pilot—that the offline model performance is a reliable indicator of online (or deployed) model performance. At this stage, pressured by the organization's rush to realize value, analytics teams may inadvertently assume that the pilot's results can be extended without question. The problem is that once a model hits the real world, the 80/20 rule kicks in and those 20% of edge cases not encountered in the pilot become 80% of the problems, and the resultant performance in these situations can all of a sudden take a serious nosedive calling the whole project into question. What do teams do then?

The Booking.com team explained that one of the key steps to ensure success is proper experimental design and, at a bare minimum, an A/B test between a treatment and control group to prove that the model is performing as desired and expected. We've discussed A/B tests and experimental design in the Technology chapter, and they are a set of techniques that require skill and know-how to get right but are critical when proving the benefit of an intervention (like a new analytics tool). The travel giant's paper showed that putting all of these pieces together requires both a mature culture and the right skills.

The second key recommendation from the paper is the importance of monitoring more than just outputs. Machine learning models are trained on historical data, so data teams must also monitor input data to discover issues before they hit the outputs.

A great example of this is one of the very common technologies used across many large enterprises, *forecasting*. Forecasting is a technique that typically uses statistical or machine learning technologies trained on historical data, e.g., time series data, to then extrapolate those trends (e.g., base, linear, or seasonal trends), based on the data at hand. Students will learn that with forecasting techniques, such as linear regression, the predictions are only truly reliable when predicting values from a range of data on which the algorithm has been trained.

When a new set of circumstances (inputs) embodied in the data are encountered by the model (e.g., COVID-19) that significantly deviates from what the model was trained on, then all bets are off. Data teams might get lucky, and the outputs resulting from the not-previously-encountered inputs could be reasonable, but more likely than not, the outputs will send the company in the wrong direction, which is known as data drift.

The key finding from the Booking.com team was that once a model is deployed to production, there is a critical need to continually monitor the input data (data drift) in addition to the output data (model drift). It is important to flag when data points are used that represent scenarios outside of the input training data distributions. The outputs from such edge cases can be more carefully treated, and even used to train the models for future predictions, improving robustness.

In summary, based on the publication, the Booking.com team recommended that before deployment, appropriate (data and model) monitoring techniques and systems must be established, and an A/B test conducted, to unequivocally prove the benefit of the new technology. For a company like Booking.com that runs thousands of analytical experiments, this capability is critical. Each new feature or technology may only improve the performance of the website by a single percentage point (or sometimes even less), however, when measured across millions of website visitors, even half a percentage point can make a huge difference. Detecting such a small change is only possible with a scientific framework like A/B testing.

For other companies that are bringing in a new analytical tool for the first time, the gain may be much, much larger. In this case, an A/B test may not be needed from a practical point of view, but will most likely make sense from a risk management one. What happens if the large change in performance is in the *negative* direction? The A/B test will limit the damage and save the company's reputation, and possibly a lot of money.

The outcomes for companies undergoing one or two major projects may be obvious and an A/B test may not be needed; however, monitoring is still necessary and important for all tools. Thorough monitoring of inputs and outputs will enable data science teams to more easily catch troublesome issues that go under the radar, and preemptively address them before they become serious problems.

Outside Influences

Throughout the book, both co-authors share lessons learned from personal stories and those from peers to illustrate the challenges facing analytically immature organizations. These aren't difficult to find and discuss due to their regularity. The failures of analytically *mature* organizations do not come to light as often and aren't as common, so sharing their stories can be truly insightful.

Upon review of the top reasons why ADSAI projects fail, lack of the right resources comes in at No. 3 for analytically immature organizations (covered in the People chapter), but this is the *top* reason for failure at analytically mature organizations. How can this make sense?

These capable organizations do have data scientists, machine learning engineers, software engineers, project managers, and more. What they *don't* have are these highly skilled resources in the *volumes* that their organization's appetite for data and analytics mandates. To fulfill the company's desire to have analytics as the primary driver of performance and value, the team is stretched across many projects. The strategic imperative to leverage analytics for a competitive advantage is one of the key characteristics of an analytically mature organization presented by Davenport in his book *Competing on Analytics* and it can lead to this type of situation.

Being the major and most common point of failure revealed by our research for analytically mature organizations, we want to share our own anecdotal experiences and findings on this topic. We'll begin with a challenge discovered by Evan in a pioneering project that delivered a nationwide pricing system for a well-known retail brand, which was to be the first such engine delivered in Australia.

The story began with an analytically mature organization that decided it needed a uniquely distinctive advantage in the highly competitive market in which it operated—the goods they sold were seen as practically identical to their competitors by consumers, so it was very difficult for the organization to differentiate their products on anything other than price. The organization's goal was to deploy an analytics tool to increase profit margins, and given the scale at which it operated, even a small improvement in its pricing strategy could lead to an enormously beneficial outcome, so the business case was solid.

This principle is best understood by a simple example. Table 6.1 shows how a 10% increase in price (assuming that sales volumes remain the same) can improve the bottom line more than a similar 10% increase in sales volume (at the same price). *Ceteris paribus*, this simple example evinces that price is a powerful lever which a company can pull to improve profits.

This powerful leverage stems from getting the price right, and it is clear why organizations target this variable, especially in a scenario in which the

TABLE 6.1

Comparisons of price and volume increases on profit

Case	Price	Volume	Unit Cost	Profit	% Profit Increase
Base	$1	100,000	$0.5	$50,000	0%
Volume lift	$1	110,000	$0.5	$55,000	10%
Price lift	$1.1	100,000	$0.5	$60,000	20%

retailer sells a commodity and doesn't have much else in its favor except for its brand identity via marketing and advertising.

When Evan launched this project into production (after admittedly experiencing some technical difficulties during the build phase), the solution was delivered as expected, and he heeded this book's advice with an A/B test at the end of the pilot before rolling out the pricing engine nationwide. The project was completed, the engine was switched on, and usage began. This was also when the challenges arose, even in this analytically mature organization.

To understand why the issues arose, let's first take a step back.

The types of challenges we face as data scientists aren't always things we have control over or can influence, but they can nonetheless beget failure. Given these issues may not be under the control of the analytics team, they most likely lie in the control of the broader company (even if they are externally driven) and organizations can take action to avoid these failures, but it may require an organization-wide effort.

This effort will sometimes need to focus on the *people* aspect—most importantly when it is a case of *missing* people. When an analytics team in a large organization is able to deliver a project for which they are their own stakeholder (i.e., it is not procured by outside departments or stakeholders), it usually succeeds regardless of whether the company is analytically mature or immature. However, this is not the way the process normally works. Analytics teams usually deliver projects for *others*, not themselves, which leads to some significant challenges involving managing the unmanageable at an organization-wide scale.

One of the things that the analytics team has almost no influence over is whether their stakeholders remain in their jobs for the duration of the project. Oftentimes, the stakeholders can change by way of transfer, promotion, leave, or even termination while a project is ongoing. Even if the client of the project doesn't move roles, due to high-level strategic considerations, they may change *priorities*, etc. What can the analytics team do?

These situations force ADSAI team members to extend themselves beyond their technical training—a topic we explored in depth in the People chapter. The most important thing that the project team can do is ensure that the activities they carry out align with the company strategy and not solely with the *individual* stakeholders' desires. By doing so, when an individual leaves, the project can continue to thrive and not fail as a "pet project" dreamt up by one person to further their career or build a personal industry relationship. Internal politics will *always* be an issue, and companies that follow an individual's agenda will suffer more than an organization in which everyone is part of a team pulling in the same direction.

In Evan's case, around the time the A/B testing was completed, a key stakeholder in the retail organization left. This person was the project champion and there were serious concerns as to whether the project could successfully continue after his departure. However, fortunately, the company for which Evan was doing the project was not only analytically mature but also generally well run, so a suitable replacement in the organization was found and the team was able to continue without any major issues.

The project rolled out successfully in spite of the key stakeholder's departure and entered production, but then Evan encountered another important challenge. Analytics tools are often a small part of a larger system as we've indicated earlier. The parts of the business that this tool touched were broad (reaching into supply chain and merchandising questions) and the project team realized it had to extend its sphere of influence, horizontally as well as vertically, to ensure long-term adoption.

For some data scientists (and teams), it can be challenging to go outside their silo and thoroughly engage across many parts of the business, especially with some data scientists seeing data-driven, model-based decision-making as the only reasonable way to make a decision. When the analytics team not only has to engage the end user in the pricing team, but the CFO as well (like Evan did), difficulties can arise.

Going vertically in the organization can be problematic because these people are usually very busy. Often, what data scientists are looking for is simply support, so the request for a meeting is not a burning priority for an executive team member. When the meeting does occur, it is often clear that the team's solution isn't the most important issue these executives need to address. At this point, maintaining their direct support can be difficult.

In Evan's case, he had the support of the CFO during the pilot and A/B tests, and the finance leader was heavily involved in the final steps before rollout. It may sound sufficient, however, in the focus on the day-to-day operation, Evan made the mistake of decreasing engagement and losing touch with this key supporter. The lack of contact resulted in the team having to specifically answer unnecessarily pointed questions months later regarding the value of the tool.

The question of value was naturally a significant concern for the CFO, who was responsible for approving the budget for the tool's ongoing usage. Were he to decide that the tool wasn't worth it (possibly simply due to not being aware of what was going on), funding would disappear and the tool would be switched off. Fortunately for the analytics team, this wasn't the case. We were lucky to work with an engaged corporate team who spent a large portion of their time continually communicating with other stake-holders within the business and ensuring that the success of the work was broadly understood.

What could have led to the downfall of the project and the failure of the rollout eventually only resulted in some surmountable challenges that were solved together as a group. One of the key factors that led to the ability of both parties to deliver a favorable outcome will be our next topic. A lack of this particular factor is one from which analytically immature organizations can surely suffer. But once there have been a few successes, the likelihood that organizations lack this factor is even higher. It can therefore breed its own dangers even for analytically mature organizations.

Humility

> One of the things I have learned well from many real-world modeling engagements is that finding the supposedly 'optimal' solution is often not nearly as important as putting the solution values into a form that the client is accustomed to seeing.
>
> **—R.E.D. "Gene" Woolsey, PhD, Professor, Colorado School of Mines, Operations Research Academic, Practitioner & Consultant**

Out of this entire book, this particular section is one very near and dear to Evan. In fact, the company he worked for while writing this chapter, Ubidy, has *humility* as one of their key company values, and the selection of this value was something he championed. The ability for people to be humble is seen as critical by both co-authors, and not just for an ADSAI team's success, but in any organization to enable people to learn, grow, and thrive. We are not alone. This belief is held by many other experts as well.

In management guru Patrick Lencioni's book, *The Ideal Team Player: How to Grow an Effective Team*, he singles out three virtues that a company should focus on to help teams work together effectively. Based on his own significant consulting experience, and that of his company, the three values he identifies are humility, hunger, and social intelligence. In fact, he lists humility first and explores this virtue before the others, clearly because of its primary importance.

In research independent of the wisdom of the management consulting industry, numerous scholars have provided evidence of the benefits of humble leadership. Although humility may be a seemingly vague and subjective concept, a 2018 paper from a team at Seattle University showed that there is "a greater consensus in definitional work than some researchers may realize"[2] leading to a way to really start measuring the benefits of humble leadership—and this is what has been happening.

For example, in early 2023, researchers at the University of North Texas and University of Northern British Columbia produced a meta-analysis of the work of 212 unique studies and came to the conclusion that:

> Humble leadership most strongly predicts followers' satisfaction with the leader and the leaders' participative decision making. We also find humble leadership does not affect their own job performance or the performance of organizations, but improves the performance of their followers and teams.[3]

In addition to creating a positive work environment, which improves the performance of the team, a level of humility can help save significant time and money, as Tesla discovered in the early 2010s. Elon Musk, then CEO, embarked upon an automation mission to create an automotive manufacturing line that was supposed to be completely run by robots. After years of effort and millions of dollars, it was decided that the automation hubris wasn't justified and the bombastic CEO announced on X (formerly Twitter) that:

> Yes, excessive automation at Tesla was a mistake. To be precise, my mistake. Humans are underrated.[4]

Apart from causing issues in team performance and challenges with leadership, a lack of humility can cause companies to become complacent. They know the ADSAI process and so don't need the checklists anymore; they can skip steps because they think they know what the outcome will be, which can result in a well-disciplined and professional function becoming lackadaisical. Key steps are missed, fingers are pointed, and projects begin failing again. As companies grow, they need to remain grounded. One company that has imbued this principle is Amazon with its "Day 1" mentality.[5] The concept inspires an attitude of being constantly curious, nimble, and experimental—one that would certainly assist with not becoming complacent, bloated, and braggart.

Ensuring that ADSAI teams have the humility not to inflate their role is important, as well as to understand that they have the tools to play a role in assisting better decision-making and resist trying to reduce everything that matters in decision-making into a quantitative value for an algorithm. This point is made well in the previously referenced book *Sensemaking* by Christian Madsbjerg. Even better, author-psychologist Gary Klein discusses the powerful capability of the non-quantitative in what is called *naturalistic decision-making* in his insightful book, *Streetlights and Shadows*.[6]

Klein's book provides many examples that should humble the nascent data scientist into realizing how much more goes into a decision than what is captured in their model, or even things that may never be captured in a model. The book provides stories of firefighters, military officers, and others who have to make quick decisions in highly stressful situations and yet are able to take a set of vague, complex, and conflicting inputs and still make good decisions based on the types of patterns they recognize, without AI tools. It is doubtful that an algorithm or robot could exist any time soon that could relieve the decision-making stress from the situations described in his research, due to the challenges of simply capturing such data and then producing extremely context-specific and novel recommendations in new situations based on unseen variations to past situations.

In addition to humility, a small dose of empathy also goes a long way in leadership and can help strengthen a person's humility. This was evidenced by perhaps the most interesting projects one of the co-authors was involved in—the seemingly successful completion of two large-scale nationwide optimization engines. These engines optimized two different things: the price of retail goods and the allocation of human resources to tasks.

Both were exciting projects spanning a number of years before they reached a stage where the major issues were resolved and the users were somewhat happy. Some, however, were still unhappy—the developers of these analytical engines!

Initially, both projects were conceived to take full advantage of the high flexibility of the situations in which they would be used. The pricing engine would explore all possible prices within reason and the human resource allocation tool would take full advantage of the interchangeable nature of the labor completing specific warehouse tasks.

However, what the development team discovered during both projects was that the users of the engines did not want the results to go too far outside their comfort zones. In fact, ideally, the sophisticated optimization tools would replicate the current decisions of the team, deviating only slightly every now and then from values that the old guard deemed similar enough to their past choices (reminding us of R.E.D. "Gene" Woolsey's epigraph at the start of this section).

What began as two high-powered, cutting-edge tools slowly morphed into deformed, mirror images of the human processes they were supposed to outclass. The development team and data scientists poured incredible ingenuity into their design and execution, only to be sabotaged by the demands of the end users to "stay within brand guidelines."

When this happened, it not only destroyed morale, but also the business case. The original business case was built on the assumption that the engines would have flexibility in their selection of optimal choices, and this had been validated in the proof of concepts. But as real-life results were produced, it was decided that they were too different from business-as-usual, and the engines were slowly constrained to the point of simply producing decisions almost identical to the human ones albeit in a faster and more consistent fashion, hardly the outcome expected by the design team.

Despite the rhetoric from upper management plus the strategic and corporate desire in both companies to leverage data science, it was the decisions made by the end users that reduced a 10x ROI to a much lower and question-able benefit. However, the twist here is that this less-than-optimal outcome arose from a lack of empathy by the analytics team for how the users wanted to operate, their KPIs, and what was important to them.

These examples should always remind the budding data scientist that there is so much more involved in the decisions they are helping inform than just their technical expertise or the data they see. It is something any team or company should bear in mind when delivering projects, and it is something that our final example of failure (perhaps better called a challenged delivery) demonstrates. It shows us that for capable companies, believe it or not, success is not guaranteed, even after a project is delivered.

Small Stumbles, Solid Outcome

If there is one thing that Australians love, it is the underdog. Watching the least-favored team kick the final goal to win in the dying minutes of a footy game is the most relished outcome for any Australian sports fan. When small Australian companies come out and deliver world-class solutions that can proudly stand on a global technical stage, it is something that the population from Down Under reveres. However, the underdog, just like in the next case we discuss, still has to fight for its victory.

This story is literally one of life and death because it involves equipping sur-geons with the implements they need to save lives. In the late 2010s, a small Australian data science organization, Max Kelsen, embarked upon a revolu-tionary healthcare project called SAVI: Semi Automated Visual Inspection.[7]

During surgery, it is of course essential that the surgeons have every piece of equipment they need. This is complicated because each person is physi-cally different and the exact implant size or tool specifications needed can be different for each operation; hospitals are unable to carry this amount of stock, so they need to order it in advance. The providers of such critical sur-gical kits are the giants of the surgical world, including Stryker, Johnson & Johnson (J&J), and similar organizations.

The hospital's strategy is as follows: A hospital plans an operation for a patient and requests a kit with all the tools and implants needed from the surgical provider. To facilitate timely delivery, the manufacturers, such as J&J, build warehouses all over the country to be able to quickly provide the tools. Once gathered, the tools are stored in a high-grade metal tray for steril-ity and easy access for surgeons. It is J&J's job to be 100% certain that all the tools are present—no duplicates, all required sizes, and all sterile. Once an operation is complete, it would be easy to throw out the remaining toolkit regardless of whether the equipment was used, but with some items costing upwards of $1,000 per unit, this would be expensive and an incredible waste.

So, what do hospitals do? They return the used kits to keep the costs down.

Here's how that typically goes: Companies like J&J receive the kit back from the hospital with leftover tools. J&J would then put the tools through an industrial dishwasher to sanitize them. An employee would print off an inventory sheet and check for each item: one scalpel (tick), two screws (tick), etc. Because some tools and sizes look very similar (e.g., 5mm vs. 7mm blades), it is a slow and difficult manual process. Before Max Kelsen intervened, this process was done by hand, with an individual recording each item and scanning the sheet. It was time consuming and error prone. For a complicated surgery, it could take an hour per tray, and for operations requiring six trays, a lot of the checks were simply mechanical.

This process can be automated with the advent of powerful computer vision systems that can provide a solution that is surprisingly user friendly. The end solution is simply a tablet with an app.

The way this works is as follows: The team at J&J scans the consignment code as the tray comes in. The code lists what is meant to be in the tray. They pull the lid off and take a picture of the tray's contents. The AI algorithm identifies which tray it is and what is expected to be there (inventory list). Because Max Kelsen is an analytically mature organization, it had reasonable expectations of what was possible for this project, and their goal was 80% recall, i.e., if 20 parts are in a tray, the AI could correctly identify 16 parts, perhaps missing four and noting them as missing. If the AI notes a part as missing, that is OK, because an employee can check and confirm. However, a scenario in which the AI notes an item as present when it is actually missing would mean the subsequent surgical operation would fail. Therefore, higher precision is the necessary key metric to determine project success (i.e., you don't want to misclassify something as being there when it isn't). The system was built with performance targets along the lines of 99.9% precision and 80% recall.

This is when various challenges arose.

Not only did J&J want to check if everything was in the right place, one of the organization's subsidiaries wanted to detect if the parts were contaminated—but how? If photos aren't taken from all sides, marks and other clues of contamination might not be visible.

At first, it wasn't clear to Max Kelsen how to find a solution for this, but because they were an extremely capable outfit by this point in time, the team backed themselves and said they would try to do it. The stakeholders that wanted this functionality also added to it a number of similar sounding checks that they supposed should be easy, but, from a technical perspective, are incredibly difficult, e.g., locating parts and foreign objects in the tray. Now, instead of the AI model only looking for 20 things, it needs to look for any type of object. For a computer vision model not trained on every possible object in the world, how could this be achieved? The model would need to be general enough to "detect other things." The internal engineering team realized this step was best left for a later stage in the project in order to have the chance to solve other, simpler problems in the meantime.

With this plan in place (to postpone the general detection), the technical team was happy to proceed; however, unbeknownst to the engineers, one of the *non*-engineers (who was part of the *commercial* team) made a commitment to bring "detect other things" into the current scope of the project. When the engineering team was told this, they immediately knew it would jeopardize the entire project because it meant other key objectives couldn't be sufficiently focused upon—and they were right. The dramatically increased scope of work hamstrung the other objectives.

This new functionality would require a very different model architecture with multiple models. Unfortunately for the engineering team, the salesperson involved did not have sufficient technical background and had agreed to the "detect other things" additional step to keep the client happy, likely not understanding its impact. This resulted in a misalignment between the engineering team and commercial team. (This unfortunately happens *far more often* than one might expect in even the most analytically mature commercial technology companies.)

With huge effort, the engineering team completed the pilot in eight weeks. The code was rushed, which meant it wasn't easily scalable for more trays. The team nervously looked at what they had achieved and were unsure that it would work in prime time. They tested three kits, but the next step was to immediately test 200 kits, and then soon after, 1,000 kits.

Although the client didn't technically experience a failure, the Max Kelsen team probably anticipated the project failing during those early stages. They also continued refactoring the rushed models for many, many months, which is an expensive game of catch-up. Even though they are an analytically mature organization, they stumbled on unreasonable client expectations complicated by a communication gap between teams. This landed them in hot water when it came to the "detect other things" request. The team should have been upfront with J&J instead of agreeing to something that they knew was technically very challenging.

The team at Max Kelsen taught us a final and nuanced lesson—a difficult one that comes right to the core of what we see as the major thesis of this book—ADSAI projects are so much more than a technical challenge. They often involve crossing company silos, dealing with egos, and in this case, being able to say "No" without losing the project by managing client expectations. Unfortunately, saying "No" in many cases will mean losing the opportunity, which is why of course there is pressure to agree. However, for cases like Max Kelsen's, perhaps saying a heavily qualified "Yes" (e.g., it will be done in a future phase at a commensurate fee) would have been the most practical answer to a request that couldn't be easily accommodated. It requires a level of people skills that may not be common among data scientists because it is typically neither a part of their training (as noted in the People chapter) nor expected in their daily work.

If a team is composed of people who are not just technically capable but also understand and have the ability to deal with the people-side of the problem, then a company is well on its way to data science nirvana.

The Journey to Perfection

As we have seen in this final chapter on failure, there will always be new lessons that confront us. Even the best can stumble at the finish line. In our journey to perfection, is it possible to reduce the failure rate of ADSAI projects to 0% or even something practically very close to it? What would it take to do this? If we assume an organization could achieve a 0% failure rate, what would that look like?

To begin, a company would no longer fall victim to AI hype and there would be a vision and strategy surrounding exploiting data and analytics. It would mean that every time the organization comes up with a good idea to leverage ASDAI, the relevant resources would be available, including the right skills and tools to execute the idea. It would mean: (1) the data is always available, (2) the business case is known from day one, (3) cross-functional capability is present, (4) there is a good understanding of data across the organization, and (5) data scientists understand their company's domain. Organization leaders would stand behind the data strategy and sufficiently understand ADSAI to have the correct expectations. Teams would have the right tools to build the products, and then once rolled out, the products would be well adopted within the organization and end users would understand how to use them.

This is not impossible and does exist in some tech companies, but it is rarely ever seen in retail, supply chain, finance, healthcare, or other companies outside of a core tech focus (and many tech companies don't even get it right either). The perfect scenario is probably an unrealistic one unless the core business is simply building software that leverages data and analytics. But flipping the script and trying to work backwards from the software domain (i.e., a tech company trying to enter the retail, supply chain, finance domains, etc.) may also not be the best strategy. We have already seen IBM, Google, and Amazon's health ventures fail to commercialize their technologies outside of their core technology domains.[8,9,10] Although they have mastered the art of technology, their inability to go beyond their core areas of focus shows us how difficult it really is to achieve in non-software domains.

As we've learned throughout this book, value-creating ADSAI projects produce technologies or insights that are typically embedded within larger organizational processes. Even if ADSAI project failure rates could be reduced to 0%, what would that accomplish if the other parts of the organization still fail to deliver on their commitments that are essential to the project's success?

Both co-authors view the challenges faced by an organization holistically. Achieving a goal of 0% failure rate would probably mean that not enough risks are being taken (and little is being learned) but more importantly, it is not a realistic target because there is no other part of a business that is as successful as this in any case. The cost and effort involved in achieving a 0% failure rate would very likely be a poor investment compared to investing in other areas that could really improve an organization's capabilities.

When it comes to bucking the failure trend and trying to achieve the coveted 0% in ADSAI, one company that seems to successfully span the tech and brick-and-mortar realms is Amazon. But even this behemoth is not without its failures, as well recognized by ex-CEO and founder Jeff Bezos. In fact, his attitude toward failing is one that mature and immature companies alike could learn from: Not trying can be the biggest failure of all. When he presented his commencement address to the Princeton University Class of 2010, he famously said: "I didn't think I'd regret trying and failing, and I suspected I would always be haunted by a decision to not try at all."

ADSAI projects are not guaranteed successes, and if we fear failure, no project would begin at all, which brings us back to FastFoodCo from the start of the chapter. How did two analytically mature organizations manage to struggle with what should have been a straightforward task?

They struggled for the very reasons we expand upon in this book and, as we wrote, although it looked like a technical failure, it was anything but. The project was complex and pushed beyond the boundaries of previous work. Having succeeded in a number of other projects, FastFoodCo was ready to innovate further. What they stumbled on is the common thread for all topics discussed here. You'll notice that the difficulties presented in this chapter did not arise from technical challenges and, even if they did, underlying these technical problems was always a deeper challenge—a people one. This challenge faces *all* projects, not just ADSAI.

For the FastFoodCo project, if they had managed to create better clarity, oversight, and communication throughout, which could have helped avoid the situation of two separate FastFoodCo teams, the financial damage for the consultants might have been avoided. This wasn't a case of poor project management or structures, or even missing team roles and responsibilities, there was simply *not enough clear communication* between the real-time and batch teams, both verbal and documented. This led to ill-matched data features and data pipelines between pilot and production.

Under normal circumstances, an ML engineer (the consultant) has less understanding of the data pipeline side, but when it comes to building data systems for machine learning, a data team won't know the issues the way an ML team does. In the usual case, the consultants or ML engineer would have designed and delivered the project end-to-end, but for a variety of practical reasons, it didn't make sense in the FastFoodCo project. Could we really fault either team for the approach taken?

Given that FastFoodCo had its own data team, it made sense to use internal teams and not outsource to consultants (saving both money and time). But it also meant that the consultants were on the *outside* and not present for FastFoodCo's standup meetings; they weren't seeing what the company was doing for the most critical resource: data. Having ML engineers who can flex into the data engineering side would be valuable. Opening up the communication and joining the standups would have allowed the ML engineers to foresee real-time data issues better than the data team.

Again, it would have cost more to have the external consultant involved in 15- to 30-minute standups every day during the pipeline development. (During the project, they only held one or two meetings every week: A higher-level scheduled status meeting and some ad hoc catch ups with the data engineers.) Involving the engineer consultants on a more regular basis would have caught the issue of incompatible data forms in time—a data team wouldn't always pick this up. If the ML engineers had been more integrally involved, they could have done the pipeline work themselves—micro-batching would have sufficed and real-time may not have been necessary.[11]

The technical problems at FastFoodCo were caused by people problems, which are always the most challenging for any organization. We may never be able to completely eliminate these types of problems. If we were able to solve all our people problems, it would truly take us to nirvana and then more than mere ASDAI failures would be avoided. We would no longer need to worry about why analytics projects fail, but any project ever. The challenge of people problems is so great that we may never reach our 0% failure rate goal. We have to accept that not every project will succeed as long as humans are at the helm and while ADSAI projects deliver results beyond their own silo. Playing on the phrase to err is human, Henry Petroski once wrote a book, *To Engineer is Human*, we believe even more that To Analyze is Human.

Critical Thinking: How Not to Fail

- Companies continually underestimate the effort required to deploy an ADSAI tool. Why do you suspect this is the case?
- What can you do if the champion of your project leaves? What should you have done beforehand to prepare and mitigate this risk?

- As problems become larger, their potential impact becomes larger and silos must be broken down. This can lead to the benefits of projects having a greater impact but also to challenges with delivering such complex projects. This is an area in which analytical maturity is key. List some of the principles you have learned in this book that are key to success.

- Humility is a leadership and organizational trait that generally leads to better employee engagement although this isn't unique to ADSAI projects. What aspects of ADSAI projects in particular can benefit from a humbler leadership?

- If you had faced a case similar to the SAVI project when it came to the scope creep, what would you have done differently?

- If we stopped failing at ADSAI projects, what serious implications could this have that are worse than trying and failing?

Notes

1. Bernardi, L., Mavridis, T., & Estévez, P. A. (2019, July). 150 successful machine learning models: 6 lessons learned at Booking.com. *KDD '19: Proceedings of the 25th ACM SIGKDD International Conference on Knowledge Discovery & Data Mining*, 1743–1751. https://doi.org/10.1145/3292500.3330744.

2. Nielsen, R. G., & Marrone, J. A. (2018). Humility: Our current understanding of the construct and its role in organizations. *International Journal of Management Reviews*, 20(4), 805–824. https://doi.org/10.1111/ijmr.12160.

3. Chandler, J. A., Johnson, N. E., Jordan, S. L., B, D. K., & Short, J. C. (2023). A meta-analysis of humble leadership: Reviewing individual, team, and organizational outcomes of leader humility. *The Leadership Quarterly*, 34(1), 101660. https://doi.org/10.1016/j.leaqua.2022.101660.

4. Aiello, C. (2018, April 17). Elon Musk admits humans are sometimes superior to robots, in a tweet about Tesla delays. *CNBC*. https://www.cnbc.com/2018/04/13/elon-musk-admits-humans-are-sometimes-superior-to-robots.html.

5. Slater, D. (n.d.) Elements of Amazon's Day 1 culture. AWS Executive Insights. Amazon Web Services, Inc. https://aws.amazon.com/executive-insights/content/how-amazon-defines-and-operationalizes-a-day-1-culture/.

6. Klein, G. A. (2009). *Streetlights and Shadows: Searching for the Keys to Adaptive Decision Making*. MIT Press. https://doi.org/10.7551/mitpress/8369.001.0001.

7. Blake, M., & Bean, C. (2023, January 6). SAVI transforms surgical instrument tracking with Google Cloud. *Google Cloud Blog*. https://cloud.google.com/blog/products/ai-machine-learning/savi-transforms-surgical-instrument-tracking-with-google-cloud.

8. Taylor, J. (2023, June 12). Jeff Bezos' most outrageous business failures. *GOBankingRates*. https://www.nasdaq.com/articles/jeff-bezos-most-outrageous-business-failures.

9. Failory. (2021, May 31). What Was Google Health and Why Was it Discontinued? *Failory*. https://www.failory.com/google/health.

10. Gainty, C. (2023, January 16). From a 'deranged' provocateur to IBM's failed AI superproject: the controversial story of how data has transformed healthcare. *The Conversation*. https://theconversation.com/from-a-deranged-provocateur-to-ibms-failed-ai-superproject-the-controversial-story-of-how-data-has-transformed-healthcare-189362.

11. It is advisable to only maintain one set of feature engineering code. A lot of orchestration of batch vs. real-time is handled by modern tools (like Apache Beam). Technology products may cost more, but it saves the data scientist from versioning features and making sure the features and data are available for batch and real time. Work can also be centralized with more sophisticated tools, such as a feature store, so that only a single version of each feature is generated and the different latency and cost requirements of the batch and real-time workloads are handled automatically at the infrastructure layer. What you can do is, instead of centralizing all the data, each part owns their data, but the features are central (i.e., a central source of truth for metrics). This is a more advanced paradigm and one that would have saved FastFoodCo a lot of trouble, but certainly not something an analytically immature organization would typically think of or be able to do.

7

Conclusion

> Investigation and research done a few years ago under the auspices of the Carnegie Foundation for the Advancement of Teaching uncovered a most important and significant fact – a fact later confirmed by additional studies made at the Carnegie Institute of Technology. These investigations revealed that even in such technical lines as engineering, about 15 percent of one's financial success is due to one's technical knowledge and about 85 percent is due to skill in human engineering – to personality and the ability to lead people.
>
> **—Dale Carnegie**[1]

As we have observed throughout this book, most of the failures and mistakes involving data science are not because of difficult technical issues or concerns, but result from a need for greater strength in "soft skills," i.e., the *human factors*. Data *science, machine* learning, and *artificial* intelligence are academic disciplines—the names of which are misleading in the context of *implementation* in real-world human settings that are, of course, determined by people, human nature, human behavior, and different types of management skills.

To illustrate this, we will now "flip the script" with a departure from failures, and end the book on a positive note with a success story about one of Doug's favorite people, whom we shall call "Rusty."

If Doug were putting up a billboard to promote this story, the sign would read "People Make All the Difference in Determining a Successful Outcome" and Rusty's likeness would be featured prominently next to the text. Doug had the good fortune to have Rusty on his Optimization Solutions team at Southwest Airlines. In Doug's professional opinion as a 30-year veteran practitioner, leader, and educator, Rusty is a *paragon of excellence* in the sense that he embodies 100% of the attributes of a *world-class, top 1% ADSAI professional*:

- A very positive "can-do," "get it done" attitude, upbeat "lean forward" demeanor, and almost always has a smile on his face. This is simply his personality.
- Educated at outstanding technical schools and displays superior technical acumen and skills in modeling and coding (i.e., BA from Rice University in computational and applied math, and Texas A&M Graduate Studies in industrial engineering).

DOI: 10.1201/9781032661360-8

- Digs deep to understand the detailed context of the business problems he is modeling.
- Creatively and energetically deals with data and systems issues.
- Focuses exclusively on his customers' highest priorities and most pressing problems.
- Excellent communication skills in all phases of his work.
- Closely partners with customers throughout the project life cycle to ease the strain of change.
- Carefully bridges the gap between the "art of the possible" and what is realistically achievable.
- Displays extraordinary project- and solution-delivery acumen, skills, and capabilities.
- Focuses on using the right tool for the job, resulting in quick delivery of value.
- Ability to lead the successful development and production deployment of multiple game changing OR solutions for his company, i.e., impeccable holistic delivery execution skills.
- Exhibits tremendous empathy for his customers in their problem-solving struggles.
- Member of the *9-figure Annual Business Value Capture Club* (to be explained later).

His story personifies our principal thesis.

Among other high-value projects he has completed at Southwest, Rusty is best known for being the architect, product owner, and team leader of their Crew Planning Optimization solution. Airline crew schedule development is, mathematically speaking, one of, if not the most difficult problems for an airline to solve. Airline crew planning is concerned with finding a minimum cost assignment of flight crews to a given flight schedule while satisfying restrictions dictated by collective bargaining (union) agreements and the Federal Aviation Administration (work rules for safety). Crew labor costs are the single greatest operating expense for most airlines, closely followed by jet fuel.

Traditionally, from a technical perspective, the problem has been modeled as a set partitioning (or set covering) problem, both of which are well known to be NP-complete (which means no polynomial time algorithm exists that is guaranteed to solve the problem, i.e., it is difficult to optimally solve real-world-sized problems in a reasonable amount of time). The problem is further complicated by myriad complex contractual and FAA work rules governing how many hours pilots and flight attendants can work or must rest in a day, week, month, and year, as well as rules governing trip length, i.e., 2-, 3-, 4-day trips, and so on.

Crew planning is an ongoing intensive and highly stressful endeavor because flight schedules are continually changing, and work rules continually evolve with each new labor contract. Each flight schedule, contract, and/or FAA rule change requires refreshing, redeveloping, retesting, revalidating, and redeploying the crew planning solution model and code base. Working nights, weekends, and holidays are not at all uncommon in order to hit mandated deadlines. There is *zero tolerance* for failure. *The crew schedule must be published on time.*

For the past 24 years, Rusty has been the primary operations research developer and Crew Planning Department customer partner for the ongoing design, development, testing, validation, production implementation, support, and maintenance of the Crew Planning Optimization solution at Southwest Airlines, known as **DPOS** (**D**uty **P**eriod **O**ptimization **S**ystem). He has formed strong, long-lasting, and unbreakable bonds with his customers. Claire Taitte, former Senior Manager of Inflight Crew Planning and Analysis, was one of Rusty's customer partners. She observed,

> Rusty was like our optimization James Bond. During each major scheduling crisis during my 20-year career working with Rusty, from 9/11 through COVID, we could count on Rusty to deliver a solution that exceeded our expectations. However, unlike James Bond, Rusty did it while maintaining a lovely family and without a huge ego.

Dr. Phil Beck, Rusty's former first line manager, confirmed, "Rusty provides tremendous value to his customers through his technical skills, thorough understanding of the customer business processes and objectives, and willingness to do whatever it takes to meet project goals and deadlines."

His commitment to excellence, customer partnership, and outstanding performance in Crew Planning Optimization earned Rusty the *President's Award*, the *highest honor* a Southwest associate can receive.

Rusty's impact and accomplishments can be summed up in the following vignette.

In the late 2010s, Southwest Airlines decided to retire its legacy internally developed crew planning system (i.e., UI, application, databases, etc.) and replace it with a new-and-improved software application platform. A request for proposal (RFP) process was conducted and an in-depth evaluation and benchmark of vendor finalists was carried out, including of the respective crew planning optimizers, against the status quo incumbent. In the comparison of optimizer modules, Southwest's own DPOS was declared the winner "hands down" because it produced lower cost and more operationally efficient and effective crew plans than any of the prospective competitor vendor bidders. After a long, thorough evaluation process and with all due consideration, Southwest's Crew Planning Department leadership decided to dismiss all of the vendor finalists and build the new system *in-house*, primarily due to the differential business impact generated by Rusty and DPOS. This would remain the core component of the new system.

As a final validation of the decision, I asked Rusty to conduct an experiment to determine the exact *annual maximal incremental business value and economic impact* of DPOS. The experiment was as follows:

1. Use DPOS to generate a *feasible* crew plan, but one that was not optimized, meaning it would be *functional* but not efficient or cost effective, as if it were generated "manually in a naive manner," and calculate the annual cost (i.e., DPOS optimizer "dials and knobs" turned down to zero).

2. Use DPOS to generate a *fully optimized* crew plan, meaning it would be maximally efficient and cost effective, and calculate the annual cost (i.e., DPOS optimizer "dials and knobs" turned up to the maximum capability).

3. Compare the *total crew labor cost* of the *unoptimized* and *optimized* DPOS crew plans.

The result was *astounding*. The annual crew labor cost differential between the naive unoptimized crew plan and the fully optimized plan was *$100 million*. That is the *additional* cost (~0.5% of annual revenue) that Southwest would incur annually *without* DPOS and Rusty.

Even with Rusty's tremendous intellect, attitude, commitment, and skill, there is no way he could have achieved that result on his own. The integral partnership and trusting relationship that Rusty developed with his Crew Planning Department colleagues working shoulder-to-shoulder for more than two decades is what made the difference and enabled the end result. Rusty is also supported by a small, but elite team of OR staff whom he has trained and developed over the years. Interestingly, confirming the Carnegie Foundation research project, it is Rusty's *personality, demeanor, behavior, and relationship* with his customer, and his leadership with his team, which make the greatest difference in his performance and DPOS outcomes. Many people "can do the math" but relatively very few embody Rusty's unfailing dedication, commitment, perseverance, thoroughness, judgment, positive outlook, and attitude in the *crucible* of some of the most intensive, time-sensitive, and deadline-driven problem solving in the airline industry.

From his tenure at Southwest as the leader of the Enterprise Data, Analytics, and Optimization Solutions team, Doug is most proud of working alongside his HR business partner to create a new position, job description, and level of *Principal OR Advisor*, so Rusty could receive a promotion from Senior OR Analyst, the point at which he had "capped out" in the organizational hierarchy. Anyone who works in big corporations knows that creating a new position is no small feat and requires a "labor of love," but no one was more worthy of it than Rusty. Principal OR Advisor remains the highest individual contributor level for an OR professional at Southwest Airlines, and, to date, multiple staff on Doug's former team have been promoted into that role.

In his position at Southwest, Doug was fortunate to have a phenomenal team of ADSAI professionals and leaders, and the list of their accomplishments is long and distinguished by multiple *President's Award* designations, industry award-winning projects, accolades from customers, with business value and economic impacts across the enterprise in crew training, event and facility scheduling, airline operations control, jet fuel and liquor inventory management, and much more. Rusty is representative of the kind of person that every ADSAI leader wants to recruit and hire onto their team, and will go to great lengths to retain. In the end, such people can make all the difference.

Continuing the Success

We tend to overestimate the effect of a technology in the short run and underestimate the effect in the long run.

—Amara's Law (Roy Amara)

Both co-authors are committed to supporting more ADSAI projects to succeed, because we have spent our careers working with complex ADSAI only to see too many of our colleague's projects fail. What is most concerning at this time is the unrealistic expectations of a society misled by hype surrounding just what ADSAI can achieve. The principle expounded in Amara's Law is as applicable to analytics, data science, and AI as it is to general technologies.

The extraordinary levels of misrepresentation surrounding AI have surpassed even that of analytics in the post-*Moneyball* era, with the promise of game-changing impacts in every industry; the threat of ChatGPT and robots eliminating millions of white- and blue-collar jobs, robot world domination, and human redundancy leading the 24-hour AI-focused news cycle. What feeds the exaggerated claims surrounding analytics and AI is the success of the few companies that are creating tremendous business value and yielding significant economic impact based on their mature AI capabilities (or sometimes just luck).

In conclusion, to temper this exuberance, we will summarize our main points to ensure they can be easily remembered and hopefully lead to change.

To reiterate our initial thesis, the greatest danger exists for analytically immature organizations to be misled by the hype. For these entities, an estimated nine out of ten projects will fail to deliver the desired outcome. To avoid this, we strongly recommend building the foundations in a pragmatic way by focusing on some small projects within your existing people and technical capabilities that will be able to deliver a commercial gain, while being aligned with your business strategy. Build from there.

The co-authors' professional experiences and insights as to why data science projects fail were consistently confirmed by our research into an inordinate amount of original source material, including:

- Published materials from fellow practitioners in blog posts, white papers, podcasts, videos, and similar "less scientific" outlets.
- Peer-reviewed articles published in scientific journals and conferences.
- Interviews with peers.
- Asking ChatGPT to reveal what it had learned about ADSAI project failures.

Despite ubiquitous best practices and helpful frameworks, it turns out that these elevated rubrics fail at the level of addressing the detail that constitutes the root of the complexity in executing and delivering ADSAI projects. These factors include:

- The necessity of understanding the business problem and ensuring it is aligned with corporate strategy instead of a void in vision or strategy being replaced by belief in the hype.
- Failure to select the most impactful problems to solve.
- Data issues such as its procurement and management.
- A lack of proper application of the model with too much focus on techniques and technologies.
- The importance of possessing soft skills to deal with the human dimensions, for example,
  - Communication
  - Change management
  - Project management (the "art" component of this)
  - Focusing on business priorities
- Setting realistic expectations as opposed to overly high, unrealistic ones.
- The existence of capability gaps arguably caused by the nontechnical inexperience of data science practitioners, which is in turn exacerbated by university education programs that are overly focused on technical topic domains and need greater focus on the realities of ADSAI project execution and delivery.

- Too much focus on the technology, manifested by treating ADSAI like an "IT project" with the resulting overreliance on software tools by practitioners.
- Insufficient engagement of business stakeholders, subject matter/ domain experts, and end users, which leads to change management roadblocks in using the resulting solution/product.
- The high complexity of production environments compared to the generalized frameworks, which may work well for the initial sand-box models but not for enterprise-wide AI tools, making the transition to business as usual rife with issues, such as:
  - (Near) real-time data pipelines
  - APIs connecting to other systems
  - Automatic data- and model-drift detection and refitting
  - Availability, reliability, performance, and fault tolerance

According to conventional wisdom, failure is often defined to encompass deficiencies in scope, timeline, quality, and budget. These are the typical metrics of project success and relevant for our context. However, we categorize success and failure as encompassing the following:

- Was the model fully implemented (i.e., deployed to production, as a decision support system that continually generates value)?
- Was the model then utilized to solve a business problem (that the business cares about), answer a key business question, or make a decision (i.e., is anyone using it, and has it improved their circumstances? Did it generate useful insights? What was the outcome relative to the original intent of the project?)
- Was significant, tangible, measurable business value and/or economic impact generated/manifested? Even better, was it then used as originally intended?

Our research determined that the failure of data science projects has many sources. We grouped them into four themes:

- Strategy
- Process
- People and
- Technology

We'll now summarize the main points from each theme.

Strategy

The most difficult part of executing ADSAI projects correctly begins with *strategy*. The main strategic failings (among others) that we discovered in our research are as follows:

- Failing to build the *need* in the organization
  - Poorly defined use case
  - No clear business value
  - No actionable insights
  - A solution looking for a problem
- Lack of, or alignment to, vision or strategy (often caused by poor data maturity)
- Not clearly measuring success (unclear deliverables, missing actionable insights)
- Lack of leadership/upper management buy-in and alignment among the senior leaders
- A culture of decision-making not grounded upon being data-driven, model-based, and analytically oriented
- Solving problems that aren't business priorities

Understanding the business problem at hand is often a point at which data science projects go awry. Sometimes business people themselves do not completely understand what the real problem is. Therefore, we should not be surprised if the data scientist needs to personally investigate, along with their business counterparts, to determine the real nature of the problem to be solved. Sometimes organizations do understand the problem, but there can be a breakdown in communication, such as a lack of clear explanation from the business, or a failure to adequately listen and ask clarifying questions on the part of the data scientist, which inhibits developing a mutual understanding of the problem. Getting to a clearly stated and mutually understood problem definition, as well as associated business process flows, data flows, and decision-making processes and criteria, is foundational to initiating and successfully completing a data science project.

There is folklore in the optimization community of a statement poignantly made by one of the greatest contributors to the field, George Dantzig. Dantzig was a pioneer in the field of operations research and invented one of the core technologies used to solve linear programming problems: the simplex algorithm. He was also a winner of the President's National Medal of Science, among many other accolades. (You may not even realize you know who Dantzig is, but if you have ever seen Matt Damon in *Good Will Hunting*, you know about him.) Few people have influenced the field more than he did.

In an interview in the 1980s, the optimization specialist was asked what his top contribution to the field was. Listeners were expecting him to respond with one of his algorithms, but he didn't. According to the rumors, Dantzig is supposed to have retorted: "My greatest contribution may have been to force business people to think clearly about what they really wanted."

Dantzig understood that his work forced businesses to clarify their objectives and think about the entire context in which their different potential decisions were operating—which was often more valuable than the solution itself.

It goes without saying that businesses and data scientists should focus on problems and data science projects that represent an agreed upon (high) business priority, i.e., projects that will realistically generate significant business value and economic impact, however you measure it. Unfortunately, that is not always the case. Sometimes, organizations do not have a clear set of prioritized projects ranked on true business values. Even if they do, sometimes data scientists, and, yes, even business people, get distracted by other initiatives that consume time and resources, causing both a lack of focus and a clear path to failure.

Process

The *process* of executing and delivering ADSAI projects is fraught with potential pitfalls that can cause failure if not properly accounted for and thoroughly addressed, including:

- Data issues
- Setting reasonable expectations
- Communication

The challenges associated with data are many and will continue to beleaguer data science projects. Historically, it involved not having enough data or not having it in one place for analysis, or proceeding with too much data in too many forms and in too many locations. Great strides are being made in the fields of data engineering and data governance, as well as the development of technology platforms that support these endeavors. The volume and dynamism of data generated by myriad enterprise systems, e-commerce, and social media platforms, IoT devices, etc., will continue to generate more data than most enterprises can realistically, let alone easily, manage. The key for successful data science projects is to focus on the data that you *must* have for the project to get to MVP/M (minimum viable product or model). Additional relevant data can always be added when it becomes available down the road. A short story will well-illustrate this point, which was told to Doug by an unnamed company's former regional CIO.

Several years ago, a global beverage and snack brand manufacturer hired a well-known global consulting company to collect, organize, catalog, index, and store *100% of the company's data* in a data warehouse, complete with data lineage, metadata, lookup tables, etc. The project was a mandate from the CEO and global CIO as part of the company's *Digital Transformation* initiative to enable the company to be more data-driven, make better and more informed decisions, faster. After more than three years of diligent effort, and exhausting the project's entire low 9-figure budget, the company and their consultants realized that they had only captured about *50% of the company's existing data portfolio, or half of the original intended scope.*

Although the company and their consultants were plowing through the capture of enterprise data sets, the data portfolio grew and grew, either in new data sources, data set additions, or refreshes to existing data, much, much faster than the project team could capture the data. The project was canceled and pronounced a failure, because the scope deficit, budget overruns, and extended timelines were deemed unacceptable. The company avoided the sunk cost fallacy and wisely decided not to throw good money after bad.

What went wrong?

Doug has faced similar challenges when leading large enterprise data organizations, however, he takes a decidedly different approach upon realizing that there is no way to successfully catch a "data tsunami" with pails, buckets, or even Olympic-sized swimming pools. His approach involves first recognizing that not all data has equal value. For example, customer transaction purchase history data that can be used to estimate customer lifetime value (LTV) is more valuable than the maintenance history data on HQ parking lot lighting. Second, before embarking on a project to collect enterprise data, the team needs to determine what data it really needs to answer the most pressing questions, solve the most complex problems, or make the most important business decisions that will generate the most business value and economic impact. For example, data for a customer 360-degree view to see how Net Promoter Scores (NPS) impact LTV over time. Lastly, data collection must be prioritized and limited in scope based on business value potential, for example, limiting initial data collection to 20% of existing data with prioritization and scope based on greatest business value potential, then prioritizing the next X% of existing data based on the next most economically impactful set of questions, problems, or decisions to address. The team can then "rinse and repeat" this process as many times as necessary, as budgets permit, to build the *highest-value enterprise data portfolio.* This three-step approach, focused on value-based prioritization of data capture, can help avoid a three-year, low-9 figure, 50% data-capture project catastrophe.

No one likes to be disappointed or fail, and the fallout that follows a failed ADSAI project can wreck relationships with colleagues and stakeholders. Everyone wants their data science projects to help their company and stakeholders, and of course their own career progression. All the more important reasons for setting realistic expectations on all of the relevant KPIs for the project, i.e., scope, timing, budget, and business value targets. Leaning toward conservatism is the best approach and usually proves successful (longer term). Stretch goals are fine, as are BHAGs (Big Hairy Audacious Goals). Epic fails, caused by over-promising and under-delivering, can ruin your career (or even get you fired). Sandbagging promotes skepticism and leaves constituents with a lack of trust the next time around.

Setting the wrong expectations is only exacerbated by the hype surrounding AI. Many vendors (and the media) would have us believe that implementing AI projects is simple—something we've touched on throughout the book. But this is wrong. Properly completing an AI project requires a lot of work on many fronts, especially the people side. In an MIT Sloan Management review report published in 2020, the authors revealed how a data science tool on its own isn't the solution: "Organizations that extensively change business processes when integrating AI solutions are five times as likely to realize significant financial benefits."[2] There's an enormous gap between those who make no changes to *any* business processes and those who make extensive changes to *many* business processes. This is influenced by realistic expectations around what an AI project really entails and the changes it can cause to people's roles.

Communication is critical between all parties involved, especially the data scientist (and AI translator) and the business manager ("customer"), as well as data engineers, software engineers, business analysts, data governance analysts, end users, subject matter experts, and potentially many others. Additional individuals who bring unique skill sets and perspectives are often required to complete a data science project. Clear, concise communication is essential for success because it fosters mutual understanding and agreement among all parties on all the critical facets of the project. If there are n people on a project, the number of possible communication links between them are $n(n-1)$, or on the order of n^2 (i.e., complexity rises faster than people may linearly expect). It's no wonder Brooks's Law states that adding resources to an already late project will only make it later… just the additional communication alone will further derail an off-track project.

Finally, the project approach can play a big role in whether an ADSAI project succeeds or fails. Beginning with a minimum viable product or model is often recommended—except when it's not. This serves to remind us of the complexity of ADSAI, and that cookie cutter approaches are a surefire way to lower your chances of success.

Project management has evolved to be considered both a science and an art. Techniques like PERT/CPM and Agile burn-down charts attempt to quantify and measure how a project is progressing and how well a team is performing. These tools are invaluable to a project manager, but they primarily *inform*. There is a disproportionate amount of additional *judgment* that must be applied to managing the scientific modeling aspect of a data science project, as well as the systems development activity.

Measuring and gauging the complexity of a task that will impact resource consumption and timelines is a skill that comes from the experience of working on numerous projects with wide ranging, high and low levels of difficulty, and learning how to approach and solve them. Measuring and gauging a team's output and productivity level as it rises and wanes over the course of a long project is a skill developed through observation, informed by data, and active interaction with team members as they climb steep learning curves and struggle to overcome a series of challenges with data, changes in scope, infrastructure issues, etc. Project managers who know when to challenge and when to relent, and by how much, are a rare and skilled breed of professional who evolve from experience over time, and not from PM certification courses alone.

Another aspect that can decrease the chances of success is not working closely with the customer, or even worse, leaving out the customers' voice altogether. Having their close involvement throughout the project is not a luxury, it is a *must* if you want to ensure the end result is used and doesn't just become shelfware.

People

As in any scientific endeavor, experimentation, data collection, and analysis are part of the process, combined with the use of advanced mathematics, sophisticated software, and computer technology. Notwithstanding the science and technology, the practice of data science takes place in the private sector (e.g., business, industry, research) and public sector (e.g., government, military, law enforcement), all of which are inhabited and operated by *human beings*.

Human involvement in data science is substantial and materially significant in every step of the process, and requires the development and application of many "soft skills" that necessarily facilitate successful execution and completion of data science projects. Of all the soft skills required, communication is by far the most critical and foundational to successfully executing data science projects and one that we covered many times. Specifically,

- Listening, to understand;
- Being heard, to be understood;
- Speaking and writing concisely, impactfully, and tailored to the target audience; and
- Gaining a deep level of mutual understanding of all aspects of a project.

As in any human endeavor involving teams of people, whether it be a co-ed softball team, an expedition climbing Mt. Everest, or delivering a data science project, *empathy* is the most important quality to embody regardless of how incredibly difficult things get along the journey. Add to that a dose of humility, and you could be like our friend Rusty. And trust us, as worthwhile as data science projects may be, things will get difficult at many, many points along the way, and you cannot afford to alienate any constituents, partners, teammates, or stakeholders. *People rarely forget heroes, but they certainly never forget jerks.* You may (barely) get through one project, but you will *never* get through another one by treating everyone involved with anything less than *The Platinum Rule (which states that you should do unto others as they'd like done unto them.)* Some of the best advice on how to do this well can be found in *The Platinum Rule* by Michael O'Connor, PhD and Tony Alessandra, PhD, as well as Dale Carnegie's book *How to Win Friends & Influence People*.[1,3]

Once good communication is underway, the next critical step, per Jim Collins' famous adage, is "getting the right people on the bus." Having the right types of resources with the right skills is foundationally critical to success, and its absence is an often-encountered point of failure in ADSAI projects. Apart from high IQ, characterized by impeccable math and coding skills, *emotional intelligence*, or EQ, is necessary to address all of the "soft skill" dimensions of being a data scientist and is even more important than IQ, according to the Dale Carnegie study.

Having the best math and code means nothing if trusting relationships and partnerships with business stakeholders are not firmly established so that everyone is in harmonious lockstep on the journey. This starts with the definition of the business problem, then includes data collection and solution design, development, testing, validation, deployment, and implementation, and finishes with all of the business process changes that go along with the solution. Out of all the unique needs for an ADSAI project, one key resource role that is evolving to become a critical one is that of analytics (or AI) translator.

University education has always played and continues to play a critical role, through rigorous coursework and theses, in establishing strong ADSAI *technical* skills. Fortunately, our research found that among the nation's best MS in Data Science programs that we surveyed, most now incorporate a combination of courses to provide students with learning opportunities that go beyond pure technical skill development and better address real-world challenges. These include:

- Capstone
- Practicum
- Internship
- Colloquium
- Storytelling and Communication
- Dialogue with real-world ADSAI professionals on project dynamics

- Managing Data Science Projects
- Co-operative education incorporating professional work and on-the-job training

Although, as flagged in the People chapter, these are often a minor component or final part of the degree, and not an integral part incorporated into the student's study throughout the degree. This is a shame. The 2021 Anaconda "State of Data Science" report (a survey of 4,299 individuals from more than 140 countries) highlights that,

> Overall, soft and business-related skills were the most significant gaps between what universities teach and what organizations need. Being involved in strategic business conversations and communicating and explaining results to stakeholders are skill sets that can bridge the gap between data literacy and decision making.[4]

The co-authors strongly believe that there is indeed an urgent need to fill this void in university education, based on our accumulated awareness of the potential pitfalls that can cause ADSAI initiatives to go awry, and on our more thorough understanding of the most prevalent, salient reasons *why* data science projects fail. There is a clear and present opportunity to enhance and extend the ADSAI curriculum and learning experience to more directly address the types of factors espoused in this book.

In addition to the outstanding technical curricula, and real-world capstone, practicum, internship, and colloquium courses offered by MS programs at universities, both co-authors strongly advocate for and recommend including the research and lessons taught by this book in a standalone seminar course, or incorporating it into one of the other practicum courses taught by industry professionals or clinical professors of practice who can also provide *their own examples* of how and why data science projects fail. We believe this vital course content would provide an invaluable perspective on the pitfalls in executing real-world ADSAI projects at scale, and how to avoid them.

A final suggestion that all courses would benefit from is less focus on the models and more focus on the data. Many university curricula simply lack the single most important course for building models—*working with data*. This is an endemic problem that is not just confined to applied mathematics degrees, but is also relevant for computer science. We introduced in the Process chapter the journal paper, "Everyone wants to do the model work, not the data work," which directly summarizes the situation:

> Lack of adequate training on AI data quality, collection, and ethics led to practitioner under-preparedness in dealing with the complexity of creating datasets in high-stakes domains. AI courses focused on toy datasets with clean values (e.g., UCI Census, Kaggle datasets), but AI in practice

required the creation of data pipelines, often from scratch, going from ground truth to model maintenance.[5]

A significant leading indicator as to whether a company will succeed or fail in their ADSAI endeavors, initiatives, and projects is the nature of the company's *culture*. Is the company truly top-to-bottom, side-to-side data-driven, model-based, and analytically inclined in their thinking and approach to strategy, tactics, problem solving, decision-making, and question-answering? Do leaders and managers "let the data speak"? Or do they rely on the HIPPO (Highest Paid Person's Opinion), who can often be relying on tried-and-true rules, potentially outdated assumptions, and historical business conditions to guide them? The balance required here is to achieve this without ignoring employee expertise.

For successful examples, consider CEO Bob Crandall at American Airlines (AA), where the CEO and CFO set the tone for the company's mode of operations based on data and analytics, or Gary Loveman, who as COO (then CEO) saved Harrah's (later Caesar's) from bankruptcy and introduced data, analytics, and loyalty card (tracking) programs to the casino gaming and resort hotel industry.[6] Capital One CEO Richard Fairbank's team runs *80,000 marketing experiments per year* to target financial products at the individual customer levels. There may be isolated ADSAI projects that succeed in a company in which the culture—and the CEO—are not thoroughly bought into and firmly aligned with data and models; nonetheless, it is highly likely that the company will *never* become an analytical competitor fully leveraging ADSAI across the enterprise to achieve strategic competitive advantage. It is all too easy for less disciplined managers and contributors to do things the way they have always done them.

ADSAI projects induce inordinately large amounts of *change*, however, as *MIT Sloan Management Review* reminds us, change needs to be embraced before it can add value. Data science fundamentally, and even radically, changes the way that problems are solved, questions are answered, and decisions are made. In general, the transition to becoming a fact-based, data-driven enterprise is transformational and thereby fraught with many dimensions of change, including moving away from the use of gut instinct supported alone by Excel-based heuristics and principles, to more rigorously rational, model-based approaches to complex problem solving and decision-making. Data scientists may lead the way, but *everyone* must go on the journey together. Data scientists may inform and teach others how these advanced techniques and technologies function, but *everyone*, from analysts to managers to executives, must "buy in" to be successful both in individual projects and in the overall transformation driven by data science methods and stakeholders.

At the risk of repetition, we can't emphasize enough that communication plays a critical role in managing change and winning over hearts and minds.

Storytelling with before-and-after comparisons including lots of data visualization to highlight the business impact generated by data science model-based solutions are crucial to demonstrating and proving the efficacy of these scientific approaches to management. (Most people love stories, especially with images included to help them understand complex topics.)

Opting into augmentation-based AI methods and iterative interactive optimization approaches can ease the transition from the exclusively human- and Excel-centered approaches to problem solving and decision-making, to the compelling alternative founded on the greater analytical rigor offered by data science. Everyone in the stakeholder/constituent group must be convinced beyond a reasonable doubt that all of the (sometimes painful) changes driven by data science are worthwhile because of the business value and economic impact that will be achieved. (That is, "the juice is worth the squeeze.")

Technology

Notwithstanding our emphasis on soft skills, or lack thereof, as a cause of data science project failure, there are myriad ways in which technology issues can present obstacles to trip up organizations.

Misapplying a model (in all senses of meaning) often occurs when faulty or improper assumptions are made about the applicability of a particular model form or its usage to solve the problem at hand. Experimental design is a critically important skill that is often lost on citizen data scientists, and some professional data scientists, and is usually attributable to a lack of training and education in the subject. Although techniques can be quantitatively applied, there is also an artfulness to a well-designed, statistically valid experiment. Predictive model bias and overfitting are also common errors that result in invalid results, but can be avoided with properly applied techniques, for example, k-fold cross-validation. When in doubt, consult with a professor or more experienced colleague, and check the textbooks and online references to ensure that the model you are employing is valid, and the experiment you are running is suitable for the problem at hand. (Google or ChatGPT is your friend because it is highly unlikely that you are the first person to encounter a given type of problem, or one that is similar. A thorough literature search is encouraged for model development.)

The final and highest hurdle to achieving ADSAI project success is advancing the model from the sandbox (of your desktop or cloud-based work area) to become a full-fledged production system (e.g., microservice or stand-alone) embedded in a high-value business process. Availability, reliability, and repeatability are necessary elements for the model/system to power the "flywheel" of continuously ongoing business value creation without regular human intervention. This process/journey requires a team to be able to realize the endgame—business people (i.e., executives for funding and political "air cover," line managers to drive change, and individual contributors to help design, develop, test, validate, and implement the solution), technology people (i.e., software, cloud, security, etc.), data people, and test/QA people. It may take months, years, or even a decade, and may cost hundreds of thousands or millions of dollars to deploy and implement completely, depending on the scope and complexity of the problem, and the level of sophistication and operational criticality of the model/system solution. The co-authors advise data scientists to make sure that the benefits delivered by their solution are proportional to the real costs of building and implementing the same, as assessed by whatever measures and metrics the finance department/board of directors utilizes (e.g., NPV, IRR, ROI, MARR).

As painful as it is to admit, after spending years and years studying, learning all of the mathematics, and learning to write and test code, you'll find that no one cares as deeply about the model, techniques, or technology as you do. People in business, and those higher up the leadership chain even exponentially more so, care more about the business value and top and bottom line economic impact of data science than the math or code. They trust that you "did the math" but they don't want to hear about it, they just want to see its impact.

Our advice is to not let yourself get "wrapped around the axle" with a lot of nuanced, overly sophisticated mathematics for its own sake when working on corporate data science projects. Please, do yourself, your constituents, and stakeholders a BIG favor, and save the math and code for the appendix of your presentation, for industry conferences and symposia, refereed academic journal publications, and data science center of excellence meetings. Always remember the Pareto principle (deliver 80% of the value for 20% of the effort), minimum viable product/model (MVP/M), and that perfection is the enemy of doneness. The model and code need to be tested, verified, and validated, but not perfect.

There is a considerable need for data and ADSAI tools and infrastructure to be available and well-managed to support the end-to-end process from model-building and experimentation through production deployment. This includes:

- Development environments and tools for professional and citizen data scientists
  - Python, also R, SAS, etc.
  - Dataiku, DataRobot, H2O.ai, Alteryx, etc.
  - Java, C#, Golang, Javascript (for UI/app developers)
- Project management and activity tracking apps (e.g., Jira, Bootcamp, Confluence, etc.)
- Data pipelines (via ETL software such as Talend, Alteryx, and more)

- APIs (for integration with enterprise apps)
- Data warehouse, data lake, data lakehouse, data mesh platforms for data integration
- Cloud computing (including server capacity and all of their MLOps, data tools)

These technologies and the science behind them are often what attract many data scientists to this field, but as erudite as they seem, it is the other factors that we've covered that are clearly more difficult to master.

Summary

To summarize, in addition to having knowledge of and the ability to apply the necessary technical skills and capabilities, data science project failure and success is largely *a function of how effectively and how closely data science strategy, people, processes, and projects are integrated and aligned with the business.* By "the business," we mean:

- *Leadership, Corporate, and Frontline Staff*, i.e., executive and mid-level leaders, as well as managers, supervisors, SMEs, and individual contributors, being supportive of fact-based, data-driven, model-based, and analytically inclined decision-making, problem solving, and question-answering as part of strategy, tactics, and operations.
- *Culture*, i.e., company belief systems and ways of thinking/working conducive to changing and evolving toward adoption of ADSAI principles, methods, and solutions, and dealing with the disruption of the *status quo* that ADSAI often causes.
- *Business Priorities*, i.e., data science projects being closely aligned to and integrated with those initiatives that are most important, relevant, and critical to the business.
- *Business Value Targets*, i.e., data science initiatives being focused on delivering value that is aimed at and aligned with KPIs, metrics that are most relevant to the business and domain at hand, and expectations that are realistically set on all phases of delivery execution, business value, and economic impact performance.
- *Business Processes*, i.e., data scientists committing to understand the way the business actually works in the domain at hand prior to attempting to improve upon the *status quo* using ADSAI, through hands-on task performance, first-hand observation and learning,

digesting annual reports, financial statements, and "tribal knowledge" shared by experienced staff.

- *Foundational Business Capabilities*, i.e., data science being closely integrated with and adhering to what are hopefully strong, well-established capabilities for communication, change management, and project management.

- *Delivering Value*, i.e., data scientists not getting overly focused on or enamored with models, techniques, or technologies, but rather focus on delivering tangible, measurable business value and economic impact using standard metrics like NPV, ROI, IRR, etc.

- *Data Engineering and IT*, i.e., data scientists and data science initiatives being closely aligned and integrated with data engineering (all departments) to ensure that high-quality data is available for all phases of ADSAI projects, and IT (all departments) ensuring that ADSAI models can be successfully developed in sandboxes and deployed into production systems to support critical business processes and operated on an ongoing basis with a high degree of availability, reliability, and efficacy (predictive accuracy performance).

Final Words

You learn nothing from success. Nothing. You learn everything from the failures.

—**Ed Sheeran (who was told he should have gotten a real job before becoming a global sensation)**[7]

The goal of the ADSAI fields of endeavor is to help solve complex strategic, tactical, and operational problems, and support and better enable data-based, model-driven decision-making. ADSAI professionals help their corporate partners answer key business questions in such a way that business value is created and economic impact is maximized. As quoted earlier in the book, Tom Davenport set the bar necessarily high when he said that "Models make the enterprise smarter; models embedded in systems and business processes make the enterprise more economically efficient." This is our desired outcome for the work of data scientists and the mindset with which we began our endeavors.

To analyze is human. Failure is feedback. Through our own failures, and those of others, we learn what is really necessary to succeed. Just ask Epic. Their failures led them to improve their ESM tool and provide hospitals with the needed caveats to prevent their own failures and dial down the ADSAI hype. By doing so, they saved lives—one of the noblest outcomes of data science—and reduced waste.

We hope this book will inspire more to see the world this way and reduce the billions in waste caused by preventable failures.

Critical Thinking: How Not to Fail

- What key characteristics did Rusty display in our descriptions of his traits and his story to help his projects avoid failure?
- What is the connection between Amara's Law and the hype we are seeing surrounding ADSAI?
- What do you see as the biggest gap in data science education leading to the greatest challenge for data scientists to long-term success in their career?
- What do you think we can do to change people's attitudes toward failure so we can exploit its valuable and sometimes expensive lessons?
- Why do you think that the success of such a technical area as data science depends so much on soft skills and people skills? Do you think this is more or less important than other functions in a business?
- Building AI projects relies on many capabilities to be in place in a business, the strategic direction, solid IT foundation, good processes, and more. On top of these foundations, we then build AI projects. What does the need for these foundations imply for the complexity of AI projects and hence their failure rates? Given this conclusion, what type of companies should be embarking on AI projects to augment their operations?

Notes

1. Carnegie, D. (2017). *How to Win Friends & Influence People*. Pocket Books. P. 18.
2. Ransbotham, S., Khodabandeh, S., Kiron, D., Candelon, K., Chu, M., & LaFountain, B. (2020). Expanding AI's Impact With Organizational Learning. *MIT Sloan Management Review*. Boston Consulting Group.
3. A few useful tenets of advice to supplement empathy and humility when times get tough:
   a. Assume positive intent.
   b. Give people the benefit of the doubt.

    c. Put yourself in the other person's position.

    d. Trust, but verify, until people prove themselves unworthy of your trust.

    e. Delete the angry e-mail before you hit SEND (better yet, don't even write the e-mail, go have a diplomatic conversation after a few deep breaths).

    f. Think, then breathe deeply, before you speak.

    g. Work the problem, don't blame the person who created or uncovered it.

    h. Read *Emotional Intelligence* by Daniel Goleman for great advice on EQ relative to IQ and the attributes of great senior executive leaders.

4. Team Anaconda. (2021). 2021 State of Data Science Report. Anaconda Cloud. https://anaconda.cloud/2021-state-of-data-science-report.

5. Sambasivan, N., Kapania, S., Highfill, H., Akrong, D., Paritosh, P., & Aroyo, L. (2021). "Everyone wants to do the model work, not the data work": Data Cascades in High-Stakes AI. *Proceedings of the 2021 CHI Conference on Human Factors in Computing Systems*, 39. https://doi.org/10.1145/3411764.3445518.

6. Loveman said to his staff, *"I am purely empirical. I am not attached to any romantic notion of how this business should be run. I am only driven where the evidence takes me"* Bloomberg - Are you a robot? *(2010, August 6)*. https://www.bloomberg.com/news/articles/2010-08-06/loveman-plays-new-purely-empirical-game-as-harrah-s-ceo and *"Do we think or do we know?"* Davenport, T., & Harris, J. (2007). *Competing on Analytics*. Harvard Business School Press.

7. Abrahams, D. (2023, October 1). *Daniel Abrahams on LinkedIn: Ed Sheeran's thoughts on success & failure: "You learn nothing from…"* [Video]. https://www.linkedin.com/posts/daniel-abrahams_ed-sheerans-thoughts-on-success-failure-activity-7114052491746430976-uGrT.

Index

Pages in *italics* refer to figures, pages in **bold** refer to tables, and pages followed by n refer to notes.

security challenges, 80
sepsis, 2–4, 11, 13; *see also* Epic Sepsis
      Model (ESM)
    mortality rate, 17n2
Siegel, Eric, 31
silos, 120
    breaking down, 102–104
    in large organizations, *121*
small and simple, starting, 104–110
Smith, Barry, 130
soft skills, 183, 194
    importance of, 188
Southern Methodist University, 127, 141
staff, 200
storytelling, 101, 198
strategy
    failings in, 190–191
        case study, 47–51
    role of, 51–75
stretch goals, 95–96, 193
success, measuring, 71–73, 190
surplus, 62

T

Tacoma Narrows Bridge failure, 6
Targeted Real-time Early Warning
      System (TREWS), 10, 13
Target Zone, 95–97, 99
task divisibility, limited, 104
teams
    capacity, overestimating, 109
    output and productivity, measuring
        and gauging, 194
technology
    fallibility of, 158–159, 198–200
    infrastructure, 159–162

overreliance on, 189
putting before business, 60–61
timeline, 33
    unrealistic, 109
Troyanos, Kevin, 67

U

universities, 122–127, 138n5, 195–196
    offering more than technical skills,
      128
University of Queensland, 127
UPS, ORION, 155
US Federal Trade Commission (FTC), 23

V

variables, project-related, 94
Vioxx, 8–9
vision, aligning, 71–73, 190

W

Walmart, 151
Waterfall methods, 31, 105
Watson Health, 28
WayBlazer, 69–71
Wigner, Eugene, 148–149
Woolsey, Gene, 99

Y

yield, 97

Z

Zolgensma, 77n15, 79n24

Printed in the United States
by Baker & Taylor Publisher Services